Should a Liberal State Ban the Burqa?

Also available from Bloomsbury

A Critical Introduction to the Ethics of Abortion, by Bernie Cantens
Contemporary Democracy and the Sacred, by Jon Wittrock
Judged, by Ziyad Marar
Traces of Racial Exception, by Ronit Lentin

Should a Liberal State Ban the Burqa?

Reconciling Liberalism, Multiculturalism and European Politics

Brandon Robshaw

BLOOMSBURY ACADEMIC
LONDON • NEW YORK • OXFORD • NEW DELHI • SYDNEY

BLOOMSBURY ACADEMIC
Bloomsbury Publishing Plc
50 Bedford Square, London, WC1B 3DP, UK
1385 Broadway, New York, NY 10018, USA
29 Earlsfort Terrace, Dublin 2, Ireland

BLOOMSBURY, BLOOMSBURY ACADEMIC and the Diana logo are trademarks of
Bloomsbury Publishing Plc

First published in Great Britain 2020
This paperback edition published in 2021

Copyright © Brandon Robshaw, 2020

Brandon Robshaw has asserted his right under the Copyright, Designs and
Patents Act, 1988, to be identified as Author of this work.

Cover design: Holly Bell

All rights reserved. No part of this publication may be reproduced
or transmitted in any form or by any means, electronic or mechanical,
including photocopying, recording, or any information storage or retrieval
system, without prior permission in writing from the publishers.

Bloomsbury Publishing Plc does not have any control over, or responsibility for, any
third-party websites referred to or in this book. All internet addresses given in this
book were correct at the time of going to press. The author and publisher regret any
inconvenience caused if addresses have changed or sites have ceased to exist, but can
accept no responsibility for any such changes.

A catalogue record for this book is available from the British Library.

A catalog record for this book is available from the Library of Congress.

ISBN: HB: 978-1-3501-2505-6
PB: 978-1-3503-0199-3
ePDF: 978-1-3501-2506-3
eBook: 978-1-3501-2507-0

Typeset by Newgen KnowledgeWorks Pvt. Ltd., Chennai, India

To find out more about our authors and books visit www.bloomsbury.com
and sign up for our newsletters.

Contents

1	Introduction	1
2	Reflections on the French ban	11
3	The liberal position on habitual public face-covering per se	27
4	What kind of liberalism?	39
5	Paternalism considered	69
6	Personal autonomy and the burqa	93
7	Adaptive preferences and the burqa	117
8	The burqa and multicultural theory	131
9	Gender and the burqa	167
10	The effect of the burqa on others: Offence	199
11	The effect of the burqa on others: Harm	207
12	Conclusion	233

Bibliography	239
Index	247

1

Introduction

1.1 Preliminary remarks

This book explores the question of whether a liberal state should – for liberal reasons – ban the wearing of the burqa in public. The problem is that liberalism appears to pull in two opposed directions on this question.

On the one hand, liberals strongly support religious tolerance, and the burqa is seen by many, including most of those who wear it, as a religious commitment. Or if it is not a religious commitment it may be a *cultural* commitment, a symbol of membership and of pride in one's culture, and liberals tend to be in favour of protecting cultural resources. And even if it is neither a religious nor a cultural commitment it may still be a personal choice, and liberals strongly support enabling personal choice.

On the other hand, covering one's face in public has effects on others, which need to be considered. Moreover, liberals are committed to supporting equal rights and freedoms for both sexes, and the gender asymmetry of the burqa (women wear it, men do not) combined with the fact that habitually covering one's face in public is liable to cause disadvantages in personal, social and professional life look like plausible reasons for being wary of it. A further consideration is that liberals value personal autonomy, which may be compromised if the burqa is worn in response to cultural pressure. The issue thus exposes a tension within liberalism.

A central element of my approach is the disentangling of a number of connected but separate strands of the problem. Thus I consider: different conceptions of liberalism and how they affect the response to the question; whether paternalism on grounds of welfare can be justified within liberalism and, if so, whether it would justify intervention in the specific case of the burqa; the value of personal autonomy within liberalism and whether a concern to safeguard or promote it could justify a burqa ban; the problem of adaptive preference and whether a socially influenced choice counts as a genuine preference; the role of multiculturalism in liberalism and to what extent it could justify exemptions; whether religion should carry greater weight than other ideologies or commitments when it comes to granting exemptions; gender issues and feminism; the problem of coerced wearing of the burqa; and the problem of how likely it would be that a ban, even if justified in principle, would prove efficacious in achieving its end.

The conclusion, which I am happy to disclose at this early stage, is that banning the burqa in a liberal state is unlikely to be justified. It could not be justified in terms of the welfare or autonomy of the individual who voluntarily wears it. It could only be justified on the grounds of harm to others. A ban might, for example, theoretically be justified if coerced wearing of the burqa were widespread. Such a ban would be regrettable, however, as it would override the free choice of those who wore it voluntarily. It would first be necessary to provide empirical evidence that such coercion was occurring; and any such ban could only be justified if there were no other, equally efficacious and better targeted means of preventing coercion.

My aim is to bring some clarity to this often heated and confused debate, and to supply clear liberal principles on which to base any decision. One thing to make clear from the outset is that I do not intend to spend any time, energy or words in second-guessing and critiquing the *agenda* of those who argue either for or against a ban. This question has bedevilled discussion on the topic at both a journalistic and a scholarly level. For example, the French sociologist Pierre Bourdieu has written: 'The apparent question, whether or not to accept the wearing of the so-called Islamic veil in schools, hides the latent question, whether or not to accept in France immigrants of North African origin' (Bourdieu cited in Gordon 2008: 42). Admittedly, Bourdieu is talking about headscarves rather than burqa or niqab here. But the tactic of calling out the latent or hidden agenda behind arguments actually advanced is all too familiar. In my view such an approach is both unphilosophical and ineffective. For even if the imputed agenda were correct (and there is no reason to suppose that everyone who opposes habitual face-covering in public has the same agenda), the arguments against the *hidden* agenda would be different from the arguments against the *ostensible* agenda. One could not counter the arguments of the latter by overturning the arguments of the former. Moreover, the accusation of bad faith carried by the 'Hidden-Agenda-Call-Out' has the effect of making the debate unnecessarily personal and ill-tempered. Throughout this book, therefore, I take the line that arguments are to be received, debated and evaluated in good faith.

1.2 Defining terms

1.2.1 What is a burqa?

Let me begin by clarifying the terms of the question. I use *burqa* throughout as a generic term for any garment worn by Muslim women – more accurately, Wahhabist women – which *covers the face*, primarily for religious reasons (because it is regarded either as a religious obligation or as a conscious demonstration of piety), although it may also be worn for cultural or political reasons. The niqab, therefore, also comes under my remit. There are differences between the burqa and the niqab, indeed: the burqa is a more enveloping one-piece garment, which in some versions also covers the eyes with gauze that can be seen through from the inside but not the outside. The niqab is a face veil which leaves a slit for the eyes; it is usually worn with a headscarf and long robe. Both types of garments, however, cover women's faces. That is the key point. Garments which cover only the hair, such as the hijab, are not relevant to my argument. They do not raise the issues that face-covering raises and as far as I can see, they are, from a liberal perspective, no more problematic than a hat. There may be other names for garments worn by women in different parts of the Islamic world. If they cover the face, then my arguments apply to them; if not, not.

1.2.2 What is a liberal state?

There are many conceptions of liberalism. My argument, however, is not tied to any particular conception. I explore different conceptions of liberalism in Chapter 4 in some detail, but here I need only state that the overall argument employs a broad concept of liberalism, which encompasses competing conceptions. I adopt the following definition of the minimal requirements of liberalism from Jonathan Quong, which all liberals, of whatever stripe, would accept:

a) Persons are free and equal, at least from the political point of view. Persons are free in the sense of being rational agents, capable of practical reasoning, with plans and projects for their own life, and with the capacity to understand and respond to moral reasons. Persons are equal in the sense that each person has the same fundamental moral status: there are no natural superiors or inferiors among us.

b) All sane adults have certain basic rights and liberties which include at least some form of freedom of thought and conscience, freedom of expression and association, rights to democratic participation and other political

rights that are essential or important for a functioning democracy, a right to bodily integrity and freedom from assault, a right to private property (however property is justly distributed), as well as equal rights under the rule of law.
c) The protection of these rights and liberties should be one of the main functions of any legitimate state.
d) Even if these rights are viewed as defeasible, they have a certain priority in our political reasoning, and are not easily defeated by conflicting considerations.

(Quong 2011: 14–15)

1.3 Why focus on a liberal state?

There are two reasons why the issue of the burqa is of especial relevance and interest to liberal states. One is a contingent reason, tied to a specific place and time. The other is a more general and timeless reason.

The contingent reason is that it happens to be a fact, in the early years of the twenty-first century, that burqa-wearing is on the rise in Western liberal states. This is a recent phenomenon and it raises questions about secularism, security, transparency, communication, multiculturalism and feminism, which liberal states must address. Some liberal states have already addressed these questions by banning the wearing of the burqa in public: France in 2010, Belgium in 2011, Bulgaria in 2016 and Denmark in 2018. In 2015, the Netherlands put into law a partial ban, whereby face-covering is not permitted in public buildings or on public transport, but is still permitted on the street (Agerholm 2016). These are all liberal democracies, which have advanced liberal reasons for their bans or restrictions on burqa-wearing.

Other European liberal states, however, have so far not followed suit, and some liberals have critiqued the bans for restricting those personal rights and liberties which liberalism ought to protect (Nussbaum 2012). Yet even in those liberal states where it is not banned, burqa-wearing causes frequent controversy and has been the subject of numerous court cases and tribunals. For example, in 2006 a British Muslim woman, Ms Azmi, who was suspended from her post as a primary school teacher, took the school to an appeals tribunal alleging unfair discrimination. The tribunal found in favour of the school, although Ms Azmi was awarded compensation for the way the dispute was handled (Wainwright 2006). In 2010, Judge Shauna Dean in a court in Perth, Australia, ruled that a witness, 'Tasneem', must remove her niqab to give evidence in a fraud trial, despite her protests and representations from the prosecution team who called her as a witness (*The Times*, 2010). In 2013, Whipps Cross Hospital in East London ruled that all employees must remove face-coverings when treating patients; the imam of a local mosque spoke out against the decision (Burr 2013). The issue, then, is a live one for liberal states.

The more general reason is that the burqa issue poses a dilemma for liberalism which it does not pose for other political positions. 'Should a theocratic state ban the burqa?', for example, is not an interesting question. The answer simply depends on the kind of theocracy. If it is an Islamic, Salafist theocracy, then of course not. If it is a fundamentalist Christian or Hindu theocracy, then of course. 'Should a (Christian) conservative state ban the burqa?' The likely answer would be yes, on the grounds that burqa-wearing would not be in line with the culture, history and traditions of such a nation, and conservatives by definition value and defend their culture, history and traditions. Whether a Marxist or self-styled Marxist state should ban the burqa is more of a moot point. Marxist ideology does not entail any specific commitment to religious tolerance and the burqa does not appear to advance the cause of the class struggle or of economic equality, so there is no principled reason why it should not. Probably whether a Marxist state banned it or not would depend upon expediency rather than principle. In most cases, then, simply naming the type of state gives a strong clue to the line that state would take on the burqa.

But for a liberal state the issue is less clear-cut. The burqa is a religious symbol and is perceived by many if not most of those who wear it as a religious obligation. Liberalism entails a strong commitment to religious tolerance. This is where the whole tradition of Western liberalism begins. As Russell Blackford puts it (citing Rex Ahdar and Ian Leigh in support), religious freedom 'is the prototypical liberal freedom, a cornerstone of modern political rights' (Blackford 2012: 1).

Historically this is true. One of the foundational texts of liberalism is John Locke's *Letter Concerning Toleration* of 1689 (Locke [1689] 2013), which argues that the practice of religion should not be under the control of the state but a matter for individual conscience (with certain exceptions justified by an appeal to state security). Since then the idea of individual freedom has widened in liberal states to include non-religious beliefs and practices: freedom of expression of political dissent and of unpopular or controversial views, freedom to make experiments in living, freedom to pursue different forms of sexuality and so on. It could be argued – and in Chapter 2 I do so argue – that religious freedom ought not to merit special status as compared to other freedoms. Nevertheless, religious freedom, as well as being no *less* important than those other freedoms, is still, symbolically, a cornerstone of liberal rights, and liberals are bound to take seriously any threat to it.

On the other hand, liberalism also entails a commitment to gender equality. The fact that the burqa is worn only by women, and could impose disadvantages on the wearer, at the very least looks like a cause for liberal concern. There is also the issue of 'living together' which was accepted by the European Court of Human Rights (ECHR) as a legitimate reason for the bans in France and Belgium; the impact one's freedom may have on other members of society is a legitimate liberal concern. The issue thus highlights a tension between important liberal principles.

Moreover, exploring reasons why a liberal state should or should not ban the burqa leads one into other disputed areas within liberalism: the role of paternalism, the value of autonomy, and the relationship between liberalism and multiculturalism. Modern liberal societies are rapidly changing. When exploring the burqa question we should remember that we are looking at a *dynamic* situation. It may be that in twenty years' time burqa-wearing will no longer be a hot button issue for liberal states. But questions about paternalism, autonomy, multiculturalism, and the tension between religion and feminism are likely to be disputed for as long as there are liberals to dispute them.

1.4 Overview of the argument

1.4.1 The argument

The argument of the book centres on whether the liberal response to face-covering per se is adequate to deal with all the issues raised by burqa-wearing. In Chapter 2 I look in detail at the French ban of 2010 and argue that the legal arguments both for and against do not, from a liberal perspective, settle the question. Chapter 3 takes a step back, to offer a thin account which focuses only on face-covering in general rather than burqas in particular – an account which in subsequent chapters will be fleshed out with contextual details, to ascertain whether the liberal response to face-covering per se should be unchanged, or should be either less or more restrictive, when the type of face-covering is the Islamic burqa or niqab. Up until Chapter 11, I shall be assuming that the wearing of the burqa is voluntary. That is because I take it as a given that liberals would naturally be against *coerced* burqa-wearing. It is *voluntary* burqa-wearing that makes for the liberal dilemma.

1.4.2 Chapter 2: Reflections on the French ban

The French burqa-ban was based on three reasons, advanced as defences when the law was contested in the ECHR: gender equality, the dignity of the individual and the requirement for citizens to live together. The position sketched out in this chapter (to be developed in much more detail later in the book) is that the ECHR were right to reject the first two reasons, subject to certain conditions that they did not acknowledge, and which need to be taken into account to settle the question. They were wrong to uphold the third; again, more detailed consideration and argument are necessary to show why. In this chapter I also argue that religious freedom should not be privileged over other freedoms, but that the liberal commitment to individual liberty is enough to make a case against a burqa-ban.

1.4.3 Chapter 3: The liberal position on habitual public face-covering per se

Chapter 3 explores the reasons why the human face is of such special significance, and why covering it raises issues that covering other parts of the body does not. I focus on the face's role in identification, ethics, empathy and communication. I examine the issue in the abstract, deliberately omitting considerations of culture, religion or gender asymmetry, in order to arrive at a liberal baseline position on the practice of habitual public face-covering per se. I conclude that although habitual face-covering in public may be disadvantageous to an individual, the liberal state would have no reason to ban it as long as it is voluntary, although restrictions on face-covering would be justifiable in certain situations. The ground is thus prepared for consideration of whether this baseline position will need to be modified in light of considerations of culture, religion or gender asymmetry.

1.4.4 Chapter 4: Two types of liberalism

In Chapter 4 I consider whether the type of liberalism espoused makes a difference in responding to burqa-wearing. I consider two varieties of liberalism often taken to be contraries: Political Liberalism and Liberal Perfectionism.

I argue that they represent extreme points on a continuum rather than a dichotomy. Liberals at any point on the continuum would agree that restricting liberty can sometimes be justified on grounds of preventing harm to others. For liberals nearer the perfectionist end of the spectrum there may also be paternalist reasons for restricting liberty. The three chapters that follow explore the place and scope of paternalism within liberalism.

1.4.5 Chapter 5: Paternalism

Here I consider whether a ban on burqa-wearing could be justifiable on grounds of the welfare of the burqa-wearer. I ask whether liberals could ever be in favour of paternalism in the first place. I argue that there is a place for paternalism within liberalism, *pace* antipaternalists like Jonathan Quong and Seana Shiffrin; but paternalism on grounds of the welfare of the burqa-wearer would not be justified. The liberal response to voluntary habitual face-covering per se need not yet be modified.

1.4.6 Chapter 6: The burqa and personal autonomy

Here I consider a special case of paternalism, likely to be favoured by liberals towards the perfectionist end of the spectrum: that is, paternalist action by the state in order to promote *personal autonomy*. My argument is that as long as the burqa-wearer has second-order autonomy (i.e. as long as she chose to wear the burqa autonomously in the first place, and as long as her choice is revocable) then despite any loss in first-order autonomy (i.e. loss of autonomy in the conditions of day-to-day life), the liberal state has no justification for intervening. The liberal response to voluntary habitual face-covering per se still need not be modified.

1.4.7 Chapter 7: Adaptive preferences

Here I consider the problem of *adaptive preferences*. If burqa-wearing is the result of a preference formed in response to social pressures and constraints, can it be said to be truly voluntary? I argue that burqa-wearing is an adaptive preference but is not necessarily non-autonomous, and that provided the choice to wear a burqa was formed under social conditions compatible with the flourishing of the individual, and provided wearing it does not make it impossible for the wearer to flourish (according to her own idea of flourishing), and provided that she is free to stop wearing it at any time, a liberal state should tolerate the practice.

However, in cases where burqa-wearing and the attendant conditions prevent the flourishing of the individual, this would be what Serene Khader (2011) terms an Inappropriate Adaptive Preference, or IAP, and the liberal state would be justified in taking measures to free women from it. For reasons of sensitivity and pragmatism such measures might well stop short of an outright ban, however.

1.4.8 Chapter 8: Multiculturalism and the burqa

In this chapter I examine first whether liberalism is compatible with multiculturalism, that is, the granting of cultural group rights by the state. I accept the form of multiculturalism put forward by Will Kymlicka (1995), in which group rights can be legitimately granted by the liberal state as long as this does not entail oppression or injustice to any members within the group. That granted, the question is whether, in the case of the cultural practice of burqa-wearing, group rights would justify loosening or removing the restrictions entailed by the liberal response to face-covering per se. In other words, should the right to wear a burqa be accommodated, rather than temporarily suspended, in situations where security, identification or communication are paramount? I argue that, although some cultural practices do merit accommodation, that is not the case for burqa-wearing. The liberal response to voluntary habitual face-covering per se need not yet be modified.

1.4.9 Chapter 9: Gender and the burqa

In this chapter I consider gender asymmetry of the burqa – women wear it, men do not – and ask if that causes problem for the liberal. I consider and accept Susan Moller Okin's (1999) argument that multicultural policies and the rights of women in minority cultural groups may conflict, and that if they do conflict it is the multicultural policies which the liberal should reject. The question is whether or to what extent the burqa adversely affects the rights of women (still assuming that the burqa is worn voluntarily). If burqa-wearing is bad for women then there is a case for a more restrictive approach than the abstract liberal position on face-covering per se. A ban might be justified, even if the burqa-wearing is claimed to be voluntary. I consider Clare Chambers's (2008) argument that where a practice is (1) the result of strong social influence and (2) disadvantageous to the person following the practice, then there is a liberal justification for a ban. I argue that this approach needs to be treated with caution. The social influence would have to be irresistible and the disadvantages very severe and irrevocable before action would be justifiable. Reprising the argument from adaptive preference, I argue that whether state intervention is justified should be decided on a case-by-case basis; and moreover, that intervention could take more nuanced and effective forms than an outright ban. The liberal response to voluntary habitual face-covering per se need not yet be modified.

1.4.10 Chapter 10: The burqa and offence

In this chapter I consider Joel Feinberg's Offence Principle: the principle that if a practice causes severe, prolonged and unavoidable offence to the senses or sensibilities, there would be liberal grounds for banning it. I accept the argument in principle and consider some ways in which the burqa might be thought offensive. I argue that none of them is so severe as to justify a ban. The liberal response to voluntary habitual face-covering per se need not yet be modified.

1.4.11 Chapter 11: Harm and the burqa

In this chapter I put aside the assumption that burqa-wearing is voluntary and ask what the liberal response should be if significant numbers of women are coerced into wearing the burqa. I argue that *if* this is so, then a ban could be justified on the grounds of preventing harm to the coerced; if there were no other way of preventing the coercion that was at least equally efficacious.

1.4.12 Chapter 12: Conclusion

Here I consider the question of efficacy and of possible unintended consequences of a burqa-ban. I explore whether there are other, more imaginative and efficacious ways of preventing coercion (supposing it to be occurring) and argue that, even if a ban were the most efficacious means at present, this could be thought of as a stopgap solution until a more nuanced solution, targeting only the coerced wearers while sparing the voluntary wearers, could be found. I end by summarising my conclusion:

1. Assuming that burqa-wearing is voluntary, a burqa-ban would not be justified on liberal grounds, but it would be justifiable to require temporary removal in certain situations.
2. But *if* a significant proportion of burqa-wearing is coerced, then a general ban would be justified, *if* no other equally efficacious means of preventing coercion could be found.

2

Reflections on the French ban

The argument

The French burqa-ban, enacted in 2010 and coming into effect in 2011, rested on three reasons, which were advanced as defences when the law was contested in the ECHR. Those reasons were gender equality, the dignity of the individual and the requirement for citizens to live together. In this chapter I explain and comment on the reasons given by the ECHR for rejecting the first two defences and upholding the third. The position argued for here (to be developed in detail later in the book) is that the ECHR was right (from a liberal perspective) to reject the first two reasons, subject to certain conditions which the ECHR did not acknowledge, but that it was wrong (from a liberal perspective) to uphold the third. I also contend that religious freedom should not be privileged over other freedoms, but that the liberal commitment to individual liberty is enough to make the case against a ban.

2.1 The story of the French ban

2.1.1 The 2010 Act

On 11 October 2010, the government of Nicolas Sarközy passed an act which effectively banned the wearing of the burqa or niqab in public places throughout France and all French territories. It came into effect in April of the following year. The act stated: 'Nul ne peut, dans l'espace public, porter une tenue destinée à dissimuler son visage' (Nobody in a public place may wear clothing designed to hide the face) (LOI n° 2010-1192).

The act goes on to exempt certain types of face-covering, such as those required for safety in certain jobs, those worn for protection in sports and masks worn during fêtes and celebrations. It is sometimes claimed that these exemptions indicate that the law was designed to target Muslims alone. For example, Myriam Hunter-Henin, in an article vehemently opposing the legality of the ban, has stated that the Act (along with an earlier Act banning wearing of the hijab in schools) is 'the legal expression of the French sensitivity to the presence of Islam in the public sphere' (2012: 615). This could conceivably be true for some of those in the Assemblée Nationale who voted for the law, or for some members of the French public who supported it, but it by no means follows that it was the only, main or true justification for the law. The exemptions are for *temporary* public face-covering, not *habitual* public face-covering. That is the crucial difference. It may nevertheless then be said that the Act clearly targets Muslims because it is only (female) Muslims who habitually cover their faces in public. However, in the first place it is only rather fuzzily true that it is Muslim women who habitually cover their faces; more accurately it is *Wahhabist* women, a strict, conservative Saudi interpretation of Islam which is not followed by the majority of French Muslims. But then perhaps the Act deliberately targeted Wahhabist women? That is the de facto effect, but the reason for the ban seems more obviously and naturally to be because they are covering their faces, rather than because they are Wahhabist.

Leaving aside any hypothetical dubious motivations behind the ban, let us look at the reasons expressly offered for it to see whether they stand up for themselves.

2.1.2 Laïcité

The French burqa-ban was not enacted for the same reasons as the earlier ban on the wearing of religious symbols, including the hijab, in state schools (2004). The 2004 ban was enacted in the name of *laïcité:* the principle that public institutions must be resolutely secular. This is a tradition dating back as far as the French Revolution, and enshrined in French law since the 1905 'Loi de séparation des Eglises et de l'Etat' (Law of the separation between church and state). According to the historian Jean Baubérot (who was personally opposed to the burqa-ban), this law is liberal and tolerant in intent, and rests on what he calls 'three pillars': 'la fin du caractère officiel de l'Eglise catholique'; 'la liberté de conscience et le libre exercice des cultes'; and 'le respect des règles de fonctionnement spécifiques de chaque culte' (A termination to the official role of the Catholic church; freedom of conscience and forms of worship; and a respect for the rules and practices of each religion) (Baubérot, 2016). Baubérot argues that the purpose of the law is not to suppress but to protect religion. The banning of religious symbols in schools and other state institutions ensures neutrality on the part of the state.

However, the burqa-ban cannot be justified on the grounds of *laïcité*, because it is not restricted to state institutions. Face-covering is banned in all public spaces, which the Act defines as 'des voies publiques ainsi que des lieux ouverts au public ou affectés à un service public' (public highways and places open to the public or assigned to public services), and it is hard to see why state secularism should prevent people wearing religious symbols when they are simply walking along the street or standing at a bus stop. As Hunter-Henin has pointed out, this cannot be seen as an instance of state secularism: 'The eradication of difference that is sought by the new law [of 2010] is alien to secularism which even in its most virulent [*sic*] forms is designed to manage rather than deny diversity of belief' (2012: 616–17).

Laïcité, then, plays no part in justifying the 2010 ban; and although Hunter-Henin expends much powder and shot attacking the idea that it could have any bearing on the matter, she states that in fact the Committee set up to consider the issue of full-face veil-wearing did not regard the concept of *laïcité* as relevant and 'the government's text which led to the 2010 law did not rely on the notion' (2012: 619). Hunter-Henin presents this as a case of the Committee having to 'admit' that *laïcité* was not relevant, as if the point was conceded with reluctance. That is misleading. The report describes *la laïcité* as '*un fondement inopérant*' (an ineffective foundation) for a ban and explicitly argues that 'ce principe [la laïcité] ne saurait être retenu dans le cas d'une interdiction portant sur l'espace public' (this principle cannot be accepted in the case of a ban relating to public space) (ANRI 2010: 173). It goes on to argue that 'l'on voit mal pourquoi, au nom du principe de laïcité, seul le port du voile intégral serait prohibé dans l'espace public' (it is difficult to see why, in the name of the principle of *laïcité*, only the wearing of the full veil [and not other religious symbols] should be banned in public spaces) (ANRI 2010: 173).

2.1.3 Gender equality, dignity and living together

If *la laïcité* was not regarded as a justification for the 2010 burqa-ban, then what was? Three main reasons were advanced: gender equality, women's dignity and the importance of living together (*vivre ensemble*). M. André Gerin, the President of the Assemblée Nationale's commissioned report into the wearing of the full-face veil on French territory, matched those three reasons up with the three principles of the French Revolution, *Liberté, Egalité, Fraternité*:

> Le voile intégral est une atteinte intolérable à la liberté, à la dignité des femmes. C'est la négation de l'égalité des sexes, de la mixité dans notre société. C'est finalement la volonté d'exclure les femmes de la vie sociale et le rejet de notre volonté commune de vivre ensemble.
>
> [The full veil is an intolerable attack on liberty, on the dignity of women. It is a denial of gender equality, of the mixing of men and women on equal terms in our society. And finally it embodies the desire to exclude women from social life and is a rejection of our communal will to live together.]
>
> (ANRI 2010: 13)

The full report, including transcripts of interviews with politicians, philosophers, anthropologists, historians, imams, Islamic scholars, representatives of feminist groups and many others, runs to 658 pages. It cannot be said that the decision to ban the burqa and niqab was taken lightly. Ultimately, though, it rests on the three reasons above cited by Gerin; and when, in 2014, the French ban was contested by an unnamed citizen known as 'S.A.R' in the ECHR, it was those three reasons – respecting dignity, furthering gender equality, and fulfilling the requirement of living together – which were advanced by the French government in defence of the ban.

By fifteen votes to two, the court upheld the ban as legal. Not for all three reasons, however. In fact only one of the reasons carried the day. The court found in favour of the French state because the ban was motivated by the requirement of *vivre ensemble* which was linked to the legitimate aim of the 'protection of rights and freedoms of others'. But the other stated aims, of furthering gender equality and respecting women's dignity, were not accepted as justifications for the ban (see ECHR Judgement in the case of *S.A.R. v France* 2014, Application 43835/11, paragraphs 119–21).

This ruling was echoed three years later, when two Belgian citizens similarly contested the Belgian ban in the ECHR in 2017. The court again upheld the ban, on the same grounds that it furthered the aim of a certain idea of living together (see ECHR Press Release 241 in the case of *Belcacemi and Oussar v Belgium*, 2017).

2.2 The ECHR judgement on the three defences of the ban

2.2.1 The ECHR rejection of the gender equality defence

The requirement to safeguard gender equality would certainly count as a liberal reason for a ban. Political equality of citizens regardless of sex is a fundamental liberal principle. It is also a principle enshrined in the French constitution. The judgement of the ECHR did not oppose this as a reason in principle, stating that the Court 'does not doubt that gender equality might rightly justify an interference with the exercise of certain rights and freedoms enshrined in the Convention [for the Protection of Human Rights and Fundamental Freedoms']' but goes on to add that

> The Court takes the view, however, that a State Party cannot invoke gender equality in order to ban a practice that is defended by women – such as the applicant – in the context of the exercise of the rights enshrined in those provisions, unless it were to be understood that individuals could be protected on that basis from the exercise of their own fundamental rights and freedoms.
> (ECHR Judgement in the case of *S.A.R. v France* 2014, Application 43835/11, paragraph 119)

In other words, as long as the practice is voluntary, freely adopted and defended by the women concerned, the state has no right to ban it; to do so would ride roughshod over the very rights and freedoms it was duty-bound to protect.

This seems, on the face of it, persuasive. Liberals do of course believe in gender equality and wish to enable, promote and safeguard it, which entails a commitment to preventing unfair discrimination against women, providing legal protection against coercive behaviour by men and ensuring that women are well-informed about their rights. But liberals do not believe that equal outcomes are to be *imposed*. If a woman freely chooses to occupy the domestic sphere, or to be deferent and obedient to her husband, then that is no concern of the liberal state. And similarly, if a woman freely chooses to habitually cover her face in public, even though this may disadvantage her in various ways as compared to men, the liberal state has no right to intervene on the grounds of preserving gender equality.

There, are, however, two important factors which the ECHR did not consider. One is the question of how free such a choice really is. The woman who makes it defends it, naturally enough: but to what extent was her choice the result of cultural pressure? (And how much cultural pressure is acceptable?) In short, how can we be sure that what is claimed to be a personal choice is not really an *adaptive preference* – that is to say, the acceptance of a suboptimal option because the other options appear even worse? This may not be an insuperable objection, but it needs to be considered. I discuss adaptive preferences in Chapter 7, and in Chapter 9 I look at the issue of socially influenced and disadvantageous choices.

The second factor is the extent to which one woman's personal choice may impact on the choices of others. If some burqa-wearing is coerced (we lack clear empirical evidence of this, but *if* it were occurring), then the willing burqa-wearers may unwittingly be facilitating this coercion. This also is a question deserving of consideration. It is discussed in detail in Chapter 11.

2.2.2 The ECHR rejection of the human dignity defence

The human dignity defence rests on the claim that habitual burqa-wearing in public offends against the dignity of the wearers. Even if they do so voluntarily, they are demeaning themselves; therefore the state may, for paternalistic reasons, intervene to protect the personal dignity of its citizens. The ECHR did not accept this defence, stating:

> The Court takes the view that, however essential it may be, respect for human dignity cannot legitimately justify a blanket ban on the wearing of the full-face veil in public places. The Court is aware that the clothing in question is perceived as strange by many of those who observe it. It would point out, however, that it is the expression of a cultural identity which contributes to the pluralism that is inherent in democracy. It notes in this connection the variability of the notions of virtuousness and decency that are applied to the uncovering of the human body.
>
> (ECHR Judgement in the case of *S.A.R. v France* 2014, Application 43835/11, paragraph 119)

The ECHR thus points to a core liberal value in its rejection of this defence: the value of *pluralism*. Pluralism, to be discussed in more detail in Chapter 3, stems from the fact that human beings, both individually and as members of cultural groups, can and do differ about what makes for a good life – which would of course include notions of human dignity. As the political liberal Jonathan Quong puts it in *Liberalism without Perfection*: 'Because we disagree about what makes life worth living, it would be wrong for the government to take sides on this question' (2011: 2).

It is true that *perfectionist* varieties of liberalism allow for the exercise of paternalism in order to safeguard or promote what are taken to be universal goods. As I shall argue in Chapter 4, *some* degree of perfectionism, and hence paternalism, is difficult to avoid within liberalism. However, allowing the state to decide what counts as a dignified way to appear in public seems a step too far in the direction of extreme paternalism, as I shall argue in Chapters 5 and 6, where I consider the issue of state paternalism and liberal restrictions upon it.

2.2.3 The ECHR acceptance of the *vivre ensemble* defence

The requirement of living together falls into two parts. The first is the protection of the public from harm by securing public order. That is not a uniquely liberal requirement. But it perhaps carries particular importance for liberal states: the liberal commitment to equal rights for citizens means that *all* citizens are to be protected equally from harm, which may not be the case with non-liberal states which recognise different levels of rights for different groups of inhabitants. The ECHR agreed that, in principle, the requirement of protecting citizens from harm by securing public order would be a legitimate aim of the state. However, they pointed out that this specific requirement was not mentioned in Paragraph 8 of the Convention for the Protection of Human Rights and Fundamental Freedoms, which the French government had used in support of the ban: and moreover,

> the Government did not refer to it either in their written observations or in their answer to the question put to them in that connection during the public hearing, preferring to refer solely to the 'protection of the rights and freedoms of others'.
> (ECHR Judgement in the case of *S.A.R. v France* 2014, Application 43835/11, paragraph 117)

For this reason, the ECHR did not consider the public order requirement as a justification for the ban, and it is left unanswered whether in this case it is a legitimate justification or not. My own view is that this would certainly be a sound liberal justification for a ban *if* there were evidence that face-covering did threaten harm to individuals by, for example, facilitating crime or terrorism. But that is an empirical question. I consider the question of harm to others in Chapter 11, but to anticipate, I do not believe there is evidence that burqa-wearing has led to increases in crime or terrorism in France or other Western liberal states.

Having put public-order considerations to one side, the ECHR goes on to consider the other part of the *vivre ensemble* requirement: 'protection of the rights and freedoms of others'. And it is on this final point that they find in favour of the French state:

> The Court takes into account the respondent State's point that the face plays an important role in social interaction. It can understand the view that individuals who are present in places open to all may not wish to see practices or attitudes developing there which would fundamentally call into question the possibility of open interpersonal relationships, which, by virtue of an established consensus, forms an indispensable element of community life within the society in question. The Court is therefore able to accept that the barrier raised against others by a veil concealing the face is perceived by the respondent State as breaching the right of others to live in a space of socialisation which makes living together easier.
> (ECHR Judgement in the case of *S.A.R. v France* 2014, Application 43835/11, paragraph 122)

I remain unconvinced that this is a sound liberal reason for banning habitual public face-covering. I argue that, although it could cause inconvenience in certain situations in the social sphere, these inconveniences could be avoided by temporary removal of the face-covering, rather than by a blanket ban. I present the case for this view in Chapter 3. For now, I merely note that the *vivre ensemble* defence rests more on a republican conception of the state than a purely liberal one.

2.3 The French republican tradition

French republicanism, though it has strong liberal elements, is perhaps better seen as a form of communitarianism. It imposes duties on its citizens which are owed not primarily to other individuals but to a republican conception of the common good. This conception depends on a social theory which, in the words of Peter Baehr and Daniel Gordon

> can be seen as a specific inflection of democratic thought that we call the elongation of the political into the sociable. The concept of citizenship is the starting point. Citizenship in modern democratic regimes enshrines the idea of politico-legal equality. According to [Richard] Bellamy, it 'is through being a member of a political community and participating on equal terms in the framing of collective life that we enjoy rights' (2008, pp. 16, 114). He also remarks that 'citizenship involves a degree of solidarity and reciprocity between

citizens' and that such citizens 'need to see each other as equal partners within a collective enterprise'.

Full-face coverings such as the burqa and niqab raise the issue of whether democratic 'solidarity' is related to citizens being visible to one another. If I can see your face but you cannot see mine, is this a politically equal encounter? That a degree of mutual visibility is a prerequisite of political equality is strongly implied by Western democratic/republican metaphors: enlightenment, openness, transparency, illumination, recognition, legibility, disclosure, accountability, publicity and, not least, public.

(Baehr and Gordon 2013: 257)

Baehr and Gordon argue that in modern democratic theory, particularly in France, the political has an inescapably social dimension. Citizenship does not merely mean participation in political processes, such as voting, but in accepting duties of reciprocity towards others, public civility, in short, the kind of obligations stressed by communitarians. And it is this set of requirements that formed the foundation for the 'living together' defence.

It is important to note that the French republican tradition differs from the American republican tradition, which, as Peter Baehr and Daniel Gordon have argued, accounts for the markedly different way in which French and American liberals see the burqa-ban (Baehr and Gordon 2013). French republicanism was born of the revolutionary struggle not only against absolute monarchy but also against the allied power of the Roman Catholic Church. American republicanism, on the other hand, has a tradition of placing a very high value indeed on religious freedom. The story of the Pilgrim Fathers leaving Southampton in the Mayflower and the Speedwell in the year 1620, to escape the strictures of the Church of England and practise their own version of Protestantism in the Land of the Free, is still a potent myth. Thus French republicanism is by its nature secular and, without being *anti*-religious, affords religion no special status; while a central purpose of American republicanism, almost its *raison d'être,* is to guarantee religious freedom. It is true that Article 10 of the French Declaration of the Rights of Man of 1789 gives a commitment to freedom of religious belief: 'Nul ne doit être inquiété pour ses opinions, même religieuses, pourvu que leur manifestation ne trouble pas l'ordre public établi par la Loi' (Nobody is to be disturbed on account of their opinions, even religious ones, provided that their manifestation does not trouble the public order established by the Law). As Baehr and Gordon point out, however, the wording of this article is significant:

Two linguistic differences from the American First Amendment are that this text does not protect the 'exercise' of religion and it explicitly posits a limit on religious rights (the First Amendment does not).

(Baehr and Gordon 2013: 268)

They might have added a third point about the wording: the use of the word 'even' to qualify 'religious', suggesting that religious opinions only just scrape into the protected zone.

All this is not to imply that French republicanism is intolerant of religion or that anti-religious sentiment was a major reason behind the burqa-ban. It is rather to point out that within French republicanism the fact that a practice is religious is no reason to grant it any special protection; whereas in American republicanism the fact that a practice is religious is a prima facie reason for accommodating it. As Baehr and Gordon argue (2013), failure to perceive this difference has led many American commentators to ascribe the French burqa-ban to racism – mistakenly, in Baehr and Gordon's view, and I agree.

The French law thus 'affirms the primacy of the social over the religious' (Baehr and Gordon 2013: 275). Baehr and Gordon state that 'the most powerful basis for opposing bans is to defend religious freedom' (2013: 273). They do not mean to suggest that religious freedom should or must trump the social obligations of citizenship; only that no other argument will do so.

I must part company from Baehr and Gordon at this point. In the first place, I strongly incline to what they have characterised as the French view, that religious freedom ought not to be privileged over other freedoms. I argue for this below. Moreover, I contend that there are other, more compelling arguments against a ban; these arguments depend on taking seriously the liberal commitment to the liberty of the individual. I argue for this throughout.

2.4 An issue of religious freedom?

Many will see the question of whether burqa-wearing should be banned as essentially an issue of religious liberty. I do not dispute, of course, that the burqa is of religious significance (though many Muslims argue that it ought not to be; see Sardar 2016). My view, however, is that a focus on its religious significance means the debate tends to get bogged down in arguments about whether one is pro- or anti-religion or, more specifically, pro- or anti-Muslim (as though either 'religion' or 'Islam' were a monolith). The burqa then comes to be seen as a symbol of Islam, and arguments centre on the supposed anti-Islamic agenda of those who support a ban. For example, in *The New Religious Intolerance* (2012) Nussbaum sees burqa-bans as part of a wider phenomenon of intolerance of Islam.

This approach runs the risk of missing something crucial: the question of how habitual public face-covering impacts on other citizens. Emphasis on the burqa as a religious obligation invites comparisons with other religious practices, which takes us away from what ought to be the central point: the *effects* of burqa-wearing, both on the individual wearer and on a liberal society. Other religious obligations, such as fasting, observing dietary laws, not working on holy days, or wearing clothing or ornaments of religious significance such as hijab, turbans, crucifixes and so on, may cause tensions and require negotiations, but they do not raise the same questions as the burqa for they do not involve the same effects. They do not entail habitual public face-covering. As I argue in the Chapter 3, this has specific and unique effects on others and on the wearer.

Habitual public face-covering could potentially cause problems both for the wearer and for a liberal society. I cover these problems in the chapters that follow. But if they can be addressed without the need for a blanket ban (as, subject to certain conditions, I argue is the case), then the issue of religious freedom need not even arise. Liberal states should not ban things that do not need banning, whether they are religious practices or not. Most discussions of religious freedom concern the right to exemptions from laws that come into conflict with religious obligations (such as the compulsory crash-helmet law clashing with the obligation of male Sikhs to wear turbans: see Barry 2011). If, however, there *is* no law against habitual public face-covering, then the question of exemption to it does not come up.

Of course, even without such a law, there may be situations in which *temporary* removal of the face-covering could be required (e.g. classrooms or courts of law). Here there might be tensions between burdens on others and religious obligations, and arguments about specific exemptions – but to *start* with those cases, each of which would have its own unique features, before having established that the default position is no blanket ban is putting the cart before the horse.

If, on the other hand, the problems for liberal societies could *not* be addressed without a blanket ban, then there is a prima facie case for one. For the right to religious freedom to overturn that case, a claim about the special or privileged status of religion would seem to be required. It is this claim, that religious freedom is of special value and significance as compared to other freedoms, that

I do not accept. But before giving my reasons, let me first explain the position of religion within liberalism, and why it might be thought to be special.

2.5 The historical importance of religion to liberalism

In Chapter 1 I noted the historical role of religion in the political philosophy of liberalism. This point is worth reiterating. Religion, and specifically Christianity, has been highly important in the development of liberalism, if not essential to it. Larry Siedentorp, in *Inventing the Individual* (2015), makes a persuasive case that the liberal ideas of individual rights, representative government, liberty of conscience and the equal worth of all human beings are direct consequences of Christian belief. Cécile Laborde in *Liberalism's Religion* notes that 'the notion of religion is central to the historical elaboration of Western liberalism, from the European wars of religion onward' (2017: 1).

The liberal commitment to tolerance first appears as a commitment to *religious* tolerance, as in Locke's foundational liberal text of 1689, *A Letter Concerning Toleration*. A commitment to state religious tolerance leads directly to a secular state (see Blackford 2012, *Freedom of Religion and the Secular State*). Thus religion – or Christianity, at any rate – was ultimately responsible for secularism.

Since Locke's time the liberal commitment to religious tolerance has widened to include tolerance of heterodox political views, unconventional lifestyles, different sexualities and so on. Nevertheless, religious freedom remains central and symbolically important to the liberal view.

2.6 Claims for the specialness of religion

Some writers, such as Sarah Song (2007) and Martha Nussbaum (2008) have argued that religious freedom is a special case. Nussbaum sees religious freedom in terms of freedom of conscience (she does not maintain that *only* religion raises issues of conscience but regards religion as the paradigmatic case). She writes:

> Conscience is precious, worthy of respect, but it is also capable of being wounded and imprisoned. The tradition [of America's religious equality] argues that conscience … needs a protected space around it within which people can pursue their search for life's meaning.
>
> (2008: 19)

Jocelyn Maclure also claims that religion is a special case and that exemption demands for religious practices carry greater weight than exemptions demanded for other cultural practices. He suggests that religion is different from other areas of life for which exemption claims or demands for special treatment can be made, because 'religious beliefs are a special type of belief that, as such, require special protection' (2011: 268). He characterises religious beliefs as meaning-giving beliefs and commitments which are central to one's identity. Such beliefs are tied up to one's sense of self-esteem and moral integrity, and the more this is so the greater the need for legal protection of those beliefs (2011: 268).

Michael McConnell offers a further argument in favour of the unique importance of religion. In his view, although conventional wisdom has it that pre-modern religious world-views were oppressive and inimical to freedom, and that 'secularization was an essential ingredient in the cultural background for liberal democracy', the truth is the other way round: 'religion, and strong protection for religion [are] best understood as allied with commitment to freedom in general' (2010: 943). For McConnell, then, freedom of religion guarantees freedom from over-intrusive state intervention, acting as a bulwark against state oppression.

2.7 A claim against the specialness of religion

The position argued for here is that we need not invoke the specialness of religion to show that a liberal state should not ban the burqa. The liberal commitment to freedom of individual choice is enough, alone, to make that case. And if it were not, the specialness of religion would not be a trump card in any case.

First, although historically freedom of religion was the parent of other freedoms (freedom of expression, freedom of association, freedom to make experiments in living, etc.), to acknowledge this fact is to say nothing about whether religion merits any special status today. Religion's temporal priority does not imply lexical priority.

Other liberal freedoms operate within limits. The right to free expression, for example, is limited by laws on libel and on incitement to racial hatred. Like other liberal freedoms, freedom of religion too must have its limits.

McConnell's argument that freedom of religion was an important defence against state oppression was no doubt true in eighteenth-century America. But there is no reason today to think that it is the only or the best bulwark against an over-intrusive state. Obviously a liberal state should guarantee religious freedom. But it is not obvious that this is more important than guaranteeing other freedoms, such as freedom of expression.

Nussbaum is particularly concerned with defending religious freedom, which she sees as currently under threat. But religion is just one example – a salient one, certainly – of freedom of conscience, and Nussbaum's argument would apply equally to other, non-religious cases where moral conscience is at stake.

Jocelyn Maclure's argument also establishes only that meaning-giving beliefs which are tied to one's sense of self-esteem and moral integrity have a greater need for legal protection than other beliefs. Maclure does not establish that *all* religious beliefs held by *all* believers are *equally* meaning-giving in this way. Nor does he establish that no *non-*religious beliefs are meaning-giving in this way. Indeed, he concedes that some non-religious beliefs, such as pacifism or vegetarianism, may be meaning-giving and tied up with self-esteem and a sense of morality (Maclure 2011: 269). Therefore, religious beliefs form part of a wider category of freedom of conscience. It is the fact that they are in that category, not the fact that they are *religious*, that is supposed to make them special.

Cécile Laborde, in her book *Liberalism's Religion* (2017), makes the case that liberalism should work with a 'disaggregated' notion of religion; that is to say, that religion should not be considered a single category for the purposes of political/legal decisions, but should be disaggregated 'into a plurality of different interpretive dimensions' (2017: 2). This reworking of the role of religion in liberal theory

> implies that religion is not uniquely special: whatever treatment it receives from the law, it receives in virtue of features that it shares with nonreligious beliefs, conceptions and identities.
>
> (Laborde 2017: 3)

In *Secularism and Freedom of Conscience* (2011), Maclure himself, writing with Charles Taylor, also acknowledges that religious beliefs are not the only type of beliefs that require to be accommodated under a principle of freedom of conscience. It is those beliefs which give meanings to one's life (as distinct from mere preferences) that deserve accommodation and these include but are not limited to religious beliefs:

> core beliefs and commitments, including religious ones, must be distinguished from other personal beliefs and preferences because of the role they play in individuals' moral integrity.
>
> (Maclure and Taylor 2011: 76)

This position, with which I am in agreement, states that there is no distinction (relevant to the question of accommodation) between religious beliefs and other meaning-giving beliefs. Laborde uses the term 'identity-protecting commitment' (IPC) for a commitment which is 'manifested in a practice, ritual, or action (or refusal to act), that allows an individual to live in accordance with how she thinks she ought to live' (2017: 203–4); and of course both religious and non-religious commitments can be IPCs.

Moreover, there is no bright line distinguishing beliefs which are meaning-giving and those which are not, but rather a continuum of beliefs ranging from those which are unconnected or tangential to one's sense of moral integrity, through those which are moderately connected to it, to those which are connected to it very strongly indeed. Maclure and Taylor acknowledge this when they say, 'the more a belief is linked to an individual's sense of moral integrity ... the stronger must be the legal protection it enjoys' (2011: 76).

When deciding whether an exemption or special treatment should be accorded to a meaning-giving practice which is a matter of conscience, the liberal state has to apply the same tests as it would to any demand for exemption or special treatment. Laborde rules out even considering exemptions for IPCs which are 'morally abhorrent'; they are to be rejected out of hand (she offers ritual infanticide as an example) (2017: 207–9). If the practice is morally acceptable in itself, or perhaps morally ambivalent (Laborde 2017), then one must proceed to weigh up the consequences of granting the exemption. Is the practice harmful? Does it impose unacceptable, unreasonable burdens on others? The specialness of the belief or practice does not bypass the need to consider those questions. Maclure and Taylor give the example of Jehovah's Witness parents in Canada who for religious reasons refused to allow their very sick child a blood transfusion; the hospital overrode their wishes and gave the treatment, and the Supreme Court of Canada upheld the hospital's decision. Maclure and Taylor endorse this judgement, because 'respect for the parents' rights was obviously too great an infringement on the right to life of a minor, namely, their child' (2011: 101).

This is a life-or-death situation, but in less extreme dilemmas, too, the right of religious or other meaning-giving beliefs has to be weighed against the consequences to others of accommodation. In particular, public laws which are there for good reasons are not to be set aside as lightly as one would set aside a mere custom or convention. As Cécile Laborde has argued:

> A democratic law which serves a legitimate public purpose should not routinely be discarded as an arbitrary customary rule, and exemptions to it should not be

allowed, even if it generates disproportionate burdens on members of minorities. I see no rationale, for example, for granting religious groups exemptions from the civil law of marriage and filiations.

(2008: 96)

I conclude that, although freedom of conscience may sometimes be a good reason for accommodation, religious conscience is not more special than other types of conscience. Not all religious believers take their religion with equal seriousness, and non-religious matters of conscience can be taken as seriously as religious matters of conscience. Moreover, moral conscience does not automatically get a free pass. The consequences for others, in terms of harms or serious burdens, have to be weighed against the right to follow one's conscience.

In the case of the burqa, therefore, requests for exemptions in institutions where the rules would normally require faces to be uncovered would have to be backed by:

1. evidence that burqa-wearing was for that individual strongly linked to their sense of moral integrity (merely stating that it was a religious requirement would not be enough). This might seem a difficult thing to establish, but as Laborde points out, '[s]incerity tests are commonly used by judges in all areas of law' and '[j]udges have, in practice, not found it hard to identify clear cases of religious fraud' (Laborde 2017: 207);
2. a convincing case that keeping the face covered would not cause harms or impose unreasonable burdens on others.

We should note that other kinds of demand for accommodation, not just those based on religious or moral conscience, must also satisfy the second of those conditions. In Chapter 8 I explore the issue of multiculturalism, and how the right to *recognition* (acknowledgement and respect for the cultural identity of minority groups), could back demands for accommodation. Here, too, recognition must be limited by the requirement not to cause harms or impose unreasonable burdens on others.

But this is to anticipate. It is first necessary to establish what the baseline liberal position on habitual public face-covering should be, before considering complicating factors. In the Chapter 3 I aim to arrive at a *pure* liberal position on face-covering, stripped of all considerations of nationality, history, republicanism, religion or any other cultural factors. The idea is to establish that, in the context-free world I sketch out, liberals would have no reason to outlaw voluntary habitual public face-covering. Obviously that is not the end of the argument. But it is a useful beginning.

3

The liberal position on habitual public face-covering per se

The argument

I consider what the liberal position on habitual public face-covering per se should be. I use a stripped-down scenario, shorn of religious or cultural context, as a thought experiment. The aim is to see what response to face-covering per se liberal principles generate in the abstract. I argue for a baseline position in which habitual public face-covering, provided it is voluntary, is to be tolerated; but certain situations might require *temporary* removal of the face-covering. This is a preliminary step; later chapters will explore whether that response still applies when cultural factors are given their due. (In fact, I shall be arguing that the abstract liberal response to voluntary habitual public face-covering per se is surprisingly durable.)

3.1 What is so special about the human face?

3.1.1 A visiting extraterrestrial

A visiting extraterrestrial would find it noteworthy that in public, in all societies, humans are allowed to cover their bodies, limbs and hands and feet, and obliged to cover their genitals, but that the covering of the face is rare, and problematic. The extraterrestrial would observe that the face is nearly always on show in public, except for temporary coverings required for protection in certain situations (welders' masks, motorcycle helmets, surgeons' masks, etc.), and that individuals who cover their faces outside of such situations tend to be viewed with suspicion: bandits, assassins, bank robbers and others of sinister intent often cover their faces, and in the films, plays and books that humans create such sinister characters are frequently depicted in this way. The extraterrestrial would observe that photographs of faces (not other body parts) are routinely used for many forms of identification – passports, driving licences, staff passes and so on. The extraterrestrial would also observe that the face occupies a prominent position in the arts across millennia and across a wide range of cultures: from ancient Egyptian sculptures and paintings to Greek and Roman busts and statues, tribal masks from all over Africa and South America, heads cast in brass and bronze from the Kingdom of Benin, representations of the face in Japanese art and in the European genre of portraiture; to representations in literature where, especially in the novel form, detailed descriptions of faces are frequent; to celebrations of the face in song ('I've Just Seen a Face', 'Baby Face', 'You're Beautiful', 'The First Time Ever I Saw your Face', etc.). In films and television programmes close-ups linger on faces, and the faces of famous stars are instantly, globally recognisable. In advertisements, joyful or amazed faces are used to advertise all manner of products. In the houses of Earth people photographs of family' members' faces are often on display, and many carry photos of loved ones' faces around in their wallets or on their phones. Would-be daters post pictures of their faces on dating websites.

The extraterrestrial would note that no other part of the body is so frequently on display and would conclude that the face must be of special significance to human beings: that covering it up is different in important ways from covering other parts of the body. And the extraterrestrial would be right.

The face occupies a special, transcultural importance in human society in a number of key ways. Emmanuel Levinas states, in *Totality and Infinity*, that ethics begins with the face-to-face encounter: 'the onset of the other, as the expression of the face ... opens a "me" to goodness' (Bergo 2017). Levinas's is a phenomenological account which I do not follow here, but a similar conclusion can be reached through a more scientific approach.

The face is far more significant for human beings than for other species. Other animals focus on the face to a much lesser extent or not at all. A peahen is more interested in looking at the tail than the face of a peacock. Dogs are more interested in scent than in visual appearance of any kind. It is only among the primates that the face is important, and among primates none have such expressive, mobile, distinctive faces as humans, or rely on them so heavily for communication.

Human babies learn to recognise faces early in life. Research by Michelle de Haan and Charles A. Nelson quotes studies which suggest that infants can recognise the mother's face 'shortly after birth' (1997: 187). The research paper

'Recognition of the Mother's Face by Six-Month-Old Infants: A Neurobehavioural Study' recorded ERP (event-related potentials – i.e. 'transient changes in the brain's electrical activity') when infants were shown videos of the faces of their mothers and those of strangers; the results showed that the infants distinguished between the mother's face and strangers' faces, but perceptual analysis took slightly longer when the face of the stranger was similar to that of the mother (1997: 209).

There is a whole region of the brain devoted to face recognition, the fusiform face area (Kanwisher et al. 1997). It is so good at its job that it often causes us to see faces in places where they are not: clouds, tree bark, pizzas and so on. This in itself tells us that there must be something important to us about other people's faces: so complex and costly a mechanism would not evolve without a pay-off, although it is still unclear exactly when this mechanism evolved or what specific selection pressures led to its evolution (Burke and Sulikowski 2013).

3.1.2 Why the human face is important: Identification and communication

There are at least two reasons why the face is so important. One is that it is the swiftest and most reliable means of identifying a person. Except for the faces of identical twins, each human face is unique. Identifying other individuals is vital for a species as social and as complex as *Homo sapiens*. A glance at another's face is enough to fix them in your social world: are they family? Friends? Enemies? Strangers? Before a word has been spoken you know your relationship with them, what duties you owe them or they owe you and what kind of treatment you can expect from them or they from you.

Second, faces express emotions. Darwin theorised in *The Expression of Emotions in Man and Animals* ([1872]1965) that the most basic human expressions are universal, and many subsequent studies have supported this (Ekman 2015). It is true that some have disputed Darwin's theory; the psychologist Lisa Feldman-Barrett has argued that facial expressions are not universal but depend for their meaning on contextual clues and thus are culturally dependent (2014). Even if Feldman-Barrett's objection holds up, however – and it is disputed by Ekman and others (2014) – it would remain true that facial expressions convey emotions in given cultural contexts.

A glance at another's face tells you not merely who they are and what their relationship is to you, but also tells you what mood they are in and what you can expect from them, or what is expected from you. For social animals like ourselves, recognising the emotions of others (and being able to express our own emotions knowing they will be understood) is vital. Seeing that someone is angry gives us a cue as to how to respond; we might get ready to defend ourselves, or hasten to mollify them. Seeing that someone is sad or in pain might make us want to alleviate their suffering; being able to convey our own sadness or pain might call forth much-needed help for ourselves. It has been found that facial expressions are the most effective triggers to empathy – far more effective than speech. Facial mirroring – imitating the expression of the face of the person before you – is often used unconsciously to convey empathy, triggered by mirror neurons in the brain (Iacoboni 2008).

The face, then, clearly signals to us that other people have emotions, needs, interests. I should like to stipulate that ethics necessarily involves paying due attention to the emotions, needs and interests of others. If this is granted, then Levinas is at least partially right when he says that ethics begins when we look into another's face. Contemplation of another's face can tell us what they are thinking and feeling, and this can be a trigger for ethical impulses. It is for this reason that charitable organisations use photographs of the faces of starving, sick or otherwise suffering individuals, especially children, in their appeals for donations.

The face is not the only trigger to ethical impulses. The voice is another. But the voice is not normally an *alternative* to the face as a signifier. They normally work in concert. And if there is a discrepancy between them – if the voice utters cheerful words while the face looks in pain – it is generally the face we trust.

Moreover, the face is a constant signifier, always there to be looked at, not turned on and off like the voice. Thus the face can reveal not just static emotions but a continuous play of them. In social intercourse with another person we are able to monitor their facial expressions, whether consciously, semi-consciously or unconsciously, and can update and modify our own speech, behaviour and facial expressions accordingly. This facility makes it possible for face-to-face ethical behaviour to be fine-tuned as one goes along. (Of course, the face is helpful in this way not just for good ethical impulses but for bad ones too, from teasing to torture.)

Faces communicate not only emotions but also age, health and well-being. It is often possible to tell from a glance at someone's face that they are tired or unwell. This, too, acts as a trigger for ethical impulses.

But the face's role in ethics is not merely that of a trigger. It is worth noting that humans have extraordinarily good memories for faces. We easily conjure up faces in the imagination or in dreams. Nor do most people have difficulty recognising a face they have seen before, even if only fleetingly, though recalling the name that goes with it tends to be harder. (Lack of facility in this area is noteworthy enough to merit a medical term, prosopagnosia: see McNeil and Warrington 1993: 1–10). The face's role in ethics is thus not confined to face-to-face encounters. The recollection of someone's face helps to mark them out as an individual, a subject and the object of ethical impulses.

I do not claim that we can only behave ethically towards people whose faces we have seen. But it is plausible to suggest that our life's experience of having recognised and responded to thoughts and feelings expressed in others' faces gives us the understanding, empathy and motivation to treat unseen others as deserving recipients of ethical consideration. We *attribute* faces to them, one might say. It seems far less plausible that a lifetime's experience of having recognised and responded to thoughts and feelings expressed in others' faces has nothing at all to do with our ethical consideration of unseen others.

For these reasons, covering one's face in public on a habitual basis is very different indeed from covering one's feet, hair or any other body part.

3.1.3 Three qualifications

There are three qualifications to add. The first is that neither identification nor gauging of emotion by the face is *guaranteed* to be reliable. 'There's no art/ To find the mind's construction in the face', says King Duncan in *Macbeth* (Shakespeare [*c*. 1606] 1987: 1002), and it is true that one can look friendly while harbouring hostile thoughts, or interested while bored. It is even possible to disguise one's face and pass for someone else, as shown by the existence of actors and impostors. Still, such deceptions would not be possible if the face were not usually a reliable guide. And an alert face reader can often detect dissembling.

The second qualification is that the face is not the *sole* means of identification, or of conveying feelings and thoughts. This can also be achieved very efficiently through speech. Blind people, after all, succeed in identifying people and do not have emotionally stunted lives, nor, clearly, are they incapable of ethics. We are able to conduct satisfactory telephone conversations without (usually) being deceived or puzzled about the identity of the caller, nor do we (usually) find ourselves in doubt about the emotional state of the person at the other end.

Nevertheless, blindness is not optimal either for recognising others, or for gauging their emotions. While it is possible to convey and detect great subtlety in speech, from word choice, intonation, stress and so on, communication would nearly always be enhanced by facial expressions. Indeed, it is noticeable that blind people use a range of facial expressions themselves, which convey information to a sighted audience. Presumably this would not be the case if *everyone* was blind, that is if we were a blind species. Then faces and facial expressions would not be of the smallest importance. But then we would have evolved very differently and our cultures would have developed very differently, and the extraterrestrial would carry home a very different report.

Finally, it is also true that, as much as would be lost by habitual public face-covering, there might be compensatory advantages for the individual. They might prefer not to be stared at; they might prefer not to be judged on their looks or to attract unwanted sexual attention. If an individual decided for these reasons to habitually cover their face in public, however, they would disadvantage themselves in certain important respects, and would be likely to cause inconvenience to other people. That is not to justify a ban, but to reiterate the point that habitual public covering of the face is a highly significant act with consequences for the self and others.

3.1.4 More than a sartorial issue

Clearly it is disingenuous of opponents of anti-face-covering laws to claim that it is all a lot of fuss about how people dress, an excessive reaction to 'a piece of cloth'. It is not a sartorial issue. This can be seen if we imagine that concealing the face could be achieved by some other means than covering it with material. Suppose there were some kind of scrambling device that caused a shimmering haze to hover in front of a person's face (without impeding their vision), so that others could not identify them or make out any facial expression. This would raise exactly the same issues as face-covering by means of clothing.

If a person were forced to cover their face in public at all times that would be a serious harm. I argue this in some detail in Chapter 11. At this point I note that it would cause difficulties in communicating emotions and state of mind, making it impossible, for example, to smile at others; and it would inhibit empathy from those around, causing the facially covered person to be overlooked and unconsidered, leading to social isolation. It hardly needs to be said that a liberal would be strongly against coercing somebody to cover up in this way. But voluntary facial covering is a different matter.

Two thought experiments aim to explore how the liberal state should react to voluntary face-covering by citizens. I have stripped the scenarios of all cultural or religious context, to identify what the liberal response should be to the practice per se.

3.1.5 Thought experiment 1: The Lone Face-Coverer

Suppose that there were no such thing as the burqa, no religious or cultural custom of women covering their faces in public. Now suppose that an individual person (their sex is immaterial) decided to wear, habitually, a garment that completely covered their face. Their reasons for doing so do not matter. Perhaps as suggested earlier they do not like being stared at or judged on their looks; perhaps they are morbidly sensitive about their appearance; perhaps they wish to cultivate a sense of mystique. But in this thought experiment there is no culture or tradition within which such a practice is normal. It is simply the personal preference of an individual (we will refer to them as the Lone Face-Coverer). How should a liberal state respond?

There does not seem to be any prima facie reason why a liberal state should respond at all. Liberals generally oppose restricting the liberty of individuals unless their actions are demonstrably harmful to others. It is not clear how the Lone Face-Coverer is harming anybody else by concealing their face. They might make others feel puzzled, frustrated or uncomfortable: but such transient feelings can hardly be characterised as harm. Perhaps some people might object that not being able to see the Face-Coverers' face caused *offence*; indeed, as I argue in Chapter 9, following Joel Feinberg (1985), there are occasions when prevention of offence would be a legitimate liberal reason for banning a practice. However, the offence in this case seems neither severe, persistent nor inescapable enough to justify a ban (a conclusion argued for in greater detail in Chapter 9).

More seriously, the Lone Face-Coverer would disadvantage themselves. They would be cut off from a great many normal social interactions, unable to communicate through facial expressions and therefore more likely to be overlooked and ignored. Certainly, as claimed earlier, if one was *forced* to cover one's face at all times in public that would be a serious harm. But this is not the case with the Lone Face-Coverer, who has chosen voluntarily to cover up. Liberals are suspicious of paternalist policies, and though I will argue in Chapter 4 for a Liberal Paternalist Principle, which permits intervention where restriction of liberty is small and the benefits great, this would not seem to be a case for it. Banning someone from covering their face, which would affect how they appear in public all the time, is a large restriction of liberty. Their behaviour would certainly disadvantage them, but it is not life-threatening or health-destroying, and it is not irrevocable. The Lone Face-Coverer could uncover whenever they liked. The liberal state therefore would not have any reason, either from the

Harm Principle, the Offence Principle or from paternalism, to prevent the Lone Face-Coverer from covering their face.

Habitual public face-covering could, however, cause inconvenience to others on certain occasions. There might be situations where for reasons of security, identification or communication, the Lone Face-Coverer would be requested to *temporarily* uncover. Banks, for example, have rules requiring customers to remove motorcycle helmets as a precaution against robbery. If the Lone Face-Coverer was requested to unmask and refused to do so, the liberal state should support the right of the bank to see its customers' faces in the interests of security, against the right of the customer to stay masked. Requiring unmasking in such a case is not treating the Lone Face-Coverer unfairly. They would be following the same rule as everybody else. Moreover, the rule is clearly there for a sensible reason. The Lone Face-Coverer has no reason of their own, other than a personal preference, to demand an exemption. And personal preference is not a good-enough reason for exemption from a rule. If it were, then the very idea of having rules would be imperilled.

Matters would be different if the Lone Face-Coverer could offer a substantive reason for exemption, based on some relevant fact about their personal circumstances. If the Lone Face-Coverer had severe scarring or a facial disfigurement which they were too self-conscious to expose in public, that could justify special treatment, and some other means of identification could be used. There would be a reasonable case for exemption based on unequal impact; the rule about uncovering would impact more harshly on this person than on others, for a reason over which they had no control. Even then it is by no means clear that the bank would be *obliged* to grant an exemption. Other factors would need to be weighed. Allowing the Lone Face-Coverer to frequent the bank with their face covered could open the way to others imitating the Lone Face-Coverer and entering the bank unchallenged with the intent to rob it.

Parallel considerations apply for other institutions where security, identity or communication are important, such as law courts, airports, hospitals, schools and so on. The liberal state, therefore, would support the right of institutions to require temporary unmasking, (absent legitimate claims for exemption, which would have to be weighed on a case-by-case basis). Apart from that, the liberal state has no reason to concern itself if an individual citizen wishes to cover their face while going about their daily business. The existence of the Lone Face-Coverer would provide no liberal justification for a general ban on public face-covering.

3.1.6 Thought experiment 2: The Face-Coverers

Let us now imagine that the example of the Lone Face-Coverer catches on. Soon there are hundreds or thousands, or tens of thousands of Face-Coverers. Let us assume there is still no religious motive for covering up. The Face-Coverers do it from personal preference. Perhaps it is a fashion statement. They include men and women in equal numbers. Is there any call now for the liberal state to intervene?

The Face-Coverers would face all the same problems as the Lone Face-Coverers, with two additional ones. First, the Face-Coverers would experience difficulty in recognising *one another* and in gauging each others' emotional states. Thus communication, and hence some forms of ethical behaviour, among the Face-Coverers themselves would be hampered. Second, the Face-Coverers would be likely to encounter greater suspicion and mistrust from the unmasked portion of the population than the Lone Face-Coverer did.

This brings us to the effect on others. The same problems arise for others as they did for the Lone Face-Coverer, but they would be multiplied by the number of people covering up. Concerns about security would be greater. Nor would those concerns be irrational; for, the greater the number of people who were masked, the greater the likelihood that one or some of them could have nefarious intent. Moreover, the existence of the Face-Coverers would make it possible for opportunists to imitate the Face-Coverers in order to commit crimes.

How should the liberal state respond? First, we can continue to rule out a ban on paternalist grounds. The disadvantages of face-covering are still not so great as to justify the major restriction on liberty of forcing someone to uncover. As before, such disadvantages are neither permanent nor irrevocable. If any of the Face-Coverers find their regime too personally disadvantageous, then they can always make the decision themselves to give it up.

But could a ban be justified on grounds of preventing harm to others? Not on the grounds of feelings of annoyance, mistrust or insecurity that unmasked people might have. Negative feelings do not qualify as harms. And although I shall later argue (Chapter 9) that the prevention of serious, intense and prolonged offence could be a good reason for a liberal state to ban a practice, the transient annoyance or mistrust occasioned by passing a facially covered person in the street does not qualify as serious offence. One can dislike or disapprove of facial covering, of course. But disliking or disapproving of someone else's behaviour or lifestyle gives liberals no right to suppress it.

But suppose the existence of the Face-Coverers led to an increase in serious crimes. Then a ban might be justified. It would depend on how events played out. If it turned out to be the case that the existence of the Face-Coverers led to a marked increase in robberies, assaults, rapes and murders by masked criminals (whether by the regular Face-Coverers themselves or by impostors), and if that increase could be definitely linked to the practice of face-covering, then there would be solid grounds for a ban. This would be hard on the law-abiding portion of the Face-Coverers. Their contribution to the crime-rise would be unwitting. Nevertheless, a ban would be justified, as preventing much greater harms than not being able to satisfy the preference to cover one's face in public (the arguments for this conclusion are presented in detail in Chapter 11).

Whether there would actually be any such crime-rise is an empirical question. In the absence of a crime-rise a liberal state would seem to have no grounds for a ban. As before, though, the liberal state should still support the right of institutions to require temporary uncovering of the face for reasons of security, identification or communication.

3.2 A question of technology

It might be that technological innovations would make the need for such temporary uncoverings less frequent. Technologies such as iris recognition, voice recognition and so on, could be used in some cases where identification was required. A liberal state should not support the right of institutions to require temporary unmasking for the sake of it, if other, equally efficacious and convenient methods of confirming identity, ensuring security or allowing communication were available. But they would have to be equally efficacious and convenient. That would have to be judged on a case-by-case basis.

Here is a final dilemma to consider. Imagine that a new kind of x-ray spectacles were invented, which allowed wearers to see straight through any facial coverings (to avoid red herrings about inappropriate use, let us also suppose that the spectacles come equipped with a block which prevents the wearer from ogling other parts of the body). In this case, officials in banks, courts, airports, schools and so on would not require temporary unmasking. The officials could wear the new x-ray spectacles. Indeed, perhaps everyone could wear them, not just officials. Would that solve all the problems? Or is that a violation of the rights of the Face-Coverers?

Let us distinguish between (1) officials wearing the x-ray spectacles and (2) ordinary individuals wearing them. Officials who wore them would be doing so to enable them to carry out their job, with its requirements of being able to identify and/or communicate with the public. That is a legitimate reason, which ought to outweigh personal preferences. The x-ray spectacles would simply be a substitute for requiring temporary unmasking (which a liberal state would support), and one might think a more acceptable form for the Face-Coverers (they do not have the inconvenience of doffing and re-donning their masks, and no one but designated officials can see their faces).

When we turn to ordinary individuals wearing x-ray-spectacles, the case is different. Members of the public who wore the x-ray-spectacles just because they were frustrated at not being able to see the Face-Coverers' faces would be doing so from personal preference. But the Face-Coverers too want to exercise a personal preference: not to have their faces looked at. If we weigh the two preferences against each other, the preference of the Face-Coverers should win out. A Face-Coverer's face does, after all, belong to them. If they do not like being stared at or judged on their looks or attracting unwanted sexual attention or if they have any other reason for covering that seems good to them, that is their own affair. For a non-official to use x-ray spectacles to see a Face-Coverer's face, simply from preference, is an unwarrantable invasion of privacy. We might think that the Face-Coverers have an extreme notion of privacy, but then it is their privacy, not ours.

3.3 Summary of the liberal position on face-covering per se

To sum up: a liberal state should support the right of individuals to cover their face in public from personal preference; with two provisos.

One, that in cases where institutions asked for temporary unmasking, for reasons of identification, security or communication, the liberal state should support the right of those institutions to require it (absent any sound reason for exemption, with personal preference not counting as a sound reason).

Two, if it should turn out to be the case that face-covering became widespread enough to facilitate a rise in anonymous actions which caused serious harms, then a liberal state would be justified in banning it. But the justification for the ban would be to remove the harms, not based on any objection in principle to face-covering.

None of this is to suggest that liberals would or should like or approve of habitual voluntary face-covering. They are free to dislike and disapprove of it and to say so. But they must tolerate it (with the provisos above) because that is what being a liberal entails. This position, arrived at without any consideration of religious or cultural issues, turns out to be the same in essentials as that argued for by Russell Blackford in the case of burqa-wearing, in *Freedom, Religion and the Secular State* (2012).

4

What kind of liberalism?

The argument

In this chapter I aim to establish three main points.

First, that there are two main types of liberal theory, best thought of as opposite ends of a spectrum, rather than two sides of a dichotomy: the types being Political Liberalism (PL) and Perfectionist Liberalism.

Second, that both types of liberal states could theoretically be justified in banning the burqa on the grounds of preventing negative impact on others. This is not to argue that either type of liberal state *would be* so justified. That would depend on whether there *was* any negative impact, and if there was, on its severity and extent.

Third, that a perfectionist state (or one towards the perfectionist end of the spectrum) could theoretically be justified in banning the burqa on paternalist grounds. No such justification is open to a political liberal state.

4.1 The liberalism of John Stuart Mill

One of the most influential of liberalism's founding texts is John Stuart Mill's *On Liberty*, published in 1859. Mill is commonly regarded as a perfectionist liberal (Donatelli 2006). However, *On Liberty* contains elements of both types of theory. Mill argues, on the one hand, that '[t]here is a limit to the *legitimate* interference with collective independence' ([1859] 2005: 7; my italics); and again that

> the sole end for which mankind are *warranted*, individually or collectively, in interfering with the liberty of action of one of their number is self-protection. That the only purpose for which power can *rightfully* be exercised over a member of a civilised community, is to prevent harm to others.
>
> ([1859] 2005: 13; my italics)

These principles are based on what is *just* or *rightful*, not on the likely beneficial effects to follow if they were put into practice, and thus form the basis for a theory of political liberalism.

Mill does also believe that putting these principles into practice would lead to beneficial consequences for individuals and for society. His argument in favour of freedom of thought and expression is based on the claim that allowing heterodox opinions to be published gives people 'the opportunity of exchanging error for truth', should a heterodox opinion be right; and, should it be false, gives them the benefit of 'the clearer perception and livelier impression of truth produced by its collision with error' ([1859] 2005: 21). Moreover, a society in which not only diverse opinions but diverse modes of life are permitted allows every individual to develop in their own way, which is desirable because

> Human nature is not a machine to be built after a model, and set to do exactly the work prescribed for it, but a tree, which requires to grow and develop itself on all sides, according to the tendency of the inward forces which make it a living thing.
>
> (Mill [1859] 2005: 72)

And again:

> It is not by wearing down into uniformity, but by cultivating and calling it forth… that human beings become a noble and beautiful object of contemplation; and as the works partake the character of those who do them, by the same process human life becomes rich, diversified, and animating.
>
> (Mill [1859] 2005: 76)

This emphasis on the beneficial effects of liberty, according to a comprehensive idea of what is good – the ideal of individuality – could form the basis for a theory of liberal perfectionism.

Mill himself, however, did not see these two elements of his theory as potential rivals, nor distinguish between them. The one was a natural and inevitable consequence of the other: allow everyone as much freedom as is just, and a diverse society of fully realised individuals with rich existences follows. Subsequently, however, the two elements have diverged, and developed into the competing theories of political liberalism and liberal perfectionism.

4.2 Political liberalism

4.2.1 The political liberalism of John Rawls

The fullest account of PL is given by John Rawls in his book *Political Liberalism* (2005). PL is an attempt to answer the question:

> how is it possible for there to exist over time a just and stable society of free and equal citizens, who remain profoundly divided by reasonable religious, philosophical, and moral doctrines?
>
> (Rawls 2005: 4)

This encapsulates three essential ideas of PL: (1) society is to be 'just and stable', (2) citizens are to be 'free and equal' and (3) pluralism of reasonable comprehensive doctrines is to be tolerated.

Together these three ideas commit PL to *neutrality* regarding reasonable comprehensive doctrines. The politically liberal state must make no attempt to favour one reasonable comprehensive doctrine over another.

What counts as a reasonable comprehensive doctrine is crucial in determining how the political liberal responds to the practice of burqa-wearing, and so the term repays closer examination. The words *reasonable* and *comprehensive* play different roles. *Comprehensive* (meaning covering every aspect of life in a unified, interrelated system of values and beliefs) is not an entrance requirement for tolerance. It is a permission. The claim is that *even if* a doctrine is comprehensive it is eligible for tolerance. This sets the bar high, for competing doctrines which are comprehensive are likely to disagree at more points, and more fundamentally, than those which are not comprehensive. If reasonable comprehensive doctrines are to be tolerated, then reasonable *non*-comprehensive doctrines – those which are composed of an unsystematic patchwork of values – are to be tolerated a fortiori. That non-comprehensive doctrines are not excluded from tolerance is made clear by Rawls's own model case of an overlapping consensus (OC), in which one of the three parties to the consensus is not comprehensive: it is

> not systematically unified: besides the political values formulated by freestanding political conception of justice, it includes a large family of non-political values. It is a pluralist view.
>
> (2005: 145)

The term *reasonable,* on the other hand, *is* an entry requirement. Only doctrines which are reasonable merit tolerance. Rawls identifies a comprehensive doctrine as reasonable if it has three features: it is an exercise of theoretical reason, that is it is a coherent system of compatible values covering the major aspects of human life; it is an exercise of practical reason, in that it provides the wherewithal for singling out and balancing values in cases of conflict, and it is based on a tradition of thought, evolving only slowly (2005: 59).

Two points need to be made. The first is that of these three features, only the first two are prescriptive. Doctrines have to be exercises of theoretical and practical reason, or they are not reasonable. But the third feature is descriptive. A reasonable comprehensive doctrine *'tends to'* evolve slowly (Rawls 2005: 59; my italics), but it is not necessary for its reasonableness that it do so. Moreover, *non-comprehensive doctrine*s may not be based on established traditions of thought at all, and may spring into being and develop rapidly, yet still be reasonable.

The second point is that Rawls's definition here says nothing about the *content* of the doctrine. However, a crucial limitation on content is entailed by Rawls's requirement that such doctrines be held by *reasonable persons*; that is by those who

> desire for its own sake a social world in which they, as free and equal, can co-operate with others on terms all can accept
>
> (2005: 50)

This entails a commitment to reciprocity: reasonable persons 'insist that reciprocity should hold within that world so that each benefits along with others' (Rawls 2005: 50). The reciprocity requirement rules out doctrines held by those who consider certain others to be natural inferiors, whose interests can be given less or no weight. It would rule out a doctrine which endorsed slavery, for example; and it would rule out a doctrine which held that women's interests count for less or are more easily set aside than those of men.

The question is how competing reasonable comprehensive views can coexist in a society that remains just and stable, and in which citizens remain free and equal. The first stage of the answer is that each comprehensive view is to be guaranteed tolerance by the politically liberal state, but *not enforced*. To take Rawls's own example (2005: 138), it is reasonable, in his sense of the term, to hold the principle of *extra ecclesiam nulla salus* (outside the church there is no salvation), and the liberal state would intervene to prevent persecution or discrimination against those who profess that belief. But the liberal state must not enforce that belief (by fining people for not attending church, for instance).

For it is equally reasonable to disbelieve it. As Rawls notes, declining to enforce such a belief does not mean the liberal state denies its truth (2005: 138). It should express no view on the matter. The point is that it would be unreasonable to enforce truth-claims on which reasonable people disagree.

4.2.2 The overlapping consensus

That is only the first part of the answer to Rawls's question. State-enforced tolerance is a modus vivendi, but not necessarily a stable one. The competing parties have as yet no reason to refrain from imposing their own doctrine on the others if they had the power to do so. Rawls's answer to this is that over time an *overlapping consensus* can and should develop, via the intermediate stage of a political consensus. In other words, each competing party will go beyond merely submitting to state-enforced tolerance and will come to endorse and feel allegiance to a liberal political conception of justice, one that lies outside their own comprehensive doctrine and under which all citizens are treated as reasonable, free and equal (Rawls's favoured candidate for this role is, naturally enough, his own conception of justice as fairness). Rawls's contention is that 'gradually, as the success of political cooperation continues, citizens gain increasing confidence and trust in one another' (2005: 168), and thus the OC is formed.

The OC is not merely a *convergence* of doctrines, like a central Lego block, to which different-coloured bricks could be attached from different sides, without actually touching each other. Although parties to the OC may each hold comprehensive doctrines which are in competition with one another, they must also *share* reasons for accepting a consensus based on principles of justice that treat all citizens as fair, reasonable and equal. This sharing of reasons is why the consensus is *overlapping*; it is not an assemblage of non-touching Lego bricks, but the sweet spot of a Venn diagram.

There are other views of the type of consensus necessary for a liberal polity. Gerald Gaus and Richard Vallier argue for a convergent consensus, where signatories need not share any of the same reasons, but need only have mutually intelligible reasons (Gaus and Vallier 2009). Thus, some people might sign up to the consensus as card-carrying political liberals; others might sign up because they have religious authority for the belief that there should be no compulsion in religion (*Koran* 2:256, trans. Arberry 2008); still others might sign up simply because, having had cause to cooperate with those holding conflicting doctrines, they have developed goodwill towards them, and have no wish to suppress the sincere if wrong-headed doctrines of their friends. These reasons would be mutually intelligible, but no one reason unites all three parties. And in this case there is no clash between the reasons. They simply do not touch. However, I think it can be shown that intelligibility is not a satisfactory criterion and that mere convergence is not enough for a stable liberal polity.

Let us imagine a person, or group – let us call them the Give-'Em-Enough-Rope Tendency – joining the OC because they believe that it allows unbelievers to persist in their unbelief and hence end up in hell, which is where they deserve to be.[1] This emerges from a sincerely held reasonable comprehensive doctrine and supplies a firm reason for signing up to the OC. Moreover it is easily intelligible and leads to a convergent consensus.

But it does not feel quite right that a group should join the convergent liberal consensus for such deeply illiberal reasons. Consider another version of the Give-'Em-Enough-Rope tendency, who locate their pay-off in this world rather than the next. Imagine an extreme sect accepting the OC for precisely the opposite reason to that urged by Rawls: they join the consensus not because they believe it makes society stable, but because they believe it makes it *un*stable. They are certain that a pluralist society carries within it the seeds of its own destruction. Therefore they embrace the OC with real enthusiasm, because it appears to guarantee that in the long run decadent pluralistic societies will collapse, riven by internal dissensions, and leave the way clear for the sect to establish their theocracy. Let us be clear that they do not accept the OC as a *faute de mieux*; they are convinced that it is the surest way, ultimately, to achieve the kind of society that their god wants, though that might not happen in their own lifetimes. Again, this is intelligible and leads to a convergence. But the reasons leading to that convergence are so *di*vergent that it does not seem to qualify as a consensus.

The Rawlsian political liberal would urge that the entry requirement for the OC is that the comprehensive doctrines of joiners must be held by *reasonable persons*; that is, by those who 'desire for its own sake a social world in which they, as free and equal, can co-operate with others on terms all can accept' (Rawls 2005: 50). Neither version of the Give-'Em-Enough-Rope Tendency values a social world of free and equal citizens for its own sake. They value it only as a

---

[1] I am reminded of the story about an old-time Scottish hellfire preacher, who declaimed in a sermon: 'And after death, the sinners and the unbelievers will be tormented in the sulphurous fires of hell, and they will cry out and say "Lord, Lord, we didnae ken!" And the Lord will reply: "Well, ye ken noo!"'

means to an end. The reasons one joins the OC *do* matter, after all. They require a shared commitment to the ideal of a society of free and equal individuals.

Moreover, when political questions are deliberated in such a polity, arguments advanced must appeal to what Rawls called *public reason*: that is to say, they offer reasons that 'are reasons that reasonable persons as free and equal citizens, drawing on their favoured reasonable political conception of justice as well as general rules of enquiry and reasoning, sincerely believe other citizens will share as reasons from the point of view of free and equal citizenship' (Watson and Hartley 2018: 40). For example, suppose in deliberations about whether the burqa ought to be banned in public, one party contended that it should not be banned because that would override personal liberty of religion and expression, while another party to the debate agreed that it should not be banned, but for a different reason: that woman ought not to be allowed out uncovered in public. Their views converge as far as the law goes, and are mutually intelligible. But only the first is a *public reason,* that is one which assumes and relies on a commitment to free and equal citizenship.

The objection might be made that Rawls offers no evidence that his hope that many different doctrines would happen to agree on a liberal political conception of justice is warranted. Jurgen Habermas has critiqued Rawls on this point, arguing that he does not provide a justification for his political conception of justice which shows that people *ought to* accept it (Habermas 2011: 25–45).

This dispute will be left in abeyance for the moment. Jonathan Quong's position, discussed in Section 4.6, seems to offer a way out of the difficulty. But whether a deeper justification for the OC is a requisite or not, it is at any rate *possible* that an OC on a liberal political conception of justice could develop, and Rawls's schema has empirical evidence in its favour. There already exist broadly liberal societies, such as Great Britain and the United States, in which religious and cultural groups holding radically conflicting doctrines seem content to coexist and to accept the liberal political conception of justice which embraces them all. Such societies are only stable to the extent that there genuinely *is* an overlapping consensus, of course. It is always possible that groups within such societies may exploit the OC as a stalking horse, pretending to sign up while seeking ways of overthrowing the liberal political conception of justice. Still, such societies appear to be holding up well so far, and Rawls's view that people will eventually come to accept and endorse the political values of the state they live and breathe and work and socialise in does not seem psychologically or sociologically implausible on the face of it, even if no state in the world has yet realised the project completely.

4.2.3 The priority of right over good

Another key feature of PL is that it requires what Rawls terms 'the priority of right' over the good (2005: 173). This means that PL is concerned only with securing institutions and laws which are *just*. It must not try to impose or encourage lives which are *good*, because reasonable persons will disagree as to what counts as a good life. As Jonathan Quong puts it,

> the state should make no judgements about the goodness of citizens' lives. It should instead be concerned only with *justice:* with the just distribution of freedom, resources, and other advantages between citizens, ensuring that each is given a fair chance to develop and pursue his or her own conception of the good life.
>
> (Quong 2011: 1)

This conception of liberalism sets a high value on pluralism. Indeed, its purpose is to accommodate pluralism. It is taken as axiomatic that there will be competing conceptions of the good and that it is not the place of the state to favour any one over any other. In Section 4.4.2 I shall argue that *some* idea of the good is necessary even to PL. But the goal of PL would be to keep that idea as thin as possible.

4.2.4 Necessity of some form of harm principle

Under PL each citizen would be at liberty to pursue their own conception of the good. But for this to be possible, the state would sometimes need to restrict liberty to prevent harm to others. This was expressed by Mill in a formulation which has come to be called the harm principle:

> The only purpose for which power can be rightfully exercised over any member of a civilized community, against his will, is to prevent harm to others.
>
> (Mill [1859] 2005: 13)

The harm principle is a limiting principle. It delimits the area of justification according to which a government may intervene to restrict the liberty of citizens. As Richard Vernon notes, 'Mill's stress falls heavily on the exclusive aspect of his statement – we cannot impose legislation on you for your own good' (1996: 625). Moreover, not every case of harm would justify state intervention. As Mill says:

> It must by no mean be supposed, because damage, or probability of damage, to the interests of others can alone justify the interference of society, that therefore

it always does justify such interference. In many cases an individual, in pursuing a legitimate object, necessarily and therefore legitimately causes pain or loss to others, or intercepts a good which they had a reasonable hope of obtaining.

(Mill [1859] 2005: 114–15)

So, harm is not in itself a criterion for when the state may intervene and when it may not. Not all cases of harm justify intervention. The point is that whenever state intervention to restrict liberty *is* justified, it can only be on the grounds of preventing harm to others.

Rawls claims that Mill's liberalism is comprehensive: it urges a comprehensive view of the good life, one of individuality (2005: 375 n. 3). Mill is thus a comprehensive liberal. But he does not advocate that the state should actively seek to promote individuality. His harm principle is a principle of pure PL. Mill states:

[A person's] own good, either physical or moral, is not a sufficient warrant [for exercising power over that person against their will]. He cannot rightfully be compelled to do or forbear because it will be better for him to do so, because it will make him happier, because, in the opinions of others it would be wise or even right.

([1859] 2005: 13)

This would prevent the state's attempting to coerce citizens into the individuality which Mill himself so prizes. It is a cast-iron prohibition against imposing any comprehensive doctrine on anyone. PL requires such a principle. For without some form of harm principle, pluralism would not be possible. A political liberal need not use the *term* 'harm principle' (as Rawls does not); perhaps they would say that the requirement of a just distribution of freedom does all the necessary work. For, if my freedom includes the freedom to harm you, that lessens the amount of freedom available to you, which is unjust. Or perhaps they would say that the requirement that comprehensive doctrines be *reasonable* would rule out comprehensive doctrines which caused harm to others. For if my doctrine entitles me to harm you, while not granting you the same entitlement against me, then it offends against the principle of reciprocity; which is unreasonable.

In any case, the recognition that preventing harm to others is a legitimate reason for the exercise of state power takes care of two essential concerns of PL: my freedom to pursue my conception of the good life must not be allowed to prevent you pursuing your conception of the good life, and I must not interfere with your freedom to pursue your conception of the good life, unless it prevents me pursuing mine.

Mill's formulation of his principle, however, requires modification. He says that preventing harm to others is the *only* rightful reason for the exercise of state power, which is unnecessarily limiting even by his own lights. In chapter V of *On Liberty* Mill states:

> There are many acts which, being injurious only to the agents themselves, ought not to be legally interdicted but which, if done publicly, are a violation of good manners and, coming thus within the category of offences against others, may rightly be prohibited. Of this kind are offences against decency.
>
> ([1859] 2005: 119)

This suggests that preventing offence to others, as well as harm, may also be a legitimate reason for the exercise of state power. Mill also appears to countenance soft paternalism when he says that it would be justifiable to forcibly prevent someone crossing a bridge which they did not know to be unsafe (2005: 117). A pure Political Liberal would be reluctant to countenance paternalism, but (as I argue in Chapter 5) it is not so easy to rule out *tout court*. Given that (as argued in Section 4.6) there is a continuum between PL and perfectionism, a more open and flexible version of the harm principle would be useful, such as the one put forward by Joel Feinberg:

> It is always a good reason in support of penal legislation that it would probably be effective in preventing (eliminating, reducing) harm to persons other than the actor (the one prohibited from acting) *and* there is probably no other means that is equally effective at no greater cost to other values.
>
> (1985: 26)

This principle is less restrictive than Mill's in that it does not make preventing harm the *sole* reason for penal legislation which would restrict the liberty of the individual. This formulation of the principle also makes explicit that if there are other equally effective means available to prevent harm, they should be preferred to penal legislation. The principle in this form is acceptable to both political liberals and perfectionists and it is the formulation I employ when considering the issue of harm to others in Chapter 11.

4.3 Political liberalism and the burqa

How then would PL respond to the practice of burqa-wearing?

The first point to note, or to reiterate, is that PL could not countenance *compulsory* burqa-wearing. If a woman is compelled by her husband or relatives to cover her face in public, against her will, then she is neither free, nor equal with her male relatives. Nor could a comprehensive doctrine which stated that women, but not men, must have their faces and bodies covered in public (whether they like it or not) be termed reasonable. Coerced burqa-wearing is a harm. Forcing someone to cover her face infringes her liberty, makes her socially isolated, shuts down career opportunities, causes physical discomfort, may lead to vitamin D deficiency and associated health problems and so on. The politically liberal state would have a clear warrant and duty to put a stop to coerced burqa-wearing.

With *voluntary* burqa-wearing, however, the picture looks different. If the politically liberal state has a duty to intervene when a woman is forced to cover up, it has a duty, at least prima facie, not to intervene when she chooses to cover up. The same principle is at stake. Citizens should be allowed to pursue their own conception of the good. The politically liberal state is not there to enforce or encourage any one conception of the good above others. It must allow citizens to make their own choice about that. The political liberal must support the right of any woman to wear a burqa of her own free will. *Unless the practice causes harm to others.* This proviso will be looked at in detail in Chapter 11. The point to note here is that PL could *only* support banning the voluntary wearing of the burqa on grounds of a harm principle. Whether it actually does cause harm to others and whether a legal ban supported by penalties would be the best means of reducing or eliminating the harm are empirical questions.

4.4 Perfectionist liberalism

4.4.1 The doctrine of perfectionism

The major alternative within the tradition of liberalism to PL is perfectionist liberalism. Perfectionism is a moral theory, or perhaps tradition, found in Plato and Aristotle and running through Kant, Hegel and Marx, to contemporary writers such as Joseph Raz and Thomas Hurka. According to Hurka, perfectionism is a moral theory that

> starts from an account of the good human life, or the intrinsically desirable life. And it characterizes this life in a distinctive way. Certain properties, it says, constitute human nature or are definitive of humanity – they make humans humans. The good life, it then says, develops these properties to a high degree or realizes what is central to human nature. Different versions of the theory

may disagree about what the relevant properties are and so disagree about the content of the good life. But they share the foundational idea that what is good, ultimately, is the development of human nature.

(1993: 3)

Perfectionism in this broad sense is not necessarily liberal. Indeed, it may be inimical to liberalism if the good life is narrowly interpreted and if it is the role of the state to promote the good life. Plato's *Republic* ([*c*. 380 BCE] 2008) is perfectionist but it is not liberal.

Our concern here, however, is with *liberal* perfectionism. Liberal perfectionists hold that

it is at least sometimes permissible for a liberal state to promote or discourage particular activities, ideals or ways of life on grounds relating to their inherent or intrinsic value, or on the basis of other metaphysical claims.

(Quong 2011: 27)

Joseph Raz states the point in more extreme terms:

It is the goal of all political action to enable individuals to pursue valid conceptions of the good and to discourage evil or empty ones.

(2009: 133)

4.4.2 The path from political liberalism to perfectionist liberalism

The two approaches appear to be alternatives. Yet there is a clear path from one to the other. Even if one's conception of political justice is restricted purely to very basic principles about what rights citizens should have, one has to make assumptions about what kind of rights are suitable – which depends on a theory, however skeletal, about what is good for people. Rawls himself in *A Theory of Justice* acknowledges the need for a 'thin theory of the good' in order for rational choosers to have any basis for choice. He imagines that choosers in the Original Position would have such a thin theory:

Other things equal, they prefer a wider to a narrower liberty and opportunity, and a greater rather than a smaller share of wealth and income. That these things are good seems clear enough… I have also said that self-respect and a sure confidence in the sense of one's own worth is perhaps the most important primary good.

(1999: 348)

But this inevitably opens the possibility of thickening one's theory of the good. If it is 'clear enough' that wider liberty and a greater share of wealth as well as self-respect and a sense of self-worth are good, then why not include other goods whose goodness is also clear enough? One might add that, other things equal, citizens would prefer longer lives rather than shorter; better health rather than worse; sufficient food rather than insufficient and so on. Martha Nussbaum, from a position of PL, argues for ten basic capabilities that a liberal state should provide for its citizens:

1. **Life**
2. **Bodily Health**
3. **Bodily Integrity**
4. **Senses, Imagination and Thought**
5. **Emotions**
6. **Practical Reason** (including liberty of conscience)
7. **Affiliation** (A: capability for social interaction, friendship and freedom of assembly; and B: protection against discrimination on grounds of sex, race, caste, etc.)
8. **Other Species**
9. **Play**
10. **Control Over One's Environment**

(Nussbaum 2001: 78–80)

It is true that these are *Capabilities* – they should be made *available*, so that all citizens are capable of benefiting from them, but there is no obligation for any citizen to do so. But the fact that it is these Capabilities and not others that are to be made available implies that they are good things for human beings to have. Nussbaum did not intend to move towards perfectionism. She intended simply to provide an improved framework for thinking about how economic policies can improve the lives of those in developing countries, and especially women, because 'the normative approaches characteristic of utilitarian economics are inadequate guides to public policy' (Nussbaum 2001: 299). Nevertheless, the capabilities approach moves liberalism in a perfectionist direction simply because it fills in more of the ingredients requisite for a good life. Nussbaum might contend that she has not really moved very far along the spectrum because the precise ways in which each capability is to be satisfied remain open. Nussbaum distinguishes capability (what a person may do) from functioning (what they actually do) and argues that

> if we were to take functioning itself as the goal of public policy, pushing citizens into functioning in a single determinate manner, the liberal pluralist would rightly judge that we were precluding many choices that citizens may make in accordance with their own conception of the good, and perhaps violating their rights.
>
> (2001: 87)

For example, although the capability to play is one of Nussbaum's ten essentials, an individual 'may prefer to work with an intense dedication that precludes recreation and play (2001: 87). For this reason, 'where adult citizens are concerned, *capability, not function, is the appropriate political goal*' (Nussbaum 2001: 87). Therefore,

> for political purposes it is appropriate that we shoot for capabilities and those alone. Citizens must be left free to determine their own course after that. The person with plenty of food may always choose to fast, but there is a great difference between fasting and starving, and it is this difference I wish to capture.
>
> (2001: 87)

Nevertheless, Nusssbaum's ten capabilities supply a much fuller account than Rawls's 'thin theory of the Good'. Moreover, simply making the capabilities available makes it more likely that they will be taken up and used – that is the point of them, after all. Providing a certain set of capabilities *encourages* certain functionings. Nussbaum herself says:

> There are some ways of life that people find deeply satisfying, and that probably do not involve unacceptable levels of indignity or capability inequality, which are likely to cease to exist in a regime of choice, simply because of social pressure, and the availability of alternative choices.
>
> (2001: 236)

The capabilities approach does embody a view, not of one particular model good life, but a fairly well-defined set of them. And indeed Nussbaum herself says that any theory of universal norms, if it is to have content at all, 'will say that some objects of desire are more central than others for political purposes, more necessary to a human's quality of life' (2001: 112). So by providing the capabilities for those objects of desire and ruling out others, the capabilities approach has moved at least some distance along the spectrum in the direction of perfectionism.

And why stop at ten capabilities? Jonathan Wolff and Avner De-Shalit in their book *Disadvantage* take Nussbaum's ten Capabilities and add four more to make fourteen:

11. Complete independence (ability to do as you wish without dependence on others)
12. Doing good to others
13. Living in a law-abiding fashion
14. Understanding the law

(Wolff and De-Shalit 2007: 190–1)

Nor does there seem any reason to stop at fourteen. Dispute about candidates for the list could continue. One could bring parameters to the dispute by stipulating that the more nearly universally valued the good, the better a candidate it is. On that basis, one might want to say that maximal development of intelligence should be on the list. Intelligence is near-universally valued. So the state would have a right, if not a positive duty, to pass laws, pursue policies and establish and regulate institutions with the aim of providing citizens with the capability to develop their intelligence. One might also press a case for including happiness. Or personal autonomy, which Joseph Raz in *The Morality of Freedom* takes as the foundation for a fully developed perfectionist position.

4.4.3 Raz's perfectionist liberalism

Raz makes the case for a liberalism which is non-individualist – that is it is not concerned with the securing and protecting of individual rights, but with collective goods. Raz's belief in some collective goods as intrinsically desirable springs from his belief that personal autonomy is intrinsically desirable (see Raz 2009: 203). For personal autonomy requires a range of acceptable options, and 'at least some of the social conditions which constitute such options are collective goods' (Raz 2009: 205). As examples of collective goods, Raz offers a society which has a legal profession, and medical and architectural professions, or a society which recognises homosexual marriage.

Such collective goods are not to be thought of as rights. Once collective goods exist, rights proceed from them: if I live in a society with recognised marriage, then clearly individuals have a right to get married; moreover it is not hard to make a case that this should include the right to same-sex marriage, absent any justification for withholding a right from homosexuals which heterosexuals enjoy. But it sounds odd to say that I have a right to live in a society with recognised marriage in the first place: for there is no one against whom I could claim that right, or who would be failing in their duty if it were not provided.

Raz's brand of liberalism, therefore, is not primarily concerned with what rights individuals have. That question comes in secondarily. Primarily, Raz's liberalism is concerned with providing the conditions for personal autonomy. Raz views personal autonomy as intrinsically valuable. And therefore it is intrinsically valuable that there be a range of collective goods – including the basic collective good of living in a society in the first place (Raz 2009: 206), since 'the provision of many collective goods is constitutive of the very possibility of autonomy' (2009: 207).

Raz's liberalism is perfectionist in two ways. First, he holds that personal autonomy is ultimately and intrinsically valuable for human beings. Let us call this Claim 1.

Second, he holds that personal autonomy 'is valuable only if exercised in pursuit of the good' (Raz 2009: 381). That is Claim 2.

If both of these claims are true, Raz's liberal perfectionism must follow, and we find ourselves moving further away from PL. I examine the strength of Raz's two claims in Chapter 6. Let us note here that Raz's perfectionism would generate a different response to the question of whether a liberal state should ban the burqa. Banning it in order to prevent harm to people other than the wearer is still an available option for the liberal perfectionist, as it is for the political liberal. (Raz himself endorses a form of harm principle, as a requirement for protecting personal autonomy – see Raz 2009: 401). In addition, however, the liberal perfectionist could countenance *other* grounds for a ban, arising from Raz's Claims 1 and 2.

Raz argues that the state should secure the conditions for personal autonomy, which means making a range of acceptable options available. But not all options will be deemed acceptable. As Raz puts it, 'some options one is better off not having' (2009: 408). Suppose that the wearing of the burqa substantially compromised one's autonomy. This falls foul of Claim 1. For the liberal perfectionist there would be a strong prima facie case for banning it.

Moreover, even if it could be shown that a burqa-clad woman retains her autonomy (on the grounds that wearing it is a conscious, authentic choice which she continues to endorse), a perfectionist might still argue that the state should not allow it, if it falls foul of Claim 2. Raz's perfectionist moral pluralism allows that many forms of life are good, but holds that some 'are worthless and demeaning, and ... political action may and should be taken to eradicate or at least curtail them' (Raz 2009: 133). A case might be made that a life lived behind a burqa is worthless and/or demeaning. I am not making that case here. But liberal perfectionism allows for the possibility that if such a case were made, a ban could be justified. Indeed, one of the reasons advanced by the French government in defence of its ban – the requirement to protect the dignity of women (ANRI 2010: 13) – is perfectionist in just this sense.

To sum up, while a political liberal has only one possible reason for banning the burqa (preventing harm to others), a liberal perfectionist has three: (1) preventing harm to others, (2) encouraging autonomy, (3) discouraging worthless/demeaning ways of life.

The question is whether Raz's two claims are true. These claims will be examined in detail in Chapter 6, on autonomy. At this stage I wish to make just two points about Raz's Claim 2.

First, it implies the possibility of constant change in the options offered, encouraged, withheld or discouraged by the state. The consensus on what counts as a good life changes over time. A liberal perfectionist in Victorian Britain might well have been against the institution of homosexual marriage, and indeed the decriminalisation of homosexual activity, deeming such activity to be 'evil or worthless'. Today's liberal perfectionist takes a different view. Liberal perfectionism is therefore dynamic in a way that PL is not. This is not to saddle the perfectionist with moral or cultural relativism. Changes may be for the better, constituting moral *progress*.

The second point to make about Claim 2 is that it entails acceptance of paternalism. Raz himself makes the point:

> One way in which the autonomy-based doctrine of freedom advocated here deviates from some liberal writings on the subject is in its ready embrace of various paternalistic measures.
>
> (2009: 422)

In Raz's perfectionist liberalism, it is the duty of the state to provide citizens with options which it deems good, and to discourage them from pursuing options which it deems evil or worthless. If citizens disagree with the state about what options are good, then they will be the objects of paternalism. I discuss Jonathan Quong's charge that Raz's perfectionist liberalism is paternalist below, and examine the general permissibility of paternalism in greater detail in Chapter 5. First, though, I explore a third liberal position, a halfway house between Rawls and Raz, which accepts Raz's Claim 1 but ditches his Claim 2: Ben Colburn's theory of autonomy-based liberalism.

4.4.4 The halfway house of autonomy-based liberalism

In his book *Autonomy and Liberalism,* Ben Colburn makes the case for liberalism 'as the political philosophy that is committed to the promotion of individual autonomy' (2010: 1). His aim is twofold.

First, he wants to 'bring order to [the] chaos' that is liberal theory (Colburn 2010: 1). What *liberalism* means is contested both among liberal theorists and by their opponents, and Colburn aims to bring clarity to the debate by deriving liberalism from one simple principle: a commitment to promoting individual autonomy.

Second, he aims to provide a guide or lodestone for liberal state *policy*. Asking, 'Will this measure promote individual autonomy or not?' provides liberal policymakers with an evaluative tool.

Colburn defines individual autonomy as 'the capacity to decide for ourselves what is valuable in life, and to shape our lives in accordance with that decision' (2010: 2). This is a useful definition, clear, concise and in line with established philosophical usage, and I am happy to adopt it, although I have some further considerations to add in Chapter 6.

Colburn thus endorses Raz's Claim 1 – that personal autonomy is ultimately and intrinsically valuable for human beings – and like Raz believes that it is the task of a liberal state to encourage autonomy. However, Colburn does not endorse Raz's Claim 2. His theory is explicitly anti-perfectionist. He sums up his position in the following two claims:

> The Autonomy Claim: The state ought to promote autonomy.
>
> Anti-perfectionism: The state ought not in its action (intentionally) to promote any value.
>
> (Colburn 2010: 43)

One wants to object that the two claims appear to contain the seeds of a contradiction. For if autonomy is a value, then the state ought not to promote it, according to the second claim; yet according to the first claim, that is precisely what the state ought to do.

Colburn's way out of the contradiction is to argue that autonomy is a *second-order* value: a value about values. (Recall Colburn's definition of autonomy: the capacity of individuals to choose for themselves what is valuable.) But anti-perfectionism is to be understood as concerned with *first-order* values – that is the values that individuals choose for themselves. And so,

> Since autonomy is a second-order value, it is consistent both to endorse anti-perfectionism (so understood) and to say that the state should promote autonomy.
>
> (Colburn 2010: 57)

Understood in this way, the two claims are not only non-contradictory, but Colburn argues that the one entails the other. Colburn calls this the Equivalence Claim: 'anti-perfectionism implies that the state ought to promote autonomy, and *vice versa*' (2010: 57). Colburn offers the following formal argument for the Equivalence Claim:

1. If anti-perfectionism is true, it must be justified.
2. If the state ought to promote autonomy, then anti-perfectionism is true.
3. Any justification for anti-perfectionism implies that the state ought to promote autonomy.
4. (From 1 and 3): If anti-perfectionism is true, then the state ought to promote autonomy.
5. (From 2 and 4): The state ought to promote autonomy if and only if anti-perfectionism is true.

(2010: 57–8)

Clearly it is premisses 2 and 3 that do the heavy lifting. Colburn argues for the truth of premiss 2 by considering the case of Harriet, who has decided that the valuable thing in life is to play Bach's Cello Suites consummately well, and if she can live according to this value, her life goes better. But this does not mean that the state should promote cello-playing, because cello-playing 'is valuable only for those, like Harriet, who consider it valuable' (2010: 59). The state *could not* promote autonomy by promoting cello-playing. It could only promote autonomy by promoting people's abilities or opportunities to decide for themselves what is valuable.

Colburn then considers a possible objection to Premiss 2. What if the state did not, itself, *decide* what was valuable, but promoted values which individuals had already decided on? Thus, suppose Harriet has decided that it is valuable to play the cello well, and so the state gets on with promoting that value for her (e.g. by texting her exhortations to practise, allowing her to claim tax expenses on money spent on music lessons and recordings, etc.). This runs into insuperable practical difficulties. If the state tries to promote Harriet's values for everyone, then it rides roughshod over the autonomy of the great majority who do not share Harriet's values: and if it tries to help every single citizen by promoting differing values directly to each individual – cello-playing for some, attendance at football matches for others, the study of philosophy for others, group-sex for others and so on – that would be a logistical nightmare. The state would need to provide personalised exhortations and the appropriate facilitating conditions for every citizen and, given that what individuals value often changes, would need to keep itself continuously informed on what each citizens' values currently were, which would inevitably involve 'drastic violations of privacy' (Colburn 2010: 59). There is the additional point, not made by Colburn, that it seems redundant to promote values to individuals which they have already endorsed for themselves.

Colburn adds that as well as the practical difficulties of the state's promoting values decided on by individuals, it would be illegitimate in principle. From the point of view of second-order autonomy, the value of cello-playing is *de dicto* – that is, it is valuable only because Harriet says it is. But for Harriet herself, cello-playing is valuable *de re* – for its own qualities. Therefore (Colburn says) to translate Harriet's first-order value into the terms of a second-order, generalised value is to risk mistranslation:

> at best we turn an unrestricted generalization into a value claim that is indexed to a particular individual at a particular time, and at worst we will translate a true sentence into one that is false.
>
> (2010: 60)

Colburn's argument works well with the example of cello-playing. Wanting to be an expert cello-player is very much the kind of value one chooses for oneself and it is a value that it is not widely shared. Suppose, however, we take a value that *is* widely shared. 'Harriet values being in good health.' Because the vast majority of people would prefer to be in good health than not, there is a closing of the gap between its *de dicto* and its *de re* values: it is valuable not just because Harriet says it but because millions of other people do so too, and they agree on this because good health is something that normal human beings value for its own qualities. If the state were to promote good health, by providing facilities for fitness and relaxation, emphasising sport and exercise in the school curriculum, regulating the food industry to restrict the use of unhealthy ingredients, keeping the public informed about medical matters and providing easy access to screenings and medical treatments and so on, such a programme would not run into practical or logistical problems that promoting individuals' hobbies, enthusiasms or career choices would run into, neither would it require drastic violations of privacy. The truth of Colburn's Premiss 2, then, is not demonstrated by the example of Harriet and her cello.

Colburn's Premiss 3 – 'Any justification for anti-perfectionism implies that the state ought to promote autonomy' – could only be proved true if all other justifications for anti-perfectionism were shown to be false. As Colburn concedes, that is an unending task. His method is to rule out the four leading alternative candidates: relativism, pluralism, scepticism and neutrality. The approach is to show that each of these alternative candidates *either* fails to give a plausible reason for anti-perfectionism *or* does so by dint of a covert appeal to the Autonomy Claim. There is no necessity to go through them all, but we can take his treatment of neutrality as exemplary.

Colburn's characterisation of the neutrality argument, based on Rawlsian PL, is as follows: 'if it is to be legitimate, a state must be neutral, and if it is to be neutral, it must be anti-perfectionist' (2010: 65).

Legitimacy requires neutrality because if the state were not neutral, then it would make laws and policies based on a comprehensive doctrine with which some citizens would disagree. Colburn contends that this is a problem because of Rawls's belief that persons are free and equal and possessed of two 'moral powers': 'a capacity for justice and a capacity for a conception of the good' (Rawls 2005: 19). Imposing a comprehensive conception of the good on unwilling citizens fails to respect the latter of these two powers: which is no different from failing to respect their autonomy. In other words, neutrality is required because it guarantees citizens' autonomy, and if it did not do so, then there would be no reason for requiring it.

Unless someone comes up with alternative grounds for anti-perfectionism – and Colburn does seem to have dealt with all the obvious candidates – then Premiss 3 is true.

However, if Premiss 2 is not true – and as I have argued, the example of Harriet and her cello is not sufficient to demonstrate that it is – then it would not be the liberal state's *sole* duty to promote autonomy. It might be the liberal state's duty to promote autonomy *and other values as well*. Once one has already made the break with PL by stipulating the promotion of one value, autonomy, as the state's *raison être,* why not others, such as health? Or perhaps the state should promote happiness, or intelligence. It is not obvious that these are less universally valued than autonomy.

Colburn would no doubt reply that, to the extent that the state performs other duties, it becomes less of a liberal state. It is the commitment to autonomy which makes it liberal; and it would be less liberal to precisely the extent that it sought to promote other values.

There are two points to make in answer. One is that if a liberal state's duties really are limited to promoting the value of autonomy to its own citizens, this is a pinched kind of liberalism which few actual liberals would wish to accept in practice. It rules out any form of *beneficence* from the state, other than autonomy promotion to its own citizens. Such a state would have no duties towards creatures which were incapable of full autonomy – brain-damaged people, or non-human animals. As Martha Nussbaum has argued in *Frontiers of Justice*, a liberal state has duties towards those with lesser autonomy, and towards those who are members of other, less fortunate states (2007). Nor would a Single-Value-Autonomy-Based-Liberal State, as I shall term it, sanction state-organised relief for disaster-stricken foreign countries, or policies to preserve a clean environment, natural beauty spots or historic buildings for future generations. These policies fall foul of Single-Value-Autonomy-Based Liberalism not merely because they are not concerned with promoting autonomy, but because they could actually restrict it. It is still a recognisably liberal position to hold that the state should promote autonomy, but that it may promote other values too; and that these values could occasionally conflict with autonomy. But if that is so, Colburn's Equivalence Claim is not sound, because Premiss 2 would be untrue. The state's promotion of autonomy only entails anti-perfectionism if the state must not promote any other values.

The second point is that even if we were to accept Single-Value-Autonomy-Based Liberalism, autonomy does not subsist in a vacuum. It is inextricably related to other values. I discuss this in more detail in Chapter 6, but here let us note that maximal personal autonomy might require physical health: chronic illness could skew one's notions of what is valuable (George Orwell pointed out in his essay 'Politics vs. Literature' that if you are suffering from toothache or seasickness it is impossible to appreciate that *King Lear* is a better play than *Peter Pan* (2000: 384). It is also difficult to be autonomous without good mental health. One cannot be fully autonomous if one is suffering from depression. Maximal autonomy, moreover, requires a fully developed intelligence. The more intelligent one is, the more options one will be aware of, and the better able to judge between competing values, and the sounder one's apprehension will be of the likely consequences of living one's life in accordance with one set of values rather than another.

Therefore, even a state which was strictly Single-Value-Autonomy-Based would find itself in practice having to promote a range of values besides autonomy. It is true that these values would not be promoted for their own sake, but because they promoted autonomy. Nevertheless, the policies of such a state would in the majority of cases be indistinguishable from those of a more perfectionist state.

On the issue of the burqa, however, there is one clear distinction to be made between Colburn's autonomy-based liberalism and Raz's liberal perfectionism. Whereas the Razian would sanction banning the burqa on three separate grounds, the Colburnian would ban it only on two: (1) preventing harm to others and (2) encouraging autonomy. The potential Razian third reason – discouraging worthless or demeaning ways of life – is not available to the Colburnian.

4.5 Quong's restatement of political liberalism

In *Liberalism without Perfection* (2011), Jonathan Quong argues against basing liberalism on the value of autonomy, or indeed any other value or set of values. Liberalism makes possible or gives rise to values such as autonomy. But it is not a liberal state's duty to favour one value or set of values above others. Quong explains his thesis thus:

> Liberal societies are crucially characterised by pluralism or disagreement regarding what makes a life good, valuable or worthwhile. Disagreement about the nature of human flourishing is a deep and permanent feature of free societies. This fact, when combined with the thesis that governments must be able to justify their actions to citizens, yields the conclusion that governments must refrain from acting on the basis of any particular conception of what makes for a valuable, flourishing or worthwhile life. Because we disagree about what makes life worth living, it would be wrong for the government to take sides on this question. Instead, the government should remain *neutral* on the issue of the good life, and restrict itself to establishing the fair terms within which citizens can pursue their own beliefs about what gives value to their lives.
>
> (2011: 2)

If Quong is right, then many standard justifications of laws and policies become inadmissible (2011: 4). Making recreational drugs, gambling or prostitution illegal on the grounds that they are disvaluable would not pass the test of 'public justification', because not everyone would agree they were disvaluable (2011: 4). And:

> Attempts to restrict or alter the way the Amish or other orthodox religious communities raise their children that are justified by claims about the value of autonomy in a human life similarly fail to be publicly justifiable.
>
> (Quong 2011: 4)

By the same reasoning, a state ban on burqa-wearing could not be justified by the claim that wearing it limits or destroys autonomy. Perhaps the wearer does not value autonomy. And it is not the state's business to tell her that she ought to do so.

Quong's restatement of PL is generally faithful to Rawls but differs from him in one important way. Quong has a different conception of the role played by the OC. His is an *internal* conception of liberalism. On this view, pluralism arises because of liberalism; pluralism is not a pre-existing problem which liberalism arrives to solve. Therefore, he does not seek to justify why one should be a liberal in the first place, but he aims rather to understand 'what kinds of arguments, if any, citizens already committed to certain basic liberal norms can legitimately offer to one another' (2011: 5). Basic liberal norms are abstract values such as 'the idea of persons as free and equal, or a general commitment to fairness in the distribution of goods or advantages among citizens' (2011: 5).

Thus the role of the OC in Quong's conception of PL is different from that implied by Rawlsian PL, which Quong terms 'the common view'. The common view regards the subject of the OC as being a principle or principles of justice. But this leads to a serious difficulty when it comes to debate about constitutional questions, which are supposed, in PL, to be settled by public reason. If different citizens hold the same principle or principles, but for different reasons, there is no common ground for them to argue on: they will simply appeal to incompatible reasons.

Quong dramatises this with a thought experiment (2011: 172). Suppose we have a Politically Liberal state in which there are two Comprehensive Doctrines. The first of these doctrines (CD1) supports Rawls's two Principle of Justice for reasons *a* and *b*. The second comprehensive doctrine (CD2), on the other hand, supports the Principles of Justice for reasons *c* and *d*.

Now suppose that 'our political society faces some constitutional question which pits the first principle against the second' (2011: 172). Quong's imagined scenario is that the government is considering a scheme called the *Occupational Policy*, which would require

> restricting people with specified scarce talents to a limited range of occupational choice at average wages for three years after they receive their first post-secondary degree … Restricting people with valuable and scarce talents in this way will, let us assume, ensure greater overall productivity, and also ensure that the additional resources generated can be distributed to the least advantaged.
>
> (2011: 172)

This policy is in line with Rawls's second Principle of Justice – the principle of fair and equal opportunities, and of removing inequalities which do not benefit the worst-off or are not acceptable to them – but offends against the first principle, which guarantees equal liberty for all, subject to the usual constraints (see Rawls 1999, chapter Two). Those citizens who endorse CD1 believe the first principle should have priority over the second, and so they reject the Occupational Policy. But those who endorse CD2 disagree. They think that the second principle should have priority over the first. Of course, those in the CD2 camp are not just disagreeing with those in CD1, but with John Rawls, who states that that the first principle should have lexical priority over the second. But so what? The OC, in the common view, does not require that people accept the same principles for the same reasons. In fact, the point of the OC, on this view, is precisely that it does not. Citizens who uphold CD2 have their own, non-Rawlsian reasons for accepting the two principles, and those reasons dictate the opposite prioritisation. But that means that upholders of CD1 and CD2 have nothing to say to each other on the subject of the Occupational Policy. Neither can offer a justification that the other would accept.

Quong's response to this problem is to state that the subject of the OC should not be a principle, or principles, at all. Rather, it should be 'the fundamental idea of society as a fair system of co-operation among free and equal people' (2011:190). This, then, would form the bedrock of agreement upon which a liberal society rests.

Moreover, in Quong's account, the purpose of the OC is not the same as in the common view. For in the common view, the OC acts as a *justification* for the principles which are the subject of the consensus: 'These principles must be reasonable – look, people agree on them'. As Quong points out, this view leads to a dilemma:

> *a)* either the overlapping consensus is superfluous within political liberalism, since reasonable people will by definition endorse the (correct) political conception of justice, or *b)* the overlapping consensus is not superfluous, and

people could (in the second justificatory stage) reject the political conception without being unreasonable.

(2011: 167)

If we go with the second horn of the dilemma, then people of illiberal views would be justified in rejecting a political conception of justice *purely in virtue of rejecting it*. For if the OC is justificatory, one can vitiate its power to justify by the expedient of not signing up to it. As Quong says, 'If we want to preserve the liberal content of our theory, it is essential that such people are excluded from the constituency of the overlapping consensus' (2011: 167).

Quong's theory avoids this dilemma, and it appears also to avoid the difficulty of legitimacy raised by Habermas (2011) referred to above. In Quong's account, the purpose of the OC is not to justify the content of the consensus. Its purpose is to supply the necessary *basis* for public reason. Without a shared commitment to the fundamental idea of persons as free and equal citizens, there would be no common ground to stand on when deliberating rival principles.

In Quong's version of PL, one *begins* with an overlapping consensus. Only those who sign up to it are included in the constituency of reasonable persons. This avoids the uncomfortable problem referred to in Section 4.2.1, where the Give-'Em-Enough-Rope Tendency might sign up to the OC for the illiberal reason that it will enable unbelievers to go their sinful way and be roasted after death in hell for eternity. In Quong's theory, one cannot sign up to the OC for the wrong reason. The reason is dictated by the subject of the consensus: a belief in 'the fundamental idea of society as a fair system of co-operation among free and equal people' (2011: 190).

Quong's development of his position involves a full reply to perfectionist critics of PL, especially Joseph Raz. I focus on one area of his argument against Razian perfectionism since it is the most relevant to the burqa question – that is, the charge of paternalism.

Quong argues that perfectionism entails paternalism. It is true that Raz has a version of the harm principle which is supposed in certain cases to rule out paternalist actions. In his version, harming others means limiting or damaging their prospects, which diminishes their autonomy, so the state is entitled to use coercion to prevent harm (Raz 2009: 416). But it is not entitled to use coercion to prevent morally repugnant actions which do not harm others, because coercion is a blunt instrument and will limit people's autonomy in more than just the targeted area; putting someone in prison does not just prevent them carrying out the morally repugnant activity but all other activities as well (Raz 2009: 418–19).

As Quong points out, however, Raz rejects state coercion of morally repugnant but non-harmful actions merely for *contingent* reasons. It happens to be a fact that using coercive measures to discourage citizens from pursuing bad options tends to cut off good options as well (Quong 2011: 54). But Quong does not agree that the harm principle should rest on this contingent fact. He considers the possibility, perhaps not technologically distant, of inserting a chip in someone's brain that would prevent bad (but not harmful) options. Not only would Raz seem to have no reason to object to the insertion of such a chip, but the logic of his position seems to demand that perfectionist states put money into scientific research so that this scheme can be realised as soon as possible. That way, citizens can be coerced away from bad options without having their good options cut off too, which is what Raz wants. Yet this seems to have profoundly illiberal implications.

Quong holds that in such a case the Millian harm principle should apply, and the state would have no right to insert the chip. His own argument for the harm principle is that

> it is fundamentally justified by an appeal to the moral status of persons ... it ensures that citizens are not treated in a certain type of paternalistic fashion, one which demeans their moral status as free and equal persons.
>
> (2011: 56)

The possibilities of technologically facilitated intervention in citizens' lives are only likely to grow in the future. Raz's position invokes the threat of unlimited state interference in citizens' lives, obliging them to choose from a menu of state-approved good options. Quong's objection to this possibility seems compelling.

At the same time, however, Quong's root-and-branch rejection of paternalism is difficult to sustain. He argues that paternalism is 'presumptively wrong because of the way it denies someone's moral status as a free and equal citizen' (2011: 74). I explore paternalism in greater detail in Chapter 5. Here I simply make the claim, to be substantiated later, that paternalism need not deny a person's moral status as a free and equal citizen. There is a distinction between *moral* paternalism, which aims to prevent someone acting in a morally repugnant way, and *practical* paternalism, which aims to prevent someone acting in a way which is likely to damage their health, ruin their prospects or end their life prematurely. The former does indeed deny a person's moral status as a free and equal citizen, and is presumptively wrong; the latter does not, and is not.

4.6 The continuum from political liberalism to perfectionist liberalism

Framing the disagreement between PL and Perfectionism as a simple dichotomy is misconceived. As argued in Section 4.4, any liberal state must operate with some general theory of the good, if it is to have any basis for enacting laws and pursuing policies. Moreover, the harm principle (in either its Millian or its Feinbergian version) involves a normative notion of the good. If we define loss of life or limb, or of bodily integrity or of liberty as harms, then we must be claiming that the possession of those things is good.

Of course there are degrees. Some liberals would argue for a very slender theory of the good indeed, others for a thicker one. This suggests that the apparent disjunction between PL and perfectionism is really a continuum. As we saw earlier, Quong defines perfectionism as the view that 'it is *at least sometimes* permissible for a liberal state to promote or discourage particular activities, ideals or ways of life on grounds relating to their inherent or intrinsic value' (2011: 27; my italics).

But this produces a skewed division between the two. PL is defined as the view that the liberal state must *never* promote or discourage particular activities, ideals or ways of life on such grounds. Then perfectionist liberalism lumps together a whole range of views, from the view that the state should *hardly ever* promote or discourage activities, ideals or ways of life on grounds relating to their intrinsic value, to the view that it should *seldom* do so, to the view that it should *occasionally* do so, to the view that it should *sometimes* do so, to the view that it should *frequently* do so, to the view that it should do so *as much and as often as feasible*.

Yet the view that the state should hardly ever promote or discourage activities on grounds relating to their intrinsic value is much closer to the view that it should never do so, than to the view that it should do so as much and as often as is feasible. Characterising the relationship between PL and perfectionist liberalism as a sharp dichotomy obscures the common ground between close-together views. The pure political liberal who believes that the state should promote or discourage activities on the grounds of their intrinsic value 0 per cent of the time is far closer to the liberal who thinks the state should do so 1 per cent of the time than to the liberal who thinks the state should do so 100 per cent of the time. Yet in Quong's terms, both the one-percenter and the hundred-percenter are classified equally as perfectionists. The image of a continuum is more helpful.

Thus, we can imagine Rawls and Quong at one end of the continuum, Colburn about halfway along and Raz at the far end.

My own view is that a position somewhere near the middle is usually optimal, avoiding the dangers of under-intervention at one end and over-intervention at the other. The pure PL position rejects paternalism or at least looks upon it with strong disfavour. As I argue in Chapter 5, however, the anti-paternalist position is not easy to maintain consistently. There are situations when paternalist intervention is justifiable and ought to be welcome to the liberal. At the other end of the continuum there is the risk of a perfectionist state over-intervening in the lives of citizens, justified by a conception of the good which not all citizens accept, to a point where it is no longer liberal at all. I consider this risk in Chapter 7, when discussing the problem of adaptive preferences.

However, my overall thesis does not depend on locating myself at any particular point on the continuum. I aim to consider the implications of the burqa question for a plurality of liberal positions.

I shall argue that even if one accepts the full Razian perfectionist position, banning the burqa on the grounds of Claim 2 is problematic; and if one adopts Colburn's halfway house, then banning it on the grounds of Claim 1 is still problematic. But there are possible justifications for a ban on the grounds of preventing harm to others, which every variety of liberal could agree on.

5

Paternalism considered

The argument

In this chapter I consider paternalist arguments for a burqa-ban. If the burqa had deleterious effects on the wearer's life, then there might be reasons to ban it *for the wearer's own sake*.

Section 5.1 defines paternalism. There are two types of paternalist argument to consider: those based on concerns about well-being, understood in quite a general sense (to include health, happiness, personal relationships and opportunities for fulfilment) and those based on concerns about personal autonomy. In this chapter I consider only the first.

Liberals towards the PL end of the continuum would tend to dismiss all such arguments from a principled anti-paternalist stance. In Section 5.2 I examine the principled anti-paternalist position and argue that it is untenable.

Section 5.3 endorses Sarah Conly's argument for at least some coercive paternalism, limited by what I term the Liberal Paternalist Principle – that is to say, paternalist policies may be justified where the restriction of liberty is small and the benefits gained or harms avoided are great.

With the general permissibility of paternalism in principle established, in Section 5.4 I examine whether specific paternalist arguments for banning the burqa on grounds of well-being are persuasive. I shall argue that they are not.

The paternalist argument for banning the burqa on grounds of preserving personal autonomy is a distinct and more complex case, and will be examined in Chapter 6.

5.1 Paternalism defined

The word 'paternalism' derives from a metaphor, implying a comparison with a father's care for his children. The comparison is with a *good* father, not an abusive, tyrannical or neglectful one: a father who makes and enforces decisions about what his children can and cannot do, in their interests, not his own, because are they not yet wise enough to make such decisions for themselves. Paternalism, then, is following a similar policy with regard not to children but to other adults. Thus, paternalist policies are:

> restrictions on a person's liberty which are justified *exclusively* by consideration for that person's own good or welfare, and which are carried out against his present will … or against his prior commitment.
>
> (Arneson 1980: 471)

Restricting the freedom of Wahhabist women to wear the burqa, for their own good, against their will, would be a clear case of paternalism.

Arneson's definition is a useful starting point, but each of its three parts requires further comment.

1. *Restrictions on a person's liberty* in the case of a burqa-ban would be likely to involve legal prohibition backed by penalties. Burqa-wearing women could be fined, and if they persisted in defying the ban, perhaps imprisoned: the same approach as is used to enforce the paternalistic banning of certain recreational drugs. The restriction could also be enforced by attempting to cut off supply, again as with drugs: importation and sale of burqas or niqabs could be made punishable by law.
2. I take the last part of the definition next as it can be dealt with more briefly than the middle one. The clause *against his present will … or against his prior commitment* narrows the definition unnecessarily. Amending it to *irrespective of that person's will* would encompass the cases where the restriction was not against the person's will, as well as those where it was. The broader definition is no less clear, and is more faithful to the spirit of the metaphor; fathers do restrict their children's liberty for their own good, but not invariably against the child's will. The child may cheerfully accept that they cannot have another biscuit, or that it is time to go to bed, or that they must practise the piano for twenty minutes, or brush their teeth for two, and might prefer the security and predictability of being told what to do and what not to do. In the adult world, many or most people prefer being forced to insure their home or car, rather than risk the consequences of their own lack of prudence if no such law was in place. It is possible that some burqa-wearing women might not object to a ban. It could remove a burden which, though assumed voluntarily, they were glad

to be rid of without having to take personal responsibility. People's desires and motivations are often mixed. (It goes without saying that women who were *coerced* into wearing a burqa would welcome a ban – but that would not be paternalist, since it would be the restoration, not the restriction of a liberty.)

3. Finally, the clause *for that person's own good* requires explication. For what is meant by somebody's own good? People differ about what counts as good. Recognition of this fact is fundamental to liberalism. Yet even political liberals need a thin theory of the good. Without being as perfectionist as Plato we can identify goods which are effectively universal for human beings, and legislators have done so. The American Declaration of Independence of 1776 famously lists 'life, liberty and the pursuit of happiness' as inalienable rights (Rosen and Wolff 1999: 391). A more granular list of goods would still command very widespread agreement: one might cite health, family ties, friendship and achievement in one's chosen field as core ingredients of a good life. Details about what *kind* of health, family ties, friendships or achievements can be left blank. But the list is normative. Being healthy does not mean one is obliged to follow any particular diet or regime of exercise; still, health means being in *good* health, and there is wide and deep agreement about what that means. Other things being equal it is better to breathe freely than wheeze, to be fit than unfit, free from pain than in it, sighted than blind, hearing than deaf or able-bodied than confined to a wheelchair.

So I am claiming, but this simple picture is not uncontroversial. Cases of Body Integrity Identity Disorder (BIID) test one's intuitions here. BIID (also called transability) is

> a rare condition characterized by an intense desire or need to move from a given state of ability to one of relative impairment, most often through amputation.
>
> (Reynolds 2016: 37)

Chloe Jennings-White of Salt Lake City is a case in point. Jennings-White, though able-bodied, wears leg-braces and uses a wheelchair, and her ambition is to be a paraplegic. She would like to have spinal surgery to render her legs inoperative, but so far has not managed to find a surgeon who will perform the operation. She is a spokesperson for the BIID movement and has appeared on CNN television to talk about her desire.

Ethicists are divided about how to deal with such cases. Sabine Müller in a 2009 article in the *American Journal of Bioethics* (cited in Reynolds 2016: 40) argued that it would be wrong to perform the surgery that Jennings-White desires; it would be treating the symptom rather than the disorder underlying it, and would offend against the medical principle of doing no harm to patients. According to Reynolds, of the seven published responses to her article, four agree with her while three support surgery for Jennings-White (Reynolds 2016: 40). Reynolds himself takes issue with Müller. He argues that Müller conflates being disabled with harm, which is ableist

> as it assumes, without evidence or argumentation, that the 'standard' able-body is, *ceteris paribus*, in and of itself better than the non-standard, disabled body.
>
> (Reynolds 2016: 40)

In turn I should like to take issue with Reynolds. First, the position of Müller and those who agree with her does not depend on conflating being disabled with harm; it depends on conflating *impairment* with harm. Reynolds himself is alert to this distinction: 'impairment' describes the condition while 'disability' refers to

> the social ramifications of a given impairment, ranging from stigma to oppression to numerous forms of inaccessibility or unequal access.
>
> (Reynolds 2016: 39)

Müller's position is not based on the stigma, oppression or accessibility problems that Jennings-White would face if she were a paraplegic. In a world where there was no stigma or oppression and no accessibility problems, it would still cause harm to Jennings-White to permanently paralyse her lower body. Being physically impaired is an objective condition. Yet as Tom Shakespeare puts it, 'Cultural Disability Studies writers may be keen to dissolve away the material effects of illness and impairment' (2014: 66). For these theorists there is no objective condition of disability, only a socially constructed one. As Shakespeare points out, however, disabled people who live with the reality of illness or impairment do not themselves tend to see it that way. Shakespeare espouses a critical realist approach to disability, which takes account of both the physical reality of impairment as well as the sociocultural aspects of how it is viewed, treated and experienced (Shakespeare 2014).

I agree with Shakespeare that impairment is real (and also that this fact does not provide a full explanation of the disability experience). That impairment is also a harm can be seen from the testimony of those suffering from impairments themselves, like Tom Shakespeare. It is also implied by the fact that to *inflict* a permanent impairment upon another person who did not desire it would be a serious harm and a serious crime, and it would not be ableist to regard it as such. Neither is it ableist to seek to cure, treat or alleviate impairments; yet without a normative model of health one would have no rationale for doing so, and no criteria for success.

Yet Jennings-White *desires* physical impairment. Does that mean it is no longer a harm? This would only follow logically if one were committed to the proposition that what one desired was by definition never harmful. But we cannot simply equate harm with 'what is undesired'. Experience tells us that people are frequently mistaken about their desires. We get what we desire and are disappointed, or we get what we did not desire and are pleasantly surprised. This is not to argue that we should be indifferent to the suffering of Jennings-White, as someone who feels she is trapped in an able body. But there are other ways of helping her, through therapy and support, rather than giving her an irrevocable impairment.

The concept of harm is indeed a slippery one, which I examine in more detail in Chapter 11. Here I simply claim that it must be a normative concept. I further claim that the normative idea of health implied by the term 'impairment', along with normative ideas of other goods that the paternalist may seek to provide, is necessary to the paternalist project. No doubt the list of goods above (health, family ties, friendship, achievement) could be extended and refined. But some normative idea of what it means for a human being to have a good life is required by paternalism.

To summarise: paternalism is the restriction of an adult person's freedom (enforced by legal penalties), for their own good (where this is understood as a normative, impersonal idea of good) irrespective of that person's will. This is a neutral definition which contains no presupposition either for or against paternalism.

5.2 The antipaternalist case considered

5.2.1 The antipaternalist presumption

The pure political liberal view is that paternalist arguments for banning the burqa can be ruled out in advance, because paternalism is wrong in principle. This view is expressed in Mill's version of the harm principle, discussed in Chapter 4: '[a member of a civilised community's] own good, either physical or moral, is not a sufficient warrant' for the state's exercising power over citizens (2005: 13).

On this view, paternalism is unjustified, not because in particular cases in the complex real world it is hard to be certain that it will work, but because it is unjustifiable in principle. Even if the opinions of others about what would make an individual better off or happier were correct, and even if their exercise of power over that individual was so finely judged as to bring about exactly the desired outcome, with no undesirable side effects, that still would not be sufficient warrant for interference.

This is an extreme PL version of anti-paternalism, to which Mill himself admits exceptions (considered later in this chapter). A slightly more moderate version holds that paternalism, though not ruled out by definition, always involves some sort of disvalue. This is the view of Jonathan Quong. He argues that paternalism is 'presumptively wrong because of the way it denies someone's moral status as a free and equal citizen (2011: 74). Paternalism might still be justified where the benefits were very great. But the loss of liberty or autonomy is always regrettable; if the benefit could be produced without sacrificing liberty or autonomy, that would always be preferable. This more moderate position suggests the possibility of a continuum. In its mildest version it could be held by a paternalist who believed that loss of autonomy and/or liberty was only slightly regrettable, and frequently outweighed by gains in welfare. In its strongest form – the form endorsed by Quong – the loss of liberty and/or autonomy is regarded as so serious as to be avoided at almost all costs; very great and certain gains in welfare would be required to justify it. I call this strong form the antipaternalist presumption.

5.2.2 The antipaternalism of Seana Shiffrin

Seana Shiffrin argues in favour of the antipaternalist presumption in her article 'Paternalism, Unconscionability Doctrine, and Accommodation' (2000). She defines paternalism as behaviour which is

(a) aimed to have (or to avoid) an effect on B or her sphere of legitimate agency
(b) involving the substitution of A's judgement or agency for B's
(c) directed at B's own interests or matters that legitimately lie within B's control

(d) undertaken on the grounds that compared to B's judgement or agency with respect to this interest or other matters, A regards her judgement or agency to be (or as likely to be), in some respects, superior to B's.

(Shiffrin 2000: 218)

Shiffrin's references to affecting B's *legitimate* sphere of influence and matters that *legitimately* lie within B's control might appear to rule paternalism out of court. However, Shiffrin argues:

> I do not think that this account *definitionally* implies that paternalism is necessarily, all things considered, wrong' [because there might be cases where] 'rights (and other forms of legitimate control) may be disregarded when a great deal is at stake'; [though others may argue that] 'rights and other forms of legitimate control are insurmountable, per se, at least as against the paternalists's sort of reasons.
>
> (2000: 220 n. 25)

She allows, therefore, some '*logical* room for dispute', but like Quong holds that paternalism is always 'morally problematic' (Shiffrin 2000: 220 n. 25)

Shiffrin states that paternalism inevitably conveys 'a special, generally impermissible insult to autonomous agents' (2000: 207). Quong agrees, claiming that state paternalism involves '*a lack of respect*' towards persons (2011: 105). As the metaphor implies, to treat an adult paternalistically is to treat them like a child. Paternalism substitutes the judgement of the government (or relevant authority) for the judgement of the person who is supposed to be benefited.

Nor would it be a defence of paternalism, according to Shiffrin, that the substituted judgement really was wiser than the judgement of the person benefited. Shiffrin offers the following example:

> Suppose an interlocutor raises his hand at a talk. He is called upon and just as he haltingly begins to articulate his point, an excited, sympathetic colleague loses self-control and interjects: 'Isn't there a better way to put this point?' She goes on to drown him out while cleverly and eloquently articulating his point. She takes over his question because she feels she has a better command of it than he does.
>
> (2000: 217)

Shiffrin uses this example to argue that such behaviour would count as paternalistic even if not intended to benefit the agent. The normal assessment of an onlooker would be that it is paternalistic, she claims, even if the aim was not to help the first speaker, but to speed up the discussion or to ensure it had more fruitful results. (It is for this reason that she inserts the 'matters that lie legitimately within B's control' clause in Part c of her definition, as an alternative to 'B's own interests').

I do not agree with Shiffrin that this would be paternalistic whether or not A really wanted to help B. Adding in cases where the motivation is *not* for B's own good attenuates the definition of paternalism (and makes it easier to argue against en bloc, which is what Shiffrin wants to do). If A interrupts B not in order to help him but for some other reason, then I would call her intervention *patronising*, rather than paternalistic. But let us leave that question to one side and suppose that A's motivation genuinely is to help B out. In that case we can agree that her action is paternalistic in intention, and also that it is insulting.

It does not follow, however, that *all* such substitutions of judgement are equally insulting. That would depend on the situation and the relationships of the people involved. If A were a boss, lecturer, lead moderator or professor rather than a colleague, B might feel helped rather than insulted. It also depends on the equability of B. Not everyone reacts in the same way to having their judgement overruled. As Peter de Marneffe says in his paper 'Avoiding Paternalism', someone may feel insulted without having actually been insulted (2006: 80). The wrongness might be located in the person who feels the sense of insult, rather than in paternalism.

Moreover, even if it were conceded that every substitution of agent B's judgement by a more authoritative or better-equipped agent A contained the seed of an insult, that is not specifically a problem for paternalism. As de Marneffe points out, non-paternalistic policies also substitute an authority's judgement for an individual's. A speed limit substitutes judgement whether imposed for paternalistic reasons ('You judge that you will be safe driving at 90, but you are wrong') or non-paternalistic reasons ('You judge that other people will be safe if you drive at 90, but you are wrong'). If paternalistic laws are wrong on the grounds that they are insulting, then so are non-paternalistic laws which aim to benefit people; which might end up meaning all laws, which is probably more than Shiffrin wanted to prove.

5.2.3 Two further antipaternalist arguments

de Marneffe also considers and rejects two further antipaternalist arguments.

One is that it is impossible to draw a line between justifiable and non-justifiable paternalism (an argument also made by Mill). de Marneffe points out that there is the same difficulty in drawing a line between justifiable and non-justifiable *non*-paternalist policies. He offers the examples of libel laws and anti-discrimination laws, where the aim is not the good of the person prohibited but others whom their actions affect (2006: 88–9). One draws a line between justifiable and non-justifiable non-paternalist policies by weighing the reasons for and against it and going with the reasons one judges to be weightier. But that is equally possible in the case of paternalist policies.

The other antipaternalist argument considered by de Marneffe is Mill's argument from the grounds of 'the permanent interests of man as a progressive being' – that is, to progress we must make our own choices and experiments in living without interference.

Without disputing the idea that we have interests as progressive beings, de Marneffe argues that not all paternalistic laws damage these interests. A law prohibiting bathers from swimming at beaches with lethal currents does not stop them swimming in other rough waters or from taking risks in general, and does not 'deprive us of valuable information about what kinds of life are choiceworthy' (2006: 87). Clearly, an *excess* of paternalism would stifle our interests as progressive beings. But *some* paternalistic laws, to the extent that they help to ensure the safety and security of citizens, could forward our interests as progressive beings.

A familiar example is the compulsory wearing of safety belts in cars. Before the law was passed in Britain in 1972, drivers and passengers often omitted to wear seat belts, and fatalities and serious injuries as a result of car accidents were much higher than they have been since. There is no sense in which this limits our interests as progressive beings. There *is* a sense in which it facilitates our interests as progressive beings, by helping us stay alive and in a condition to progress.

Here is a perfectly clear example of restricting people's liberty against their will for their own good (I take it as uncontroversial that being spared from death, paralysis, serious injury or permanent scarring caused by going through a windscreen at high speed is a good). Those who take a principled antipaternalist position must explain why such an obviously beneficial and widely accepted paternalistic law should be repealed; or, if they think it should not be repealed, they must explain why it is not paternalistic; or, if they can do neither, they should cease to be principled antipaternalists.

Seana Shiffrin takes the second of these options; that is, she undertakes to show that at least some laws which restrict liberty of individuals and benefit those same individuals are not, despite appearances, paternalistic. For it all depends on the precise nature of the reasons the law is instituted. Her exemplary case is not the seat belt law, but the Unconscionability Doctrine – that is, the doctrine in contract law which 'enables a court to decline to enforce a contract where terms are seriously one-sided, over-reaching, exploitative, or otherwise manifestly unfair' (Shiffrin 2000: 205). This doctrine is accepted by liberals, and society at large, and Shiffrin herself; it is also widely seen as paternalistic, because by it the state 'unravels a voluntary agreement between responsible agents'. Shiffrin claims that 'it is commonly cited to *exemplify* paternalism in the law' (2000: 206). Since Shiffrin is antipaternalist, and since she accepts the Unconscionability Doctrine, she must attempt to show that the doctrine is not, despite appearances, paternalist.

Shiffrin argues that the Unconscionability Doctrine can be justified by the motivation behind it, which need not be paternalistic: 'The motive may be a *self-regarding* [my italics] concern not to facilitate or assist harmful, exploitative or immoral action' (2000: 224); she calls this a 'self-regarding refusal' (2000: 227), rather than an other-regarding refusal (to enforce the contract) based on a desire to benefit B.

Thus the justification for the Unconscionability Doctrine would rest entirely on the motivation of the agent. In Shiffrin's view, the same act would be justified if the motivation was self-regarding, and (almost certainly) unjustified if the motivation was other-regarding.

Shiffrin holds that the state can legitimately refuse to accommodate certain behaviours for self-regarding reasons. On this reading, it might not be paternalistic to ban smoking or to attach punitive taxation to cigarettes or to deny smokers health care for their smoking-related diseases. It could be self-regarding: a case of the state's saying, as it were, 'We refuse to support this behaviour, not for the sake of smokers, but because we do not choose to facilitate or assist harmful actions.' Note that, although in this particular case one could frame an argument for not supporting smokers based on preventing the harm done to others (through passive smoking), Shiffrin's argument does not require that added weight. The state could apply the Unconscionability Doctrine, not to benefit others (there are no others involved), nor to protect B's welfare, but because it chose not to soil its hands by enforcing an unfair contract.

Shiffrin's final move is to limit the scope of self-regarding actions, laws or policies which deny accommodation. Before the state decides not to accommodate a choice, it should ask itself certain vital questions:

Is the decision highly personal and critical to one's sense of self? Is it a highly personal [choice] involving the body? [Will] the denial of accommodation … engender significant harm or loss of agency?

(Shiffrin 2000: 248)

The law on seat belts would almost certainly get through such an interrogation, and therefore compulsory seat belt–wearing could be justified as a denial of accommodation, without resort to paternalism.

If Shiffrin's argument is sound, it would permit or enjoin many of the same policies that a paternalist would urge. It is a similar tactical move to the doctrine of double effect, first formulated by Thomas Aquinas in the *Summa Theologica* (MacIntyre 2014), and employed by many Roman Catholics to justify medical treatment which shortens the life of a suffering, terminally ill patient: if the treatment is designed to relieve pain but also has the effect of shortening life, so long as the relief of pain is the true motivation, then the treatment administerer is not guilty of euthanasia.

The difficulty is that there is considerable scope for dishonesty or self-delusion about this. The same difficulty attends Shiffrin's approach. As Peter de Marneffe argues, just because a policy *need* not be motivated on other-regarding grounds is no evidence that it is not in fact so motivated (2006: 70). It seems odd that a law making the wearing of seat belts compulsory (for instance) should be motivated by the state's *self-regarding* desire not to accommodate risky behaviour by drivers. In the first place the state is not a self; it is hard to see how it could be motivated by personal feelings such as a desire not to soil its hands. But even if one concedes that the state might be thought of as a collective self and that it is appropriate to impute feelings to it, it is still implausible that the real motivation behind the seat belt law is simply that the state did not 'want' to accommodate the behaviour of seatbeltless drivers. The real motivation is that the law prevents fatalities and serious injuries to seatbeltless drivers. Put the two motivations side by side and it is obvious which is the stronger. Not only that, the weaker motivation is *logically dependent* upon the stronger. The state would have no reason to wish not to accommodate risky behaviour, if the risky behaviour did not result in fatalities and serious injuries. 'Well, but the fatalities and serious injuries entail financial and emotional costs on *others*' (the state might reply). But it seems impossible to be confident that this, rather than the welfare of the drivers themselves, is the true motivation for making seat belts compulsory. Nor do the two motivations exclude each other. A paternalist could happily endorse both. An antipaternalist seems committed to the view that saving the lives of the drivers themselves adds nothing at all to the justification for having such a law.

Shiffrin's project of reconciling an antipaternalistic position with support for (some) paternalistic-seeming laws thus seems problematic. As de Marneffe argues, one cannot prove that this reconciliation project is impossible to achieve (2006: 90). There may be other, better non-paternalistic reasons than those identified by Shiffrin. But one can at least point to particular policies which are widely endorsed by both paternalists and antipaternalists and show that they seem to be better justified by paternalistic than by non-paternalistic reasons.

To summarise: the antipaternalist presumption is rejected. Even if one concedes that restricting liberty or autonomy of an agent is always a disvalue, there seems no reason to presuppose that this disvalue will always or usually outweigh any benefits to the agent.

5.3 Weak/strong and soft/hard paternalism

5.3.1 Two distinctions

Within paternalism two distinctions can be made. They are between soft and hard paternalism, and weak and strong paternalism. Soft paternalism is characterised by Gerald Dworkin as 'the view that the only conditions under which state paternalism is justified is when it is necessary to determine whether the person being interfered with is acting voluntarily and knowledgeably' (Dworkin 2017). Mill in *On Liberty* supplies a famous example of soft paternalism, although he does not use that term: forcibly preventing somebody crossing a bridge which they do not know to be unsafe (presumably it is impossible to warn them; perhaps they do not speak English). This would not infringe their liberty: 'for liberty consists in doing what one desires, and he does not desire to fall into the river' (Mill 2005: 117). Hard paternalism, on the other hand, means preventing fully informed and voluntary actions for the agent's own good.

Weak paternalism legitimises restriction of liberty in cases where the agent has chosen the wrong means to achieve their ends. So, as Gerald Dworkin puts it, 'if a person really prefers safety to convenience then it is legitimate to force them to wear seatbelts' ((Dworkin 2017). Strong paternalism, on the other hand, would legitimise forcing a driver to wear a seat belt even if they did not value safety over convenience; because in the view of the strong paternalist the driver is mistaken about the ends they should be pursuing.

Even those who support the antipaternalist presumption ought to accept both weak and soft paternalism. Such cases seem unproblematic. Mill accepts that the state or authorities have a right and duty to intervene in such cases. So, presumably, would Shiffrin and Quong.

Soft paternalism substitutes the judgement of the state or competent authority for the judgement of a person whose judgement is acknowledged to be underinformed or impaired. There is nothing insulting or disrespectful about that.

Weak paternalism does not violate liberty or autonomy. It may safeguard them. In the first place, such intervention can preserve the life or health of the agent, allowing them scope for liberty and autonomy in the future. Moreover, it does this only by compelling them to do what they would choose to do anyway, if they fully understood the best way to achieve their ends.

Those of the antipaternalist presumption would require firm guarantees that, in the case of soft paternalism, the agent's judgement genuinely was underinformed or impaired, and that the restrictions placed on them genuinely were for their own good; and, in the case of weak paternalism, that the course of action (or non-action) imposed upon the agent genuinely was what they would choose for themselves, if they had a more accurate idea of how best to achieve their ends.

A straightforward position is thus available to the antipaternalist: weak and soft paternalism are permitted, but hard or strong paternalism are not.

One problem for this position is that it rules out such hard paternalist policies as the compulsory seat belt law, considered in Section 5.2.3, which deliver benefits we would not willingly forego. Consideration of beneficent hard or strong paternalist policies which do not impose too great a cost in terms of loss of liberty but deliver very substantial benefits may alone be enough to undermine the weak-/soft-paternalism-only position.

In Section 5.3.2, however, I challenge it from another angle, by questioning whether there is an insuperable line between soft/weak and hard/strong paternalism.

5.3.2 Questioning the distinctions

Let us conduct two thought experiments, stemming from Mill's example of soft paternalism – that is, preventing an unwitting person from crossing an unsafe bridge.

Thought experiment 1

Suppose we manage to stop the person from crossing the unsafe bridge and explain to them, by means of an interpreter, that it is in danger of collapse. But they reply that even though they now know the risk, they are willing to take it as they are late for a very important appointment.

Now the bridge-crosser is informed about the condition of the bridge so the remit of the soft paternalist might be thought to be at an end. Yet perhaps the soft paternalist can still find reasons to detain them. Perhaps the bridge-crosser does not know exactly how much weight the bridge will bear; perhaps they do not even know, accurately, how much they themselves weigh, nor how likely they are to die if the bridge does collapse. They are not in a position to evaluate the extent of the risk. Moreover, perhaps they do not know with certainty the consequences of being late for, or missing their appointment. And perhaps they are not fully aware of how their death would impact on those close to them. It would still seem to be within the purview of soft paternalism to detain them longer while remedying their ignorance on these matters. As long as one knew more about the facts of the situation than the bridge-crosser (imagine an intervener with the same kind of omniscience as the angel who saves the James Stewart character from drowning himself in *It's a Wonderful Life*) soft paternalism would justify one in detaining them, because in allowing them to cross the bridge in a state of comparative ignorance, one might be allowing them to take a course of action which they themselves, if more fully informed, would repudiate. There is thus a slippery slope from soft paternalism to hard paternalism, for the intervener could continue to say (with justification as long as they were better informed than the agent), 'I must prevent you from doing what you think you wish to do, because when you are fully informed, you will no longer wish to do it.'

There are two natural blocks to this slippery slope. One is that in practice the state, or relevant authority, would not necessarily be better informed than the agent. They might be worse informed. The other is that once the agent *is* fully informed, or as fully informed as possible, the role of the soft paternalist is at an end. Nevertheless, the remit of soft paternalism might be extended much further than might first appear.

Thought experiment 2

The following thought experiment is designed to question the bright line between weak and strong paternalism. Suppose that the bridge-crosser, when informed of the state of the bridge, says: 'Good – I now want to cross more than ever, because I have been planning to kill myself for some time, and this is the ideal opportunity.'

Let us also suppose that the bridge-crosser is not suffering from any mental illness or incompetency. They have made a settled, rational decision to end their life, for reasons that appear good to them. A weak paternalist ought to allow them to plunge to their death, for the bridge-crosser knows what they want and they know how to get it. Yet the weak paternalist might entertain worries about whether the agent's choice really was in their own interests; whether, whatever was troubling them, there might be some better means to address it than by suicide. The weak paternalist might feel impelled to try to stop them killing themselves at that point in order to buy them time to reconsider. If the desire to die was the agent's overriding will and purpose, and continued unabated for a long time, finally one might accept that this was not a case for any kind of paternalism, since keeping someone alive against their sincere and settled will is not for their own good. But most of us would think it justified to give strong paternalism a go and save their life at least once before it reached that stage, simply because of one's normal duty of beneficence towards others. A duty of beneficence does not usually require us to prevent another person from carrying out their own will. But where their own will is self-destructive, the duty of beneficence might require us to intervene. This is evident in cases where the agent is not fully competent (soft paternalism). But competent agents make mistakes too (Romeo taking poison because he thinks Juliet is dead, when she is only unconscious). Minor mistakes are the agent's own business. We refrain from interfering where the agent is capable of learning from their mistakes. But killing oneself is irreversible. If we do not intervene they will never have the chance to change their mind.

5.3.3 An additional objection to the weak–strong distinction from Derek Parfit

The fact that an agent may change their mind – that what they desire now may be different from what they desire tomorrow and very different indeed from what they desire in a year or a decade – leads us into another problematic area. The distinction between weak and strong paternalism is based on a snapshot or cross-section of an agent at one moment in time, when they desire one particular goal and a paternalistic intervener desires, on their behalf, another. But we are temporal creatures. We live and change through time. Just as a child may resist or resent paternalistic interference from a parent but be grateful for it in later life, so too an adult might wish to reject an imposed goal but later come to accept it.

Derek Parfit takes this line of thought much further in *Reasons and Persons* (1987). He argues for a Reductionist view of the self – that is, that selfhood is no more than physical and psychological continuity and connectedness (there is no 'deep further fact' (Parfit 1987: 312)). Since on Parfit's view selfhood is a matter of degree – that is to say, the psychological and physical connectedness between past, present and future versions of a self can be expressed (in principle) in percentage terms, rather than in the all-or-nothing relation of numerical identity – it is possible to be extremely specially concerned about myself tomorrow (a self to whom I am strongly psychologically connected) and considerably less specially concerned about myself in forty years' time (a self to whom I am comparatively weakly connected).

What, then, shall we say about acts of imprudence? On this view, imprudence should not be criticised as irrational. For 'it cannot be irrational for me to care less [about my future self], when there will be less connectedness' (Parfit 1987: 318). Instead, imprudence can be criticised from a *moral* direction.

There are two ways of doing this. One is a consequentialist criticism: my imprudence now harms my future self, which is wrong, in just the same way that other acts of mine which harm other people are wrong (and the less connected I am to my future self, the closer are such future-self-harming to acts that harm others).

The other way is to think of our acts as 'agent-relative' – that is, we have 'special obligations to those to whom we stand in certain relations, such as our parents, children, pupils, patients, clients or constituents' (Parfit 1987: 319). On this view, as we have a special relation to our future selves, so we have special obligations to our future selves.

In either case, but especially on the Consequentialist view (which holds good even if one denies or refuses special obligations) a case for hard, strong paternalism can be made, though Parfit does not spell this out. Just as it is legitimate to intervene to prevent individuals harming others, it is legitimate to intervene to prevent individuals harming their future selves, who, Parfit points out, cannot defend themselves (1987: 319).

If the argument is sound, then the distinction between weak and strong paternalism again becomes blurred: the gap between what the agent wants and what they ought to want may well narrow as the agent slowly becomes a different person. Indeed, the distinction between paternalism and *any* kind of morality that seeks to prevent harm and foster good to others begins to melt away.

Note that even if one does not go all the way with Parfit's conception of personal identity, the general line of argument still destabilises the weak-only paternalist position. For whether my future self has the same identity as my present self or not, my future self will certainly have different ideas, goals and desires from my present self. It is, perhaps, an open question whether I am a different person from my childhood self. But that I have different ideas, goals and desires from that childhood self is a fact. That I am now grateful for (literal) paternalist intervention which I then resisted and resented is also a fact. Such changes of mind do not cease when one becomes an adult, although their rate slows down. An intervention that I resentfully regard as strong paternalism now may look like weak paternalism a few years hence.

5.4 The paternalist presumption

5.4.1 Conly's coercive paternalism

Those who think of human beings as primarily rational agents, consistently able to make choices which will help them realise their well-chosen goals, will not extend the remit of weak or soft paternalism very far. Sarah Conly, however, in her book *Against Autonomy*, argues that in general human beings are poor judges of their own good. Therefore almost all paternalism is effectively soft paternalism. Moreover Conley argues that human beings are poor practical reasoners, too, not skilled at working out how to get what they want, so that most paternalism is also weak. Her view is thus the opposite of the Anti-Paternalist Presumption. We could call it the Paternalist Presumption. Sarah Conly argues for what she calls coercive paternalism – the view that:

> We may, and indeed are sometimes specifically morally obligated to, force people to refrain from certain actions and to engage in others' [for their own good, as has been established by Conly's preceding discussion of what paternalism means].
>
> (2013: 17–18)

The argument runs as follows. Conly believes that the high value placed on liberty in the liberal tradition rests on a false claim about human rationality.

> The ground for valuing liberty is the claim that we are pre-eminently rational agents, each of us well-suited to determining what goes on in our own life. There is ample evidence, however, from the fields of psychology and behavioural economics, that in many situations this is simply not true.
>
> (2013: 2)

Conly is right that in many circumstances human beings are poor reasoners – not, indeed, compared to other animals, but compared to the standards of rationality we set ourselves. We are prey to a range of cognitive biases identified quite recently by psychologists and social scientists: we are irrationally influenced by the way options are framed; our calculations are swayed by wishful thinking; we are poor at analysing risk; we over-value things we already have and under-value those we do not (the Endowment Effect); we are prone to making judgements based on stereotypes; we are more influenced by experience and anecdote than by statistics, and so on (see Kahneman 2011).

Allowing people maximal liberty, therefore, is simply allowing us 'to struggle with our own inabilities and suffer the consequences', as Conly puts it (2013: 1). Those consequences may be life-wrecking or life-ending, as in Conly's favoured example of smoking cigarettes.

Conly identifies two standard responses to this problem. Liberals are not indifferent to the harm caused by bad choices. What they seek to do is minimise that harm without coercion, by ensuring that citizens are *well-informed*. Thus, if citizens are fully informed about the dangers of smoking (by health warnings on cigarette packets, public information broadcasts, posters in doctors' surgeries, etc.), they are less likely to adopt the habit, or more likely to give it up. Such campaigns have had some success. But only some. Conly says:

> It's true that a smaller percentage of the population smokes now than did before it was discovered that smoking causes cancer. On the other hand, more than 20 percent of the American population does smoke, despite the millions of dollars spent in schools and the unmissable warnings on cigarette packages.
>
> (2013: 25)

Smoking is a clear-cut case. As Conly points out, if it is difficult to get everyone to respond appropriately to the fact that smoking is dangerous, how much more difficult would it be to get them to be alert to their own cognitive biases? Conly therefore rejects this approach. Giving people the right information is not enough, alone, to ensure wise choice-making.

An alternative is the Libertarian Paternalist approach, as advocated by Thaler and Sunstein in their 2003 paper 'Libertarian Paternalism Is Not an Oxymoron', and subsequently in their best-selling book *Nudge*. Instead of or in addition to informing people about the consequences of choices, the state (or relevant authority) makes beneficial choices more likely by exploiting people's cognitive biases, in the way options are presented or framed in any given situation. An example Thaler and Sunstein give is putting fruit before sugary desserts in cafeteria lines; customers are more likely to choose the healthy option if they encounter it first, and less likely to do so if they have to run a gauntlet of cakes and puddings first (Thaler and Sunstein 2003).

Conly has two criticisms of this approach. First, although it seeks to respect liberal belief in free choice by eschewing coercion, it uses manipulation instead. But manipulation obstructs free choice as surely as coercion, though more subtly. An antipaternalist liberal would be against both in principle. Conly is against neither in principle, but points out that manipulation is often less effective than coercion. This is her second and main criticism of the Libertarian Paternalist position. Putting the sugary desserts last reduces the likelihood that they will be chosen. But they will still be chosen by some people, because 'the option to err remains in place' (2013: 32).

Conly's position of coercive paternalism allows removal of the option to err:

> Rather than leaving us to sink or swim, as does liberalism, or engaging in mental manipulation, as does libertarian paternalism, the coercive paternalist will simply say some things are not allowed.
>
> (2013: 32)

Let us apply these approaches to the burqa question (assuming for the sake of argument that burqa-wearing does have harmful effects on the life of the wearer). The liberal position would be to inform its citizens loudly and clearly of the harmful effects and then leave the decision up to them. The Libertarian Paternalist position would be to devise policies that subtly discourage burqa-wearing. And the Coercive Paternalist position would be to remove the burqa-wearing option by making it illegal.

Note that this is a disagreement about means, not ends. All three positions would aim to reduce and, ideally, eliminate burqa-wearing, for the sake of the wearers (still supposing burqa-wearing to have harmful effects). The difference lies in what means are considered permissible. Conly's argument is that, human beings being what they are, only the coercive approach is likely to prove efficacious.

Conly argues that her position is not as controversial as it may appear:

> The paternalism I promote here is not a paternalism about ultimate ends; that is, I do not argue that there are objectively good ends, or objectively rational ends, or ends objectively valuable in any way, which everyone should be made to pursue. I am arguing for intervention in cases where people's choices of

instrumental means are confused, in a way that means they will not achieve their ultimate ends. If my subjective end is happiness, and I think playing the lottery will promote that, not because the suspense gives me some evanescent pleasure, but because I really think I have a reasonable chance of winning, I am mistaken about my means … [I]f we constrain action only to get the person to do what he would want to do if he were fully informed and fully rational, this may seem unproblematic.

If the position I am taking here is uncontroversial, I am quite willing to have it be so: we could proceed with crafting paternalistic legislation!

(2013: 43)

Of course, coercion is not always the most effective way of restricting self-harmful choices. In some cases manipulation, because it does not arouse opposition, may work better. In principle, though, I agree with Conly that coercive paternalism can be legitimate, and acceptable to liberals. There is no insuperable line between weak/soft and strong/hard paternalism.

5.4.2 The Liberal Paternalist Principle

Yet there must be some limits to paternalism if anything of a liberal position is to remain. The limiting principle I propose is the Liberal Paternalist Principle: where the restriction of liberty is small, and the gain in welfare great, then paternalism can be justified. Where the restriction of liberty is great, and the gain in welfare small, then paternalism cannot be justified.

This is a rule of thumb – there is no precise way to measure smallness and greatness in such matters. But it is clear that restricting a person's liberty in a well-defined area which does not intrude into every aspect of their life would count as a small restriction. Saving them from death or serious injury would count as a great gain in welfare.

Here is an example of a paternalist policy which seems to pass this test. In 1998, the government of the United Kingdom passed legislation to restrict the pack size of paracetamol tablets to thirty-two tablets in pharmacies, sixteen tablets in other retail outlets. The aim of the law was to reduce death by suicide; previously it had been possible to buy packs of one hundred tablets, sufficient for a lethal dose. The result, according to research by the British Medical Journal published in 2013, was a 43 per cent reduction in the number of deaths by overdose in the 11.25 years since the law was passed – or 765 fewer deaths than would otherwise have been predicted (*British Medical Journal* (*BMJ*) 2013; 346).

The restriction of liberty involved here is very small. People are still able to buy paracetamol for the purpose of pain relief. The only restriction is that they cannot buy bumper-sized packs. And the gain is very great. Hundreds of lives have been saved. This policy, then, is consistent with the Liberal Paternalist Principle.

Where the gain in welfare is more minor, and/or restriction of liberty is more major, paternalist policies become harder to justify, until a point where justification is no longer possible. Imagine a law which stipulated that all persons should wear a padded suit when out in public, to protect them from bruising if they fell over. Here the restriction of liberty would be great and the harms avoided very small. Such a policy could not be justified under the Liberal Paternalist Principle.

5.5 Paternalism and the burqa

If the Liberal Paternalist Principle is granted we can proceed to ask whether it would justify banning the burqa.

One paternalist argument is the argument from health. This is one of the most common and widely accepted types of paternalist argument. The restriction of pack sizes of paracetamol and the enforcement of the wearing of safety belts in cars have already been discussed. Such laws do not feel uncomfortable for a liberal to justify, as the damage to health avoided is very great, and the restriction of liberty small.

Applying this to the burqa, the following question arises: Does burqa-wearing pose a serious threat to health? Martha Nussbaum notes that 'one frequently hears the argument that the *burqa* is per se unhealthy, because it is hot and uncomfortable' (2012: 129), and describes this as 'perhaps the silliest of the arguments'. Certainly as she presents it is less than compelling. As she goes on to point out, 'Clothing that covers the body can be comfortable or uncomfortable, depending on the fabric' (Nussbaum 2012: 129). In hot weather, covering the body may be healthier than not, diminishing the risk of skin cancer. Moreover, being hot and uncomfortable is not a risk to health anyway. It is simply being hot and uncomfortable, which is certainly not a major enough harm to justify paternalist intervention.

There are stronger versions of the argument, however, not considered by Nussbaum. Direct skin contact with the sun's rays is our main source of vitamin D, and habitual all-body covering leads to its deficiency, a condition that causes bone abnormalities, rickets and muscle weakness. This fact might suffice to make a case for a paternalist burqa-ban, if a ban were the only way to remedy the matter.

But it is not the only way. Burqa-wearers could remove the burqa in their own gardens or other private spaces and soak up some sunshine. Vitamin D supplements in tablet form are available. A government concerned about vitamin D deficiency in burqa-wearers could publicise the condition and its causes and consequences, and make supplements available to correct it, without recourse to the blunt instrument of a ban, which has many other effects besides counteracting vitamin D deficiency.

It is also a requisite that any paternalist policies pursued by a liberal state be consistent, treating all citizens equally. Nussbaum argues that the arguments commonly advanced for a burqa-ban are ethically inconsistent:

> All five [arguments] are made inconsistently, in ways that tacitly favour majority practices and burden minority practices. They are thus not compatible with a principle of equal liberty. Hence, in turn, they are not compatible with the idea of equal respect for conscience from which that principle springs.
>
> (2012: 105)

As we shall see, I do not agree that all the five arguments discussed by Nussbaum are always made inconsistently. But Nussbaum is right to insist on ethical consistency as a requisite test for taking such arguments seriously, and she is also right that the argument from health fails to pass it. For the burqa is by no means the only form of clothing which can have adverse effects on health. Nussbaum asks:

> Would the arguer really seek to ban all uncomfortable and possibly unhealthy female clothing? Wouldn't we have to begin with high heels, delicious as they are? But no, high heels are associated with majority norms … and so draw no ire.
>
> (2012: 130)

Moreover, clothing which leaves large areas of skin exposed to the sun could lead to skin cancer, a more serious condition than vitamin D deficiency, and no one is arguing for a bikini-ban.

But perhaps burqa-wearing entails other losses in well-being, besides possible health problems, which require paternalist attention? Wearing a burqa cuts one off from a great deal of social intercourse, making it impossible to smile at other people, for example. It prevents the wearer from feeling the breeze or the sun on her face. Another point to consider is whether burqa-wearing could adversely affect mental health. Communicating with facial expressions is so deep-rooted a human instinct that the inability to do so in public spaces might plausibly lead to mental health problems such as loneliness, stress or depression. If this were so then a case for paternalist intervention might be justified.

However, there seems to be no evidence to date that burqa-wearing does lead to mental health problems. Inability to express oneself via the face has not been found to cause mental health problems in those who suffer from Moebius syndrome. Moebius syndrome is a rare congenital condition in which the sufferer is afflicted with permanent facial paralysis. Sufferers find social interaction difficult as a result. However, a 2009 study by Bogart and Matsumoto found the following:

> People with Moebius syndrome reported significantly lower social competence than the matched control group and normative data but did not differ significantly from the control group or norms in anxiety, depression, or satisfaction with life.
> (Bogart and Matsumoto 2009)

If even sufferers from Moebius syndrome do not suffer mental health problems as a result of not being able to communicate through facial expressions, it seems unlikely that burqa-wearers should do so. It is true that people with Moebius syndrome report lower social competence, but since one of the purposes of the burqa is to reduce the incidence of social interaction, this would not seem to count as a problem for burqa-wearers. Besides, burqa-wearers have plenty of opportunity to communicate through facial expressions in private, with their own family or female friends, so there is no reason to suppose social competence in those situations would be reduced.

Finally, one might consider the effects that burqa-wearing has on life chances. It drastically limits career opportunities. No woman wearing a burqa is going to get a job as a teacher, a doctor, a barrister, a TV presenter, a Member of Parliament, an actor or an athlete. But a monk or a nun in an enclosed order, or a recluse, also has drastically limited career opportunities. If burqas were to be banned on the grounds that they restrict life and career opportunities, then ethical consistency would require that becoming a monk, a nun or a recluse should also be banned.

Any possible risk to health or well-being brought on by voluntary burqa-wearing is more than matched by risks to health or well-being brought on by other types of activity and lifestyle – smoking, unhealthy eating, doing dangerous sports and so on – and ethical consistency would require that if we want to ban the burqa for paternalist reasons we should ban those things too.

Banning the burqa to safeguard health and well-being fails to meet the test of the Liberal Paternalist Principle. Preventing a devout Muslim woman from wearing a burqa is a major restriction of liberty, affecting every aspect of her daily life. To justify that, the benefits would have to be very great. But though burqa-wearing might lead to some (remediable) health problems, and some discomfort, it certainly does not endanger life, nor impair vital functions. There are social and professional disadvantages, but not such as would prevent the burqa-wearer enjoying family life, friendships, and satisfactions and achievements within her community. In short, a burqa-ban on grounds of health and well-being would be a major restriction of liberty for fairly small benefits, and could not be justified by the Liberal Paternalist Principle.

A paternalist ban on the grounds of supporting personal autonomy, however, is less easy to dismiss. This will be considered in Chapter 6.

6

Personal autonomy and the burqa

The argument

This chapter considers autonomy-based paternalism: that is, paternalist action in order to secure or promote not welfare in general but personal autonomy. This form of paternalism has at first blush a paradoxical air. There seems something odd about the state's propelling citizens towards autonomy, when the whole point of autonomy is that one decides for oneself what one values. However, the paradox is only apparent. For if persons have no autonomy to begin with, then paternalist actions cannot take it away. Moreover, as Colburn has argued (see Chapter 4) if the state promotes second-order autonomy, then first-order autonomy is not inhibited, but enabled (Colburn 2010).

In this chapter I argue for a conception of personal autonomy which is (1) *relational* and (2) *content-neutral*. I argue that autonomy should not be the sole value of importance to a liberal state. It would be the duty of a liberal state to protect or enable personal autonomy, but not to enforce it. The same would be true of other goods such as development of intelligence. This position is in line with Nussbaum's capabilities approach (2001).

If it is the case that burqa-wearing is incompatible with personal autonomy, then the liberal state would have a justification for preventing burqa-wearing. However, I argue that burqa-wearing is not necessarily incompatible with second-order autonomy. The crucial factor is whether the choice to wear a burqa is *revocable*. If it is, then second-order autonomy is preserved. Following Colburn and Nussbaum, and in contrast to Clare Chambers (2008), I prioritise second-order autonomy over first-order autonomy. Therefore, as long as the choice of burqa-wearing can be revoked at any time by the wearer(s), the liberal state has no justification for intervening on grounds of autonomy-protecting paternalism.

6.1 Defining personal autonomy

Let us begin with a brief explanation of the term *autonomy*. It is a quality which is normally dependent on freedom, but is not synonymous with freedom. Freedom is a condition: the absence of relevant restrictions or of interference, as well as the presence of whatever resources are necessary to make acting freely feasible. Autonomy is a quality which enables a person to make a certain kind of use of that freedom.

The basic definition of autonomy is simple. It means 'self-rule', from the Greek *autos-* meaning 'self' and *-nomy* meaning 'rule' or 'law'. Words often part company from their original meanings over the centuries, but in this case 'self-rule' still captures the essential sense of the concept. An autonomous nation, for example, is one which rules itself, deciding upon its own aims, policies and laws. It is not a satellite nation, obedient to the dictates of another, stronger, controlling power. This usage is faithful to the original Greek meaning, when the word was used to denote the political independence of city-states (Dworkin 2007: 333). The word has since extended its semantic reach to describe individual persons who rule themselves, deciding on their own aims, policies and laws.

Kant regarded this quality as necessary to morality. A moral person is one who is 'subject *only to laws given by himself but still universal*' (Kant [1785] 2008: 40). He calls this principle 'the autonomy of the will' (Kant [1785] 2008: 41). Autonomy is the property of rational beings, and in virtue of it, one is a member of 'the kingdom of ends': that is, a moral realm where everyone is to treat themselves and all others '*never merely as means* but always *at the same time as ends in themselves*' (Kant [1785] 2008: 41). The characteristically liberal feature of this formulation is that *all* rational beings are included under it. Personal autonomy was valued in the ancient world for kings and emperors, but not for slaves or the general populace. In Kant's system, every rational being is equally accorded the dignity of being an autonomous moral agent. It is true that Kant had some racist ideas (Allais 2016) and might not have admitted all races to be fully rational, but this is a feature of his thinking that we can dispense with. The ideal of universal moral autonomy does not depend on qualification by race.

The importance of personal autonomy is well captured by Isaiah Berlin in his characterisation of 'positive liberty' in his essay 'Two Concepts of Liberty' (1998). Berlin explains positive liberty as that which is possessed and exercised by a person able to satisfy the wish to be a subject, not an object; to be moved by reasons, by conscious purposes, which are [their] own, not by causes which affect [them], as it were, from outside... deciding, not being decided for, self-directed and not acted upon by external nature or by other men as if [they] were a thing, or an animal, or a slave incapable of playing a human role, that is, of conceiving goals and policies of [their] own and realising them.

(Berlin 1998: 203)

Although Berlin invokes at least two other senses of positive liberty in the essay (see Swift 2001: 52–68), this particular characterisation is an apt description of the idea of personal autonomy, and a good explanation of why it is valued. It underpins an ideal of human dignity, attainable by all rational beings. As far as we know, no other creatures on earth are fully rational in the sense that humans are. Autonomy is thus something that is 'distinctive and valuable about human life' (Colburn 2010: 2).

6.2 Autonomy-based paternalism

Paternalism is often held to be in direct opposition to personal autonomy. Marina Oshana describes autonomy as 'the good that paternalism fails to respect' (1989: 82), and in the majority of scenarios that is true. However, there is one case in which the two are compatible: where paternalist policies are required to provide or promote personal autonomy.

This sounds contradictory, but is not. Paternalism is easy to justify when its object has no autonomy in the first place, because then its exercise does not fail to respect autonomy (there is none to be disrespected). For instance, babies lack autonomy, and it is not merely justifiable but necessary that we act paternalistically towards them. It is this paternalist care which enables them to grow into individuals with personal autonomy.

There is, then, a possible autonomy-based paternalist argument for a burqa-ban in a liberal state. If burqa-wearers lack autonomy, then the state may be justified in restricting their liberty to wear burqas, irrespective of their wishes, in order to restore their autonomy.

Whether the argument works depends on two questions. (1) Is it the goal of liberalism to promote personal autonomy? (2) Is wearing the burqa incompatible with personal autonomy? If the answer to both questions is 'Yes', then the autonomy-based paternalist argument could justify a burqa-ban.

To anticipate: in Section 6.4 I argue, contra Raz and Colburn, that it is not the sole goal of a liberal state to promote autonomy. Autonomy, though valuable, does not automatically have primacy over other values. However, that does not of itself invalidate the autonomy-based paternalist argument. It could be *one* of the goals of a liberal state to promote personal autonomy, as a valuable thing among others.

In Section 6.4 I shall argue that in extreme cases – like the situation of a burqa-wearer in Taliban-controlled Afghanistan – a ban could theoretically be justified on the autonomy-based paternalist argument. Although, of course, in that case there is no liberal state in place to enforce a ban. On the other hand, in liberal states where a ban could be enforced it would be far less likely to be justified.

6.3 The value of autonomy in liberalism

The controversy for liberals is not over whether personal autonomy is valuable, or whether everyone has an equal right to it. The answer to both those questions is yes. The controversy is over what place it should occupy in liberal theory: whether autonomy is a welcome side effect of liberal principles, or the underlying justification for those principles.

6.3.1 The side-effect view

On an extreme PL view, guaranteeing equal and extensive liberties for all is the only essential thing. Brian Barry (2011) is representative of this position. He argues that a liberal state has no duty to promote autonomy. On his view, personal autonomy is a side effect of liberalism rather than the justification for the liberal project, which rests simply on principles of equal freedom. A liberal state should *allow* personal autonomy, but not promote it as an ideal:

> Contemporary liberals can, and do, regard it as an argument for liberalism that a liberal society makes individual autonomy possible. But that in no way commits them to the proposition that states should engage in the compulsory inculcation of autonomy – an expression whose strangeness calls attention to the peculiarity of the whole project.
>
> (Barry 2011: 120)

He does, however, concede that the philosophy of doing so would qualify as a form of liberalism: the ideal of autonomy 'is not a violation of neutrality between conceptions of the good' because 'autonomous people can have any substantive beliefs they like' (Barry 2011: 123). But this is not a form of liberalism that he himself endorses.

6.3.2 Autonomy as underlying justification

On this view, as we have seen, achieving personal autonomy for all is the sole reason one wants to guarantee liberties in the first place. Joseph Raz's version of this view is fully perfectionist, in that he argues autonomy 'is valuable only if exercised in pursuit of the good. The ideal of autonomy requires only the availability of morally acceptable options' (Raz 2009: 381).

As discussed in Chapter 4, Ben Colburn also argues for the primacy of autonomy, but without any such limitation of options: it is up to the individual to decide what is valuable in life (Colburn 2010). His view of liberalism is similar to the one that Barry accepts as a form of liberalism but does not endorse: the primacy of a content-neutral autonomy.

6.3.3 A third way: Autonomy as a value but not an ideal

The two approaches reviewed thus far are disjunctive. Either autonomy as an ideal is essential to the liberal project, or it is entirely unnecessary. But there is a third way, articulated by Clare Chambers:

> Barry, argues, rightly, that liberals do not need to be and perhaps cannot be committed to what he calls 'the ideal of autonomy'. However, liberals must be committed to the *value* of autonomy.
>
> (Chambers 2005: 166)

Chambers argues that although the liberal state should not seek to inculcate autonomy in its citizens, it must value autonomy if it is to justify liberal institutions as the most just way of dealing with disagreement. Certainly, liberal institutions could be justified in different ways, for example, by appeals to peace or prosperity (Chambers 2005). But if, as Barry does, a liberal maintains that it would be *unjust* to inflict criminal penalties on those who reject the beliefs of their community, or to discriminate against them in other ways (Barry 2011), this implies an appeal to the value of autonomy. A non-liberal need not agree; a non-liberal might well hold that dissidents should be forced to conform by means of penalties. But that is precisely because such a non-liberal does not value autonomy. To (1) support liberal institutions and (2) hold that liberal institutions are the most just way of dealing with disagreement is necessarily to invoke the value of autonomy.

I agree with Chambers's reasoning on this point. The upshot is that liberals ought to protect autonomy and to be prepared to intervene where it is compromised or denied. This does not commit one to autonomy as an ideal. The point is not that everyone should be autonomous, but that nobody should be prevented from being so.

If this is correct, we have established that, at the least, autonomy is a necessary value (though not necessarily the only necessary value) for liberals. We have not yet established that it is not an ideal as well. To argue that it is not an ideal, I make a comparison between autonomy and intelligence.

6.4 Autonomy and intelligence

6.4.1 The purpose of the comparison

Intelligence is valuable in similar ways to autonomy and for similar reasons. Yet it sounds implausible that the ideal of a liberal state should be to secure maximal intelligence for all.

This is not a knock-down argument against perfectionist liberals such as Raz. It is rather a perspective which makes thorough-going liberal perfectionism appear implausible, because a more natural and less demanding way of thinking about autonomy is to hand: we can think about it in the same way that we think about intelligence.

There are three main ways in which intelligence is analogous to autonomy: both are personal qualities; both are valuable; and both are content-neutral. I shall discuss these one by one.

6.4.2 An objection forestalled

First, however, a likely objection should be forestalled. It may be said that intelligence itself is not a simple concept: there are disagreements about how to measure it or whether it is even measurable, whether it is a single quality or a multidimensional set of qualities and, if it is multidimensional, what are those dimensions? Do musical ability, or a sense of humour, count as dimensions? Is intelligence a state or a process? Is intelligent behaviour based on a settled disposition, or is it to be understood situationally – that is, does one's level of intelligence depend largely on the situation one is in, as social psychologists like Lee Ross and Richard Nisbett theorise is the case with personality (Ross and Nesbitt 2011)? And then there is the venerable debate about whether, or to what extent, or in what sense intelligence is either innate or the product of environment. If intelligence is not a clearly defined concept, then how effectively can it be deployed as an analogy?

There are two answers to this challenge. The first is that, despite the controversies, there is enough of a working consensus on what counts as intelligent behaviour, or an intelligent person, to speak meaningfully about intelligence. But there is a second, more interesting answer, which is that the controversial nature of intelligence is itself another parallel with autonomy. Autonomy is also the subject of dispute, found in a variety of related forms (personal autonomy, moral autonomy, political autonomy, group autonomy), it is hard to measure, and could be understood either dispositionally or situationally. There is also room for discussion about the extent to which having an autonomous character is the product of nature or nurture (though that aspect of the debate has been little explored). Just as it would be hard for a state to make maximising the intelligence of all citizens a primary goal, because intelligence is such a slippery concept, so, too, it would be hard to make maximal autonomy of all citizens a primary goal, for the same reason.

Let us now turn to the three main points of the analogy, beginning with the point that both autonomy and intelligence are personal qualities.

6.4.3 Personal qualities

Freedom is a condition. So are other goods which the state can provide, such as security and welfare. These are things one has, not things one does. Intelligence, on the other hand, is a personal *quality* (or set of qualities), rather than a condition. It is reliant on background conditions: full flourishing of intelligence requires liberty of thought, and enabling conditions like a decent education system. The liberal state can, should and does provide those background conditions. But after that its job is over as far as intelligence is concerned; it has led the horse to water, but it is no part of its task to force the horse to drink. Some people may prefer to devote their lives to excelling at physical pursuits rather than spending their time studying, or they may prefer sitting in a pub to sitting in a library, and a liberal state has no reason to object.

The same considerations hold with regard to autonomy. Like intelligence it is not a condition but a personal quality, that one can be more or less skilled at deploying, and more or less disposed to deploy.

Both intelligence and autonomy are matters of degree; neither is an all-or-nothing quality. Actually both are better thought of as sets of interrelated qualities. Personal autonomy requires at least three qualities: rationality, independence of mind and motivation (one must *want* to choose one's own values and direct one's own life). Not everyone will possess all these qualities to an equal degree. The perfectionist might respond that ideally everyone should possess them to the maximum extent they are capable of. But that suggests a rather illiberal programme – the interference with individual independence deprecated by Mill in *On Liberty* ([1859] 2005). Perhaps some people prefer a quiet, unadventurous life based on accepting societal or communal norms without a great deal of scrutiny. It ought not to be within the purview of liberalism to insist on the development of certain personal qualities at the expense of others.

We would think it both illiberal and impractical if someone claimed that the task of the state was to ensure that everyone developed all the qualities associated with intelligence to a maximal degree. It is the task of a liberal state to guarantee the conditions for development of intelligence, but it is not the task of the state to force people to develop their personal intelligence to a maximal degree if they do not choose to do so. I contend that the same position holds with regard to personal autonomy.

6.4.4 Value

As argued in Section 6.3, personal autonomy is a valuable quality. The characteristically liberal position is that everyone should have equal liberty to develop and deploy it. But it is a big step from there to say that the state ought to encourage everybody to develop and deploy it to a maximal degree. What is it about autonomy that should make it, alone, *the* personal quality that the state must foster above all others?

It might be said that autonomy is instrumentally extremely valuable. It helps us to achieve all sorts of other goods. A person's autonomous decision to pursue a particular career, for example, may result in personal happiness or material well-being. Moreover, happiness and material well-being, as well as personal relationships, success in achieving goals and so on, depend on autonomy for a good deal of their meaning. They all have far more significance to the agent if they are attained through the agent's autonomous choices and actions.

But all this could equally be said of intelligence. Intelligence also helps us achieve other goods, resulting in happiness and well-being; and successes earned by our wits are more satisfying than those achieved by chance (and in fact we observe that successful people seldom do attribute their success to chance, preferring to give the credit to their own intelligence).

What is special about autonomy, though, the perfectionist liberal might urge, is that it is *intrinsically* valuable. Even when autonomy does not lead to success and happiness, we would still rather be the masters of our fate and the captains of our souls, as W. E. Henley put it (Henley [1888] 2016: 268). We prefer to direct our own lives. We resent the interference when others try to direct them for us. Being autonomous brings a dignity to our lives. It is true that in most societies throughout history the mass of people have neither expected nor got much autonomy. Autonomy was the privilege of powerful men; the idea that everyone should have it would once have been regarded as strange, indefensible and impossible. It was, we might say, a positional good. But it was always a good. The notion that everyone, not just kings, should have the liberty to achieve this good is the essence of the liberal view.

Autonomy is also, as far as we know, a uniquely human quality. With the possible exception of the other great apes no other animal is capable of it, and even great apes could only be capable of it in a severely limited sense.

Again, however, all the same things could be said of intelligence. It, too, is intrinsically valuable. A lively apprehension, a grasp of complexity, appreciation of nuances, the pleasures of learning and of problem-solving are all aspects of intelligence which we value purely for their own sake. And even when the exercise of intelligence is not enjoyable in itself, we would still prefer an intelligent understanding of a bad situation to the option of living in a fool's paradise. Intelligence, too, is a more or less uniquely human quality, with the same partial exception of the great apes and a handful of other mammals, none of them capable of approaching anywhere near the heights of human intelligence.

Neither can it be said that autonomy is a more fundamental quality than intelligence, for a certain level of intelligence is one of the essential conditions for autonomy: a baby's intelligence is not sufficiently developed for it to be autonomous, and as its intelligence grows so does its autonomy; and someone who is brain-damaged or severely mentally handicapped will never achieve full autonomy.

6.4.5 Content-neutrality

Another key feature of autonomy is that it is content-neutral. The actual content of the choices one makes is irrelevant in the question of whether one is autonomous. This naturally makes it attractive to liberals. In championing autonomy they are not championing any particular way of life. (There is an opposing view, held by some perfectionist liberals such as Marina Oshana, that autonomy is substantive. I do not accept that view, and argue against it in section 6.5.1). A commitment to personal autonomy does not imply favouring any particular values or choices. All that is relevant is the manner in which those choices are made and those values subscribed to. It is the content-neutrality of autonomy that makes Barry willing to accept autonomy-based liberalism as genuinely liberal (2011: 123).

Intelligence, equally, is content-neutral. Intelligent people display an unlimited range of beliefs and behaviours. Two highly intelligent people may believe directly contrary things (Heraclitus believing that everything changes and Parmenides believing that nothing changes). An intelligent person may even find reasons to renounce the use of intelligence: in *Candide* Voltaire recommends that we should 'Travaillons sans raisonner: c'est le seul moyen de rendre la vie supportable' (Work without thinking; it is the only way to make life bearable) ([1759] 1962: 106). Nor is there any one belief or behaviour that an intelligent person must exhibit in order to qualify.

Intelligence is also without *moral* content. If somebody employs their intelligence in planning terrorist attacks, or devising and testing instruments of torture, we do not therefore conclude that they must be unintelligent. We think it is a shame that they use their intelligence in ways so pernicious to the rest of us, and try to put a stop to their evil activities.

One might object that if we understand autonomy in a similar way then we lose our reason to value it. This seems to be Raz's view. He states that freedom, of which he takes autonomy to be 'a concrete form' (Raz 2009: 394), is 'not an independent separate ideal … freedom consists in the pursuit of valuable forms of life, and … its value derives from the value of that pursuit' (Raz 2009: 395). Yet specific instances of intelligence allied to malevolence do not make us cease to value intelligence in general. Intelligence seems to be intrinsically valuable. I contend that personal autonomy is intrinsically valuable in the same way.

A liberal state, then, should view personal autonomy and should form policies regarding personal autonomy in the same way that it views intelligence and forms policies regarding intelligence. Stunting a person's intellectual development by denying them education or stimulation and compromising or denying another person's autonomy must both be proscribed by the liberal state. The state must also ensure the requisite conditions for the development of each (which are in many ways similar: a decent education and state-guaranteed liberty of thought, expression and lifestyle are requisite for both). But there seems to me no sound liberal reason to go beyond that.

It is always open to the perfectionist liberal to accept the analogy and say, yes, the goal of a liberal state is to foster maximal development of both autonomy *and* intelligence. But this seems a move too far towards the extreme perfectionist end of the spectrum. Such an over-intervening state would compromise the freedom of choice that liberals value.

6.5 Autonomy and irrevocable choices

6.5.1 'Taliban Woman'

In her book *Personal Autonomy in Society* (2006), Oshana considers the possibility of a burqa-ban grounded in autonomy-based paternalism, through means of a case study, which she calls 'Taliban Woman':

> Suppose that this woman has embraced the role of subservience and the abdication of independence that it demands, out of reverence, a sense of purpose, an earnest belief in the sanctity of this role as espoused in certain passages of the Qu'ran … She is not permitted to support herself financially. She does not have legal custody of her children … She has no voice in the manner and duration of any schooling that her children, particularly her daughters, may receive. She must remain costumed in cumbersome garb – a burqa – when in public … [Nevertheless her life is] consistent with her spiritual and social values, provides her with a sense of worth, and satisfies her notion of well-being.
>
> (2006: 60)

Oshana argues for a social-relational account of autonomy. On her view, whatever 'Taliban Woman's' personal preferences, she cannot be autonomous if her social relations with others preclude her from directing her own life. She has given up the capacity to direct her own life. All decisions are taken for her by men. Therefore she is not autonomous. Paternalist intervention on her behalf – changing the laws of the country, giving her legal rights equal with those of men, banning the burqa, making school compulsory for girls and so on – would not violate her autonomy, since she has none.

Oshana also argues that a socio-relational account of autonomy must be a substantive one; in other words, autonomy must be of a certain kind, which does not include unthinking obedience to the will of others, or allowing oneself to be demeaned.

I should like, *contra* Oshana, to argue two things. First, that a socio-relational conception of autonomy need not be a substantive one. Second, the key point in deciding if 'Taliban Woman' is autonomous (and I agree with Oshana that she almost certainly is not) is whether her decision to live a life of unthinking obedience is *revocable*.

In discussing Oshana's case study I shall draw on work by John Christman and Joel Anderson. They offer an account of personal autonomy consistent with its being social-relation, but which is content-neutral, not substantive. They stipulate two conditions for autonomy: *authenticity* and *competency* (Christman and Anderson 2005: 3).

The Authenticity Condition requires that the choices made by the agent are such that, given the opportunity to reflect, the agent would endorse the aims, values and desires that drive those choices. Their choices authentically belong to them.

'Competency' requires that the agent must have 'various capacities for rational thought, self-control, self-understanding and so on – and … they must be free to exercise those capacities, without internal or external coercion' (2005: 3).

On Christman and Anderson's proceduralist account, then, autonomy is not substantive and to say that an act is autonomous is to say nothing about the content of that act. It is just to say that the required conditions were in place: that the agent is competent and their choice authentic. Characterising autonomy as socio-relational does not contradict the proceduralist account. My argument is that the Competency Condition comprehends the socio-relational character of autonomy, without committing one to a substantive conception.

But let us look first at Oshana's criticisms of the proceduralist account.

6.5.2 Oshana's critique of the proceduralist account of autonomy

Oshana responds at length to Christman, and others who hold a proceduralist view of autonomy, in *Personal Autonomy in Society* (2006). The point where she most directly differs from the proceduralist account is her disagreement with Christman's view that people can be autonomous 'despite having desires for subservient, demeaning or even evil things' ('Autonomy and Personal History', pp. 2–3, quoted in Oshana 2006: 42).

However, Oshana's objection mischaracterises what it is to lack autonomy. A desire for evil things might indicate an unusual amount of autonomy – suggesting a determined, self-willed flouting of conventional morality. If the agent's carrying out their evil desires would harm the rest of us then we should prevent the agent carrying them out. But this is an argument for thwarting their autonomous choices, not denying that they had them in the first place.

Subservient or demeaning desires, on the other hand, *could* supply evidence of a lack of autonomy. This would depend on the nature of the desire. There seem to be three possibilities: (1) an autonomous choice to relinquish one's autonomy temporarily; (2) an autonomous choice to relinquish one's autonomy permanently; and (3) a non-autonomous choice to relinquish one's autonomy (whether temporarily or permanently makes no difference).

For Case 1, imagine a businessman who works very hard during the week and who relaxes at weekends by being chained up in a dungeon and humiliated and abused by a dominatrix. Imagine also that the businessman is fully competent mentally, is not coerced in any way and that this is an authentic choice which he endorses whenever he reflects on it (and he reflects on it a lot). His choice of recreation is subservient and demeaning (as it is intended to be). But I see no reason to doubt that it is autonomous. Not only is the choice itself autonomous, but it does not lead to any long-term diminution of his autonomy.

For Case 2, let us look at Oshana's own example of the Voluntary Slave, from her 1989 article, 'Personal Autonomy and Society'. She argues that a person who has voluntarily entered into a condition of slavery cannot be autonomous. Their *choice* to become a slave could have been autonomous, if made in accordance with the Competency and Authenticity Conditions; but the *consequence* is a total, irrevocable loss of autonomy (if it is not irrevocable, then the slave is not really a slave, but play-acting). One would do one's best to prevent someone making such a terrible choice, for their own sake. This would be a clear case where autonomy-based paternalism would be justified. (It would also, incidentally, be supported by good non-paternalist reasons: the corrupting effect of power on the slaveowner, the potential for abuse, and the damaging effects on society's values and morale.)

Case 3 would be where the agent's choice to be subservient and demeaned failed to satisfy the Competency and/or Authenticity Conditions in the first place. Perhaps the agent was not of sound mind, or was threatened or otherwise coerced into the choice. In such a case the agent would not be autonomous, but that would not be because of the *content* of their choice. It would be for procedural reasons: because they did not meet the Competency Condition.

Thus the content-neutral, proceduralist account is sufficient to rule on whether cases of subservient or demeaning behaviour are or are not autonomous.

Oshana claims, however, that consistent content-neutrality is impossible. She argues that proponents of content-neutral accounts cannot 'avoid introducing substantive claims into their theories, in spite of their desire not to do so' (Oshana 2006: 43). This, she says, is because the conditions of authenticity and competency depend on facts that are not content-neutral: 'facts about the social situation of the agent and facts about the character of the agent's desires' (Oshana 2006: 43).

This is beyond dispute. But it does not seem to be a problem for the proceduralist. Pre-existing facts do make authenticity and competency possible. But what then? Oshana states that 'when pressed to specify those facts, we cannot help but be selective' (2006: 43). That is true, but then we are being selective about the conditions that make autonomy possible, not about which desires count as autonomous. Oshana has found evidence of substantiveness among proceduralists, but not where she needs to find it.

Oshana's next point has more bite. She says that '[we] also need to know which pro-attitudes – desires, values, interests – are consonant with an unimpaired critical psychology' (2006: 43).

A proceduralist might disagree. One has an unimpaired critical psychology if one is able to critically reflect on and embrace one's desires and values. What those desires and values actually are need not come into it. However, being able to critically reflect on one's desires and values depends on a normative idea of a healthy, functioning psychology. If an individual held bizarre, delusional or incoherent beliefs, or was in the grip of a phobia or obsession, this might be apparent in their expressed desires and values, which would be taken as evidence of a lack of capacity for the appropriate critical reflection (the case of Chloe Jennings-White, discussed in Chapter 5, might be an example). This amount of substantiveness, I think, the proceduralist must admit to. Yet it is not substantiveness about the desires themselves, but about the mental state which they may reveal.

Oshana continues:

> It is plausible that a desire for drug addiction (for example), or for enslavement, for systematic deception, for brainwashing, for the restraint of civil liberties, or for browbeating and threatening gestures on part of others is inconsonant with procedural independence and is inconsonant with a person's autonomy.
>
> (2006: 43)

It is not possible to state in advance that any one of these strange desires is definitionally inconsonant with procedural independence, without knowledge of the context. (One might imagine someone desiring to experience drug addiction so that they could write a book about it.) But if the full context suggested mental derangement and hence a lack of competency, then yes, such a desire – or rather, the incapacity of which the desire was a symptom – would indeed be inconsonant with procedural independence (and hence autonomy). To this extent, Oshana is right.

However, this does not call for a large admixture of substantiveness to the proceduralist account. There is a distinction to be made between the capacity for critical reflection and the content of desires. For the proceduralist it is the capacity for critical reflection that is crucial. The content of a desire or value is relevant only insofar as it may be symptomatic of incapacity for critical reflection. In any case, the content would be only one factor among others in making that diagnosis. Other factors would include the origin of the desire/value, its duration, its relationship with other desires/values of the agent, reasons offered in support of it, its instrumentality in achieving long-term goals and so on.

But what of 'Taliban Woman'? She is not mentally deranged; she is capable of critical reflection; she made her choice in a procedurally independent manner. Yet I agree with Oshana that she is not autonomous. If it is not the content of her choice that makes her non-autonomous, then what is it?

For proceduralists the case allows three possible responses.

1. They can maintain that, despite all appearances, 'Taliban Woman' is autonomous.
2. They can agree that she is not autonomous but find an explanation for this within the proceduralist framework.
3. They can admit that Oshana is right and adopt a substantive view of autonomy.

Response 3 is always available if responses 1 and 2 fail. But let us try responses 1 and 2 first.

Trying to maintain response 1 seems to make a mockery of the concept of autonomy. The concept is stretched to absurd limits if a woman with no power to direct her own life with regard to such matters as career, parenthood, dress, personal relationships, freedom to travel, access to education and political choices, and without power ever to change this, qualifies as autonomous. That she was autonomous when she chose that life makes does not make her autonomous after the choice has been enacted, any more than the fact that someone was alive when they chose to kill themselves means they are alive after doing so. Let us grant, then, that 'Taliban Woman' is not autonomous.

Opting for response 2 entails showing that 'Taliban Woman' fails to meet the conditions laid down by proceduralists. It is clear that as described by Oshana she meets the Authenticity Condition. She owns her choice. It is consistent with her values. She is able to reflect upon it adequately and she endorses it.

But what of the Competency Condition? Let it be granted that 'Taliban Woman' has the required capacities for rational thought, self-control, self-understanding and so on. But the Competency Condition also requires that the agent be 'free to exercise those capacities, without internal or external coercion' (Christman and Anderson 2005: 3). 'Taliban Woman' is not free in this sense as she would be swiftly and harshly punished if her capacity for rational thought led her to decide she no longer wanted to live a subservient life. She has not decided this as yet, but would not be free to do so if she did.

As Christman has stressed, although a person is constituted by interpersonal and social relations, these interactions are 'alterable and shifting' (2004: 144). But such shifts and alterations are ruled out by 'Taliban Woman's' position. If she changes her mind she is likely to be punished very severely. Therefore she is not free to exercise her rational capacities, and not only because she would not be allowed freedom if she desired it, but because awareness of the brutal sanctions hanging over her might prevent her from even desiring it. Therefore the Competency Condition is not satisfied, and Christman could agree with Oshana that 'Taliban Woman' is not autonomous – but for proceduralist reasons. There is no need for recourse to response 3.

There is a large area of common ground between Oshana and Christman. Both agree on the importance of social-relational factors, in defining autonomy as well as in thinking about actual social policies that further it. But an understanding of autonomy as social-relational does not in itself entail a substantive position of *values*. It does, however, require a substantive view of the social conditions – laws, institutions, education, welfare and so on – which make possible and encourage autonomy.

The point I want to bring out is that, on a proceduralist account, any choices that surrender control over one's life to others must be *revocable*, if the agent is to continue to count as autonomous. To be able to rule oneself entails that one is able to adopt one course of action over another. Otherwise one would be in the position of the king in *Le Petit Prince*, whose rule over the stars consists in ordering them to come out at night, knowing perfectly well that they will do so in any case. It is because he knows this that he issues the order. If the stars behaved differently, if they did *not* come out on certain, known nights, then on those nights he would order them not to. Similarly, if a person has only one option and, knowing that, 'chooses' it, this cannot count as self-rule. For the 'self-rule' is driven by the option available; the non-existent options are disvalued for sour grapes reasons. I will address this further aspect of the argument in Chapter 7.

6.6 The burqa-wearer in the West

Whether or not one agrees with Oshana that a substantive conception of autonomy is required, we can agree that 'Taliban Woman' is not autonomous. But the burqa-wearer in a liberal state is not in the same position as a woman in Taliban-controlled Afghanistan. In the first place, the burqa-wearer in the West is not subject to the same restrictions. She may still be able to choose to attend university, for instance (in East London a burqa-clad woman on a university campus is not an unusual sight). In the second place, and more importantly, her decision to wear the burqa is revocable. If she decides to doff it after a period of experiment, the liberal state will support her right to do so.

6.6.1 An objection

At this point I must acknowledge and bracket off an objection. Perhaps, despite the official protection of the state, the burqa-wearer in the West will not find her decision as easy to revoke as she thought. Perhaps within her community there are powerful forces of disapproval, backed up by the threat of ostracism or violence, which would make it too risky to revoke her decision and seek the liberal state's protection. I consider this possibility in Chapter 11. At this point, however, let us accept that the burqa-wearer in the West has the freedom to cease wearing the burqa whenever she likes and see if the case for an autonomy-based paternalist ban has anything to recommend it.

6.6.2 First- and second-order autonomy

I argue that an autonomy-based paternalist ban could not be justified, by analogy with the case of a Roman Catholic nun who has made the autonomous decision to join an extremely strict order. This choice entails surrendering much of her freedom. Once inside the convent, she must give up certain things: she cannot drink alcohol, smoke cigarettes or marijuana, have friends over to stay or have sex; she is restricted as to her mode of dress and is not permitted to wear make-up; she is not allowed out of the convent unaccompanied and only with the permission of the Abbess; she cannot lie in bed in the mornings but must get up at 4.00 am to pray and so on.

The nun would say that the freedoms she has renounced are freedoms she no longer desires, or no longer desires to desire. She is still free to do the things that are most important to her: to worship, pray, sing hymns and meditate; freer than before, in that opportunities are more plenteous. The *Book of Common Prayer* refers to God as one 'whose service is perfect freedom' and that, one must guess, is how the nun would see it. Still, from a neutral point of view, she undoubtedly has far fewer freedoms than before. The question is whether she has also surrendered her autonomy.

Clare Chambers (2008) draws a distinction between first- and second-order autonomy. First-order autonomy means being able to evaluate and question the rules by which one lives one's daily life for oneself, with the ability to reject or change them if unsatisfied and to endorse them if satisfied. The nun in the strict convent has first-order autonomy as long she can evaluate the rules by which she lives and endorse them. In this she is the same as the burqa-wearer in the West, who also has first-order autonomy in that she can endorse the rules she lives by.

Second-order autonomy is the condition of being able to choose to live or not to live in accordance with those rules in the first place. The nun had second-order autonomy in the days before she became a nun, when she made the willing, unconstrained choice to join the order, and she still has second-order autonomy if she continues to endorse that choice.

It is not even necessary for either the nun or the Western burqa-wearer to endorse every single rule by which she lives, in order to retain autonomy. As Chambers points out (2008), it is possible to have second-order autonomy without full first-order autonomy. For suppose that the nun does not endorse all of the rules by which she has to live. Perhaps she does not like the rule about rising at 4.00 am. She would change it if she could and rise at 8.30 am. She follows the existing rule unwillingly, only because it is a condition of her remaining a nun, a choice which, as a second-order autonomous agent, she continues to endorse. Again there is a parallel with the Western burqa-wearer. She might find some of the restrictions associated with burqa-wearing onerous, but accept them because they are inseparable from the way of life she has chosen and continues to choose.

The question is whether the nun and the Western burqa-wearer are truly autonomous. Clare Chambers (2008) notes that there are four possible combinations of the first- and second-order autonomy distinction. One might have both, one might have neither, one might have second- but not first-order autonomy or one might have first- but not second-order autonomy. Obviously, liberals would be happy about the first of these combinations and unhappy about the second. The difficulty is in determining, if only one order of autonomy is present, which the liberal should prioritise. In other words, is one more truly autonomous if one has only first-order autonomy, or only second-order autonomy?

The case of the nun is an example of the latter. For the former, Chambers offers the example of 'a child who has not chosen to attend a progressive school but who, once there, is required by the teachers to question rules and to find out answers for herself' (2008: 164).

Chambers makes the claim that Martha Nussbaum and others who define themselves as political liberals prioritise second-order autonomy over first-order autonomy (Chambers 2008). On Nussbaum's account, according to Chambers,

> Second-order autonomy must be protected, but individuals must be free to use their second-order autonomy to alienate their first-order autonomy, for example by joining a convent.
>
> (2008: 165)

Therefore the nun poses no problem for those who prioritise second-order autonomy, and if my analogy holds, neither does the woman who makes a second-order autonomous choice to wear a burqa.

The position argued for here is in line with Nussbaum's prioritisation. Autonomy of its very nature seems to have something of the second-order about it. It depends on the second-order ability to reflect and decide for oneself what is valuable in life (Colburn 2010). Ronald Dworkin (1988) sees second-order reflection and preference as an essential part of autonomy. Indeed, one could ask whether the idea of autonomy does not lead to an infinite regress, in which first-order autonomy submits to the priority of second-order autonomy, which submits to the priority of third-order autonomy and so on. Dworkin (1988) accepts this possibility and argues that whichever is the highest level of autonomy is the one that should have priority:

> Might we not have preferences about our second-order preferences? Could I not regret the fact that I welcome the fact that I am not sufficiently generous in my

actions? I accept this claim, at least in principle. As a theory about the presence or absence of certain psychological states empirical evidence is relevant. It appears that for some agents, and some motivations, there is higher-order reflection. If so, then autonomy will be thought of as the highest-order approval and integration.

(1988: 19)

As Dworkin states, human beings seldom actually do proceed far or for long beyond second-order autonomy (1988), but whichever is the highest order of autonomy that we reach should have priority over lower orders.

6.6.3 Chambers's disagreement with Nussbaum

Chambers, however, does not agree with Nussbaum's prioritisation. She objects that the very possibility of second-order (let alone higher-order) autonomy is problematic, because preferences – including second-order autonomous ones – are socially formed:

> The social formation of preferences casts doubt on [Nussbaum's] position in two ways. First, it suggests that people may be less autonomous than they appear, since their decisions are profoundly shaped by their contexts. Second, if autonomy is (always) limited, a choice or outcome cannot be rendered just by the mere fact of having been autonomously chosen.
>
> (Chambers 2008: 171)

The real issue, according to Chambers, is whether the social influence which produced the second-order autonomous choice is inimical to equality (a foundational liberal value) and whether the choice itself causes or entrenches inequality (Chambers 2008).

We are now approaching the problem of *adaptive preferences*, to be considered more closely in Chapter 7. To anticipate, I shall argue that the adaptive preference objection is not fatal to the possibility of personal autonomy. At this point, there are two points to be made in reply to Chambers.

First, if we reject as truly autonomous those choices which are the result of social influences which do not favour equality, we find ourselves in the strange position of approving the choice to become a nun from a woman who comes from a family of freethinkers, while disapproving of (perhaps preventing, if we put Chambers's strictures into practice) the choice to become a nun from a woman who comes from a devout Roman Catholic family with strict views about women's subordinate role. One can defy social influence to become a nun, but not go with the grain of social influence to do the same thing. The result would be an absurd double-standard: women would be allowed to become nuns if their families and communities disapproved, but not if their families and communities approved. This would be to deny the relational character of personal autonomy. Or more accurately, it would mean that the only relation between the agent and their family, friends and community that would count as autonomous would be one of opposition.

Second, Chambers bolsters her case by pointing to a seeming inconsistency on Nussbaum's part. Nussbaum holds that female genital mutilation (FGM) should be banned, because it is unjust. However, Nussbaum would ban the practice even if it were chosen autonomously by adult women, which, Chambers argues, '[undermines] her claim that, for a political liberal, second-order autonomy is sufficient for justice' (2008: 176).

Chambers agrees with Nussbaum that FGM should be banned. But the reasons Chambers has for banning it do not rest on its violating second-order autonomy, for under certain conditions it need not do that. Chambers's reasons for banning it are that it is (1) the result of an unjust social structure which makes women subordinate to men, and their sexual pleasure and fulfilment of no importance; and (2) harmful to the women who undergo it. And indeed Nussbaum cites both of these reasons herself, in her list of eight reasons why the practice should be eliminated (Chambers 2008: 177).

What, then, could Nussbaum say in reply? One possible response would be to say that FGM need not be banned after all – as long as it were not carried out by force, not performed on minors, only performed under anaesthetic by qualified surgeons with proper instruments in sterile conditions and were chosen autonomously by educated, informed adult women who had thought about their choice long and hard. After all, under those conditions one would approve of gender reassignment surgery, which could also cause loss of sexual function and pleasure. In this way Nussbaum could preserve her prioritisation of second- over first-order autonomy.

However, Nussbaum need not be driven to such a volte-face. On her list of eight reasons to eliminate the practice Nussbaum includes: '5. FGM is irreversible' (in Chambers 2008: 177). This seems a crucial difference between FGM and other practices which may be chosen at a second-order level of autonomy.

Chambers points out that certain other practices are also irreversible: 'so are most tattoos, male circumcisions, abortions, precautionary mastectomies or hysterectomies, and many sterilisations' (2008: 178). That is certainly true. But those practices do not seem harmful to the individual to the same extent as FGM. Tattoos, for example (which in any case are not altogether irreversible), do not cause bodily harm; male circumcision if correctly carried out does not cause long-term harm and, although it may cause some local loss of sensitivity, does not diminish sexual desire, sexual function or the intensity of orgasm; abortion, like precautionary surgery, is chosen because it causes less harm to the agent than the alternative. Irreversibility per se does not provide a reason for banning an action or practice. Losing one's virginity is irreversible but is not on that account a candidate for banning. The practice must also be harmful (or more harmful than alternatives) if it is to be a candidate for a ban; and the greater the degree of irreversible harm the stronger the reason for banning the practice. FGM is both seriously harmful and irreversible: it is the *conjunction* of these two facts which provides a reason to ban it. Therefore, Nussbaum's Reason Number 5 for banning FGM could simply be amended to 'FGM is both irreversible *and* seriously harmful'; and her prioritisation of second- over first-order autonomy in general can be saved by amending the principle to 'practices which cause serious harm to the individual (including loss of first-order autonomy) can be acceptable if second-order autonomously chosen, as long as the choice is *reversible*'.

Under this formulation, both the nun and the Western burqa-wearer retain their autonomy, even if their first-order autonomy is compromised, as long as they retain second-order autonomy, which relies upon the freedom to revoke their choice at any time. If the nun could leave the convent whenever she ceased to endorse her choice, and if the Western burqa-wearer could throw off her burqa whenever she ceased to endorse hers, then they are both autonomous. Possessing second-order autonomy requires having one's liberty protected by the state, and in liberal states, unlike in Taliban-controlled Afghanistan, this condition is met.

If autonomy-based paternalism does not justify banning enclosed religious orders in a liberal state, then it does not justify banning the burqa either. Of course it is open to anyone to argue that religious orders should indeed be banned in order to restore the autonomy of nuns. A ban on these grounds would have been justifiable (from a liberal point of view) in medieval Italy, where convents were frequently used as prisons in which to immure errant daughters. But it is hard to see how it could be justified in a modern liberal state, where there is nothing to stop a nun renouncing her vows and leaving the convent. Just so, autonomy-based paternalism could not justify banning a burqa which was voluntarily worn and could be relinquished at any time.

6.7 Conclusion

Let us return to the analogy between personal autonomy and intelligence. It was argued in Section 6.4 that a liberal state has no business trying to make every one of its citizens maximally intelligent. Not only would this be impossible (is *anyone* maximally intelligent?), but it is not for the liberal state to stipulate that cultivating one's intelligence is the chief end of life. For the same reasons, it is not for the liberal state to try to make every one of its citizens maximally autonomous.

But it is the task of a liberal state to allow everyone equal right of *access* to widely recognised goods of life, which would include autonomy (as well as other goods such as intelligence, health, sexual fulfilment, etc.). An irrevocable choice may deny such access permanently. Thus the liberal state is justified in banning FGM and may be justified in banning practices highly likely to cause premature death.

Or consider the following scenario. A religious sect doles out to its followers a certain drug, which has the effect of permanently reducing their intelligence, making them docile, cheerful and obedient to the sect's leaders. The followers take the drug voluntarily, but after taking it they can never recover their former level of intelligence. A liberal state would certainly be justified in banning this practice on paternalist grounds. The irrevocability of the choice justifies a ban. A ban on practices which temporarily reduce intelligence, such as getting drunk, would not be so justified.

In the same way, an autonomy-based paternalist burqa-ban could only be justified if wearing the burqa entailed irrevocable loss of personal autonomy.

7

Adaptive preferences and the burqa

The argument

Clare Chambers argues that choices are the result of social influence (2008). Therefore, one should not give a free pass to practices merely because the agent has chosen them. For the choice may not be truly autonomous. It may be the result of an *adaptive preference*.

In this chapter I argue that not all adaptive preferences are incompatible with personal autonomy. If the choice to wear a burqa was formed under social conditions compatible with the flourishing of the individual, and if wearing it does not make it impossible for the wearer to flourish (according to her own idea of flourishing), and if she can stop wearing it whenever she wishes, then it is compatible with autonomy (in particular, it is compatible with a relational concept of autonomy), and a liberal state has no reason to ban or discourage the practice.

However, in cases where burqa-wearing and the attendant conditions are sufficiently oppressive to prevent the flourishing of the individual, this would be an unacceptable adaptive preference – an Inappropriate Adaptive Preference, or IAP, as Serene Khader terms it (2011) – and the liberal state would be justified in intervening to free the women from their adaptive preference. Any such state intervention would have to be sensitively judged, however, and a burqa-ban might prove too crude an instrument for the task.

7.1 Defining the problem

7.1.1 The problem of adaptive preferences

Thus far I have considered burqa-wearing as a voluntary practice: a choice of the individual for reasons that appear good to her. Such a choice is in principle compatible with personal autonomy, even if it compromises first-order autonomy, as long as we prioritise second-order autonomy, which means that the choice must be revocable. I have not made claims about whether, or to what extent, burqa-wearing actually is voluntary, but I have tried to establish that *if* all or most burqa-wearing is voluntary then liberals have no cause to restrict or prohibit the practice (always assuming it causes no harm to others).

However, suppose that burqa-wearing is *not* voluntary. I put to one side the question of outright coercion. Obviously, liberals would want to prohibit that. (How liberals should deal with coerced burqa-wearing is discussed in Chapter 11.) Suppose instead that burqa-wearing is the result of an *adaptive preference* – a possibility raised in Chapter 6.

Natalie Stoljar points out that many contemporary feminist philosophers (herself included) value the notion of personal autonomy, because absence of autonomy is a good way of characterising the oppression of women (Stoljar 2015). In response to criticisms that the traditional conception of personal autonomy is atomistic, they have sought to produce conceptions of autonomy which recognise its social character – forms of 'relational autonomy', that is to say, accounts which 'deny that autonomy requires self-sufficiency' (Stoljar 2015). Instead these accounts stress that autonomy is compatible with the agent being in and valuing social and familial relationships. Voluntary burqa-wearing would be compatible with such a conception of autonomy, as argued in Chapter 6. But burqa-wearing as the result of an adaptive preference – that is, where 'choices and preferences are accommodated to oppressive social conditions' (Stoljar 2015) – looks like a failure of personal autonomy. Stoljar quotes Taylor's claim that adaptive preferences are 'paradigmatically non-autonomous' (Taylor 2009, in Stoljar 2015).

The problem, then, is that if adaptive preferences are by definition non-autonomous, and if burqa-wearing is an adaptive preference, then burqa-wearing cannot be autonomous. The liberal state could have grounds to take action against burqa-wearing. Far from being a case of an individual's free choice it would be a case of systematic social oppression.

My approach will be first to examine the concept of Adaptive Preferences. I shall identify different conceptions and attempt to show that not all of them are paradigmatically non-autonomous.

I shall then argue that burqa-wearing as an adaptive preference can be compatible with personal autonomy. I demonstrate this with a case study (Case Study 1).

The notion of relational autonomy depends upon and is in tension with adaptive preference. In some cases the social pressure is very strong, leaving less space for personal autonomy. Nevertheless, I argue that even in these cases some personal autonomy could exist and any state intervention should be sensitive and not extend to a ban. I demonstrate this with Case Study 2.

Finally, I will argue that in cases where the pressure to adapt one's preferences is so strong as to amount to coercion, the liberal state would have a clear right and duty to intervene. I demonstrate this with Case Study 3.

7.1.2 Defining adaptive preference

One of the earliest accounts of adaptive preference is provided by Jon Elster (1983). He quotes the well-known La Fontaine fable about the fox and the grapes in a chapter epigraph: Renard, on the point of starvation, sees some grapes above a high wall which he cannot reach; his reaction is to say that they were too green anyway, and fit only for *'goujats'* (boors). The sour grapes phenomenon, Elster says, is an example of *adaptive preference formation* (1983: 110). In this case, the fox had only two choices: going without the grapes and lamenting it, or going without the grapes and convincing himself he did not want them anyway. He takes the latter course and is commended by La Fontaine for doing so. And, indeed, perhaps the fox was wise to spare himself the misery of pining for the unattainable. Nevertheless, his preference has been distorted by his circumstances. Elster's conclusion is that social justice should not be grounded purely on 'given wants' (1983: 140); 'there is also the alternative possibility of changing the wants through rational and public discussion' (1983: 140).

Elster distinguishes adaptive preferences from *character planning* (1983: 117). Both are responses to a tension between what one would like and what one can have. But whereas character planning is a reasoned, self-aware process of adjusting to one's circumstances, and a matter of upgrading accessible options rather than downgrading inaccessible ones, adaptive preferences occur, as it were, 'behind one's back'; they are an automatic, unreasoned and often excessive reaction to constraints. Moreover, character planning is flexible and quickly responds to changes in circumstances, and is indeed on the lookout for them. It follows that choices formed by character planning are free in a way that adaptive preferences are not (Elster 1983).

Amartya Sen examines the implications of adaptive preference for work in international development. He argues that

> deprived people tend to come to terms with their deprivation because of the sheer necessity of survival, and they may, as a result, lack the courage to demand

any radical change, and may even adjust their desires and expectations to what they unambitiously see as feasible.

(Sen 1999: 62–3)

Therefore, we should seek to expand people's *freedom* to judge the kind of lives they would like to lead, a goal which takes in other objectives too, such as reducing poverty and improving education (Sen 1999). Sen argues for a *Capabilities Approach:* providing people with the capability to make life choices, rather than seeking to satisfy expressed preferences.

Martha Nussbaum is in agreement with this approach and has developed Sen's Capabilities idea into ten specific Central Human Capabilities (previously referred to and listed in Chapter 4): viz: (1) Life, (2) Bodily Health, (3) Bodily Integrity, (4) Senses, Imagination and Thought, (5) Emotions, (6) Practical Reason (including liberty of conscience), (7) Affiliation (A: capability for social interaction, friendship and freedom of assembly; and B: protection against discrimination on grounds of sex, race, caste etc.), (8) Other Species, (9) Play, and (10) Control over One's Environment (Nussbaum 2001: 78–80).

This approach requires only that citizens have the capability to access these goods, not that they actually do access them. Nussbaum captures this point by pointing to the difference between starving and fasting (Nussbaum 2001). In a liberal state which fully enacted the capabilities approach, no citizen need starve, but citizens would be entitled to fast if they so chose. Just so, in such a state no woman should be obliged to cover her face in public, but she would be entitled to do so if she so chose.

Michael Watts argues that the approach of Sen and Nussbaum is 'counterfactual' – that is, it is concerned with what individuals *would* want if it was available, rather than what they actually do want (Watts 2009). In such an approach, the role of education is of crucial importance, for two reasons: it enhances capabilities, and it also enhances the ability for critical reflection (thus facilitating a move from AP to character planning, in Elster's terms).

Serene Khader, responding to Sen and Nussbaum, offers a 'deliberative perfectionist approach' to public intervention in the lives of people with adaptive preferences (APs) (Khader 2011: 5). Public institutions have a duty to help people flourish, so they should intervene when people accept oppressive social conditions through AP: but they should do so sensitively, not simply imposing coercive measures without thought or sympathy (Khader 2011).

Khader notes that APs have been characterised in many different ways: as conscious, as unconscious, as resulting from a lack of options, as resulting from a lack of awareness, as undermining the sense of self or as not necessarily doing so (Khader 2011). Khader also argues that seeing APs as a problem necessarily involves perfectionism, for it requires some kind of normative idea of what a human life ought to be like (Khader 2011). Nussbaum's ten Capabilities, for instance, are designed to be suitable for all human beings – we all want, or would want if we were healthy and normal, to have them. Khader argues that

> the idea that a person can experience satisfaction with her form of life and yet not be doing well requires a criterion of well-being other than pleasure or desire-satisfaction. Second, seeing well-being-inconsistent preferences as evidence of inauthentic choice requires a view of human beings as having a natural tendency towards flourishing.
>
> (2011: 49)

Building on this idea of human flourishing, Khader offers the following definition of AP:

> An adaptive preference is a preference that (1) is inconsistent with a person's basic flourishing, (2) was formed under conditions non-conducive to her basic flourishing, and (3) that we do not think a person would have formed under conditions conducive to basic flourishing.
>
> (2011: 51)

I accept and employ this definition. Khader claims that it is perfectionist. As already argued, however, I do not accept a simple dichotomy between political liberalism and perfectionist liberalism. There is a continuum between them. The more fully and the greater the specific detail in which the idea of flourishing is defined, the more perfectionist the account; but it is possible for the elements of flourishing to be very general (as Nussbaum's capabilities are). I shall argue in section 7.2.2 that it is possible to be *too* perfectionist in judging whether an AP is consistent with flourishing.

All preferences are of course adaptive in a broad sense. No preference is formed in a cultural or social vacuum. Any preference we have is inevitably a response to the culture we live in, and the opportunities it allows, promotes or condemns. Moreover, our preferences are also formed in response to our limitations as frail, human, time-bound creatures with limited physical and mental capacities. Nussbaum notes that as children we may ache to be able to fly like birds, but we soon adapt to the fact that we can't, and are probably the better for that adaptation (Nussbaum 2001). Preferences which do not prevent our flourishing are no cause for concern. But preferences which do inhibit our flourishing are a problem. To capture this distinction Khader refers to the problem forms of APs as IAPs; they are those preferences which are harmful to the bearer and were formed under bad social conditions.

7.2 Dealing with adaptive preferences

7.2.1 Deliberative intervention

How then is a liberal state to intervene to help those who are saddled with the wrong sort of APs? Khader argues that the rule must be to work on changing the conditions, not the preferences directly (2011); a rule fully consistent with Sen's and Nussbaum's approach. If conditions are changed then the preferences will change accordingly – unless they are very deep-rooted, but in that case nothing could be done anyway. It is always possible that an agent 'is committed to a conception of the good that does not value human flourishing and that will not change even under better social conditions' (Khader 2011: 53). But that is not very likely; it is more likely that she is just managing 'a bad option set' and her preferences will change when the options improve. The latter is much more likely because 'people have a tendency to value their basic flourishing' (Khader 2011: 53). Khader calls this claim 'the Flourishing Claim' (2011).

Khader does not offer a precise definition of human flourishing, nor provide evidence that people do indeed value it. She does say that flourishing is not the same as satisfaction with life, and also that it involves exercising 'valuable human capacities' (Khader 2011: 49). The claim does not seem to be based on any scientific theory about human nature; Khader does not refer to any experiments or observations which support it. The Flourishing Claim, though, must rely on certain ways of living *counting* as flourishing, and others not counting, otherwise the claim would fail to distinguish what it is that people value; and this requirement must in turn rely on some kind of claim about human nature, which must in principle be capable of being corroborated (or falsified) by scientific investigation. Perhaps Khader's claim is a legacy from the Aristotelian view that the end of life is eudaemonia or 'happiness' in the sense of living well (Aristotle [*c.* 340 BCE] 2004), although Khader explicitly says she does not endorse Aristotle's views on what constitutes a flourishing life (Khader 2011: 49). In any case, it seems a plausible claim, in line with both experience and intuitions about human nature. A human being who was determined *not* to flourish would seem to be a pathological case, requiring explanation. Khader's claim, while not explicitly resting on scientific observation, is not incompatible with a scientific understanding of human nature and could in principle be corroborated (or falsified) by observation or experiment. Moreover, the idea of flourishing is sufficiently broad and flexible (Khader does not follow Aristotle in identifying flourishing with virtue, or the contemplative life; there is no single golden road to flourishing) that accepting it does not push one uncomfortably far towards the perfectionist end of the PL-Perfectionist spectrum.

Khader, then, justifies state intervention in order to create the conditions conducive to flourishing. An important qualification is that such intervention needs to be *deliberative* – that is, not coercive, abrupt, sweeping or heavy-handed; not taken without investigation and consultation; and sensitive to women's needs (all the cases considered by Khader concern the APs of women). Intervention must respect the agents' autonomy.

It has been claimed that APs are paradigmatically non-autonomous (Taylor, 2009). Khader contests this. She argues that APs cannot be defined as 'autonomy deficits' (2011). There are other types of autonomy deficits which are not APs. Moreover, not all APs are autonomy deficits. Khader analyses three different accounts of procedural autonomy deficits and argues that APs do not necessarily fall into any of them. For example, not all APs are deficits in rationality. It need not be the case, for example, that an individual with an AP is incapable of critical reflection on their decisions: 'most deprived people make reflective decisions on a daily basis – even if they are sometimes decisions among rotten options' (Khader 2011: 81). Khader also argues that one cannot identify all APs with a lack of a life-plan or a lack of agency (85–95). Khader's argument appears to show, at any rate, that APs and autonomy deficits are not entirely coterminous (2011).

Khader's claim is that when an AP is inappropriate – when it is an IAP – this is not because it is an autonomy deficit, but because it is a preference 'inconsistent with human flourishing developed under conditions unconducive to flourishing' (2011: 106). Nevertheless, it is possible if not likely that some types of AP do involve autonomy deficits. And indeed personal autonomy, in at least some degree, has to be one of the valuable human capacities that Khader says must be exercised for an individual to flourish. That it need not be the only one is agreed.

Where does this leave us with regard to burqa-wearing? The test for whether burqa-wearing is an IAP (we know that it is an AP) is whether it prevents flourishing (which ought to include the possibility of the exercise of personal autonomy). But not all burqas are worn under the same conditions. The justification, if any, for intervention and the type of intervention required has to be decided on a case-by-case basis. Below I examine three case studies of burqa-wearing, which differ in terms of how far they are IAPs, how far they involve loss of autonomy and what kind of intervention would be justified.

7.2.2 Case study 1: The convert

The first case study comes from an autobiographical account by Na'ima B. Robert, a Muslim convert who describes how she came to wear the burqa (more accurately, a full jilbab with niqab) in London in the twenty-first century.

Robert recounts how, as a convert, she first took to wearing the hijab and loose-fitting clothes. She describes this as a 'tonic' and says it freed her from her 'reliance on her looks'. Presently, under the influence of a friend, Umm Tasmeen, she graduated to a more enveloping garment, the full jilbab. But soon that no longer seemed enough either. The final step was to cover her face. She writes:

> I came to the realization that wearing the *niqab* was the least I could do as thanks to Allah who had done so much for me. It was on an afternoon that I remember as if it were yesterday: the buzz of busy streets of Whitechapel, the thought of my new marriage and wonderful husband, all the years that Allah had protected me from every danger, the good life He had given me, the blessing of guidance, of good friends, of security, and now, love – all these things were rushing through my mind. The *niqab* was not something I disliked – in fact, I quite liked it; it was not difficult for me to wear it – I was living in the East End, after all, and my husband was supportive.
>
> (Robert 2006: 193–4)

This is clearly an AP. It is an adaptation to the Wahhabist Muslim community that she lives in ('I was living in the East End, after all'). The question is whether it is an *inappropriate* adaptive preference. To answer that question we need not rely on her interpretation of how and why she came to have that preference. Since it is adaptive she may not be aware of the real reasons. But whether it is inappropriate or not depends on the objective facts of her situation. Assuming then, that the *facts* are as she reports them – which is a separate issue from the story of how her preference came to be formed – there is no evidence from this account that the choice was the result of coercion, harassment or intimidation from others; nor that her choice is irrevocable. She says elsewhere in her book that she still has female friends who do not cover their faces. If she were to change her mind and uncover again, her account offers no reason to think she would suffer unpleasant consequences. She therefore retains full second-order autonomy.

Robert's case also does not appear to meet Khader's criterion for an IAP, that it prevents or inhibits flourishing. Robert's account makes it clear that in terms of the life she has chosen, she *is* flourishing. She is exercising valuable human capacities, such as forming fulfilling relationships with her community, friends and family, finding love and sexual fulfilment with her husband, and immersing herself in a religion which she finds spiritually rewarding. She has written a book to celebrate these facts, exercising the valuable human capacity of creativity and self-expression. This does not therefore seem to be an IAP. It seems rather closer to what Elster called 'character planning' (Elster 1983).

Some might feel tempted to retort: 'Oh, but she only *thinks* she's flourishing. In fact she is deluded. She would discover what real flourishing was if she got rid of that *niqab* and explored life outside her enclosed community.'

A liberal is certainly entitled to believe this. But a liberal state is not entitled to act upon it. Just as the liberal state has no warrant to prevent people voluntarily joining enclosed orders of monks or nuns, it has no warrant to prevent people outside of such institutions voluntarily following strict religious lifestyles. A liberal state which sought to impose one particular model of flourishing on all citizens would be at the extreme perfectionist end of the PL-Perfectionist spectrum, and would violate the Liberal Paternalist Principle: very great restrictions on liberty would be imposed for gains which would not be accepted as such by the individual affected. The individual's freedom would be overridden completely. At this point perfectionism ceases to be liberal. A *liberal* state could not ban the burqa on the grounds that it represents the wrong kind of flourishing.

This is assuming that we can take Robert's account of the facts at face value. One problem with autobiographical accounts, especially those whose purpose is to defend or champion a way of life, is that one can never be sure how accurate, impartial or free from self-deception they are. Perhaps there was more pressure on Robert than she admits. Perhaps she *would* suffer reprisals if she were to change her mind about burqa-wearing. Perhaps her husband, who is supportive of her choice to cover her face, would not be supportive of her choice to uncover it. Thus it is wise to seek independent corroboration of autobiographical accounts where practicable. But in the absence of testimony that conflicts with Robert's account, the liberal state has no good grounds for intervention.

Any pressure upon her takes the form of carrot, not stick. She writes that wearing the *niqab* has earned her approval in her community: 'My husband was chuffed and Umm Tasneem and other friends were pleased' (Robert 2006: 196). She also feels content with the results of her choice:

> In the mini bubble that was the East End, I felt comfortable and confident – Bengali women were often seen around with *niqab* on so I didn't stick out like a sore thumb.
>
> (Robert 2006: 196)

If she were to doff her *niqab* she might lose some of this approval and sense of belonging. The liberal state can punish acts of violence, intimidation, harassment or persecution. But it cannot punish acts of approval. A liberalism that favours relational autonomy must favour the possibility of individuals making choices in order to please others and to be in good standing within their families and community – as long as (to reiterate) no coercion is involved, flourishing (in terms acceptable to the individual) is not compromised, and choices are not irrevocable.

7.2.3 Case study 2: The Pirzada women

My second case study is the common practice of veiling among the conservative Sufi Pirzada community of Old Delhi, discussed by Uma Narayan (2002). The women are expected by their communities to veil their faces on their rare public excursions. Many complain about this. Many of the younger women hope to marry into less conservative families where they will have fewer restrictions. Yet at the same time many feel that

> the burqa is an integral part of their social identity and sense of self, and the social discomfort they would feel without it outweighs its physical inconveniences.
>
> (Narayan 2002: 420)

However, there is an element of coercion as well:

> Some younger Pirzada women acknowledge that they veil because of the insistence of strict family elders or because their community would disparage their reputation, hurting their prospects for a good marriage, were they to go unveiled.
>
> (Narayan 2002: 420)

Yet Narayan claims that

> these reasons, individually and collectively, demonstrate that these women differ from the prisoner of patriarchy, who is forced to veil under *literal coercion*.

> These women recognize that they have real practical and emotional stakes in the approval of their family elders and in maintaining their reputation in the community.
>
> (2002: 420)

I cannot agree with Narayan that strict insistence on compliance, or having one's reputation disparaged if one does not comply, means that no coercion is occurring. It is not clear what Narayan means by *'literal coercion'* – physical violence? If that is what she means we should reply that physical violence is not the only form of coercion, and moreover that in this case, the threat of it may well hover in the air even if it is not made explicit. Acts of violence against women are far from unknown in India and must form the background to women's preferences.

I discuss the issue of coercion more fully in Chapter 11. For now, I can agree with Narayan that it is *possible* to make an autonomous choice as a form of 'bargaining with patriarchy' (2002: 421). Suppose the pressure were less: suppose that the choice was between active approval and mere tolerance. In such a case, the woman who chose to veil – though doubtless her preference would be adaptive in that it was tailored to the norms of the culture she lived in – *could* be autonomous, for the reasons that Narayan goes on to give:

> The decisions many women make with respect to 'cultural practices' ought, I think, to be understood as a choice of a 'bundle of elements', some of which they want and some of which they do not, and where they lack the power to 'undo the bundle' so as to choose only those elements they want. Much of what individuals in general want in life comes in such 'mixed bundles' that require resignation to certain tradeoffs as a means to secure goods one values, and it would be both incorrect and dangerous to ignore that choices were in fact being made by women.
>
> (2002: 422)

Narayan agrees with Nussbaum that

> women's preferences are often deformed by their patriarchal socialization and limited opportunities. Nussbaum correctly insists that such deformed preferences should not count against social policies that that will enable them to make choices that are currently inconceivable or unappealing, since women can reconsider what they are entitled to and what they can aspire to as the options available to them increase.
>
> (2002: 425)

The question then is, what state action should a liberal feminist support in order to address cultural practices such as veiling, purdah and arranged marriages, which 'contribute to maintaining women's second-class social status'? (Narayan 2002: 425)

Narayan says where outright coercion is taking place the (liberal) state 'ought to intervene to protect women' (2002: 425). Again, Naryan does not define coercion. The kind of intervention she seems to mean is to 'protect their ability to exit from the coercive situation', which would presumably mean punishing the coercers as well as providing refuges for the women to exit to. I agree with her that this is unproblematic in principle.

Narayan also argues that the state should actively foster legal and social changes (such as access to education) so that women are empowered to rethink and modify or reject oppressive practices (Narayan 2002). In other words, this is a version of a capabilities approach, and shares with it two essential principles: first, there is a norm underlying it – the legal and social changes go in a certain direction. The implicit claim is that women's lives go better for them when they have such goods as education, employment and so on. Second, this approach assumes that preferences will readapt when new capabilities are made available. On this reading preferences are *plastic, alterable* and *evolvable*.

The case of the Pirzada women is a case of an IAP. The liberal state would therefore be justified in intervening. However, the nature of the intervention needs to be carefully considered. Banning burqas in cultures where the practice is well established simply does not work very well, because the coercive effects can be no less oppressive than the practice which the ban aims to eradicate. Narayan gives the example of the effects of banning the veil in Iran in the days of the Shah: many lower-class women did not feel able to go out unaccompanied, and some lost their jobs, because veiling was not allowed in the workplace (Narayan 2002).

I have argued (Chapter 6) that autonomy is both procedural and relational. If it is procedural, then there must be genuine alternatives to any preference: the Competence Condition requires both critical reflection and *ability to act on it*. But it is also relational: that is to say, any autonomous choices must take account of the agent's relationships, her position in her family and social circle and society in general. It is not non-autonomous to take those things into account when forming preferences and making decisions. All that is necessary when squaring these two is that there genuinely are options (which means that outright coercion for or against a certain choice has to be outlawed). Then the capabilities approach takes care of the rest.

In the case of the Pirzada women, the answer would be to (1) strictly enforce laws against violence, harassment and intimidation, including or especially within the family, while also providing refuges to escape to if necessary and (2) to provide the requisite capabilities for freedom, such as education, employment opportunities, the right to own property, and full knowledge of their rights and the state's commitment to enforcing them. Then in time we might expect to see the women's preference for veiling change.

7.2.4 Case study 3: Malak Hifni Nasif

Malak Hifni Nasif (1886–1918) was an Egyptian feminist, a contemporary of the modernising intellectual Qassim Amin, who published *Tahrir Al-Mara* (The Liberation of Women) which advocated, among other things such as reform in education, polygamy and divorce laws, that women must unveil (see Ahmed 1992: 144). Yet Nasif was opposed to unveiling. Her preference was to remain veiled, for the following reason:

> How can you men of letters … command us to unveil when any of us is subjected to foul language if she walks in the street, this one throwing adulterous glances at her and that one bespattering her with his despicableness so that the sweat of shame starts from her brow.
>
> (Nasif, cited in Ahmed 1992: 180)

This is a clear case of an IAP. Nasif's preference to wear the veil is nothing to do with her flourishing. She explicitly states that it is the behaviour of men in the streets that makes veiling necessary; there is no suggestion that she wears the veil for any other reason than protection from harassment. Moreover, there is an element of physical intimidation; it is not unreasonable to fear that verbal harassment could lead to actual sexual assault. If the harassment and intimidation ceased then so would Nasif's preference for burqa-wearing.

Nasif would not be helped by a ban on the burqa alone. The remedy here would be to change the situation to make Nasif's preference unnecessary, as well as or rather than outlawing the preference. It would thus be necessary to change the culture; which may not be not as hard as it sounds. Cultures can change very rapidly. Such a change could be instituted or helped along by a liberalising state, by education and by inflicting strict penalties on men found guilty of harassing or intimidating unveiled women. And indeed Egypt did liberalise in this respect in the first half of the twentieth century, especially under the modernising influence of President Nasser, so that burqa-clad women became an unusual sight; see, for example the 1959 graduation photograph from Cairo University (Malverde 2014), though subsequently, for complex political reasons, this liberalisation went into reverse.

One can sympathise with Nasif's desire to carry on wearing the veil as a protection against the persecution of her day. It would have taken considerable personal courage to unveil in such circumstances. Face-covering is, for the *individual*, a solution to the problem of harassment. Yet continuing to wear the veil perpetuates the culture which produces such persecution, and isolates those women who choose not to wear it, exposing them to abuse or assault. IAPs reinforce the very culture which makes them necessary. For the liberal the course of action here is plain. The state should ensure that all women have the capability to walk the streets without fear of harassment, and IAPs such as Nasif's would swiftly disappear.

8

The burqa and multicultural theory

The argument

In this chapter, I consider whether the liberal position on face-covering per se – namely, that voluntary habitual face-covering in public should be tolerated, in the absence of any demonstrable harmful consequences to others such as a rise in crime, but that certain institutions might legitimately require temporary removal of the face-covering to facilitate identification or communication – is altered when multicultural considerations are taken into account. The liberal position on face-covering per se deliberately excludes cultural factors. It avoids mention of the fact that burqas are worn only by Muslims and only by women. When we allow such considerations back in, does that change the position? I consider three main forms of multiculturalism: 'maximal' tolerance, the granting of group rights and the politics of recognition. I shall argue that the latter two of these should in some cases be taken into account by liberals when formulating public policy, for good liberal reasons; but that burqa-wearing is not one of those cases. The liberal position on face-covering per se is by itself adequate to deal with burqa-wearing.

8.1 Defining multiculturalism

The term 'multiculturalism' has more than one meaning, so it will be helpful to pin down what is meant by it here. It can be used to describe either a state of affairs or a political programme. If one says, for example, 'Multiculturalism is a fact in Europe and North America', one is describing a state of affairs – the fact that nations in these parts of the world have culturally diverse populations – with no suggestion that anything should be done about it. It is multiculturalism as a political programme that we are concerned with here. By multiculturalism in this sense I mean the idea that distinct cultural groups within a larger society should, at least in some cases, receive special treatment. I accept Susan Moller Okin's characterisation of multiculturalism as involving the claim that

> minority cultures or ways of life are not sufficiently protected by the practice of ensuring the individual rights of their members, and as a consequence these should also be protected by special *group* rights or privileges.
>
> (1999: 10–11)

I should add that it is only *liberal* multiculturalism that I am concerned with. Non-liberal or illiberal multiculturalism could of course endorse privileges for favoured cultural groups and fewer or no privileges for disfavoured ones, but that has no bearing on the question of whether a *liberal* state should ban the burqa.

I consider three theories of soi-disant liberal multiculturalism. The first is the theory that liberal states should simply tolerate the practices of all the different minority cultures that may exist within them, provided that those practices are not unjust to anyone outside the minority culture, as advocated by Chandran Kukathas.

The second is the granting of group rights to minorities. The case for group rights is based on the claim that 'minority rights are not only consistent with individual freedom but can actually promote it', because 'freedom is intimately linked with or dependent on culture' (Kymlicka 1995: 75) – with the proviso that group rights must not override the freedom and equality of individual citizens.

The third is that liberal states have a duty to *recognise* minority cultures – to show not just tolerance but acceptance and respect to minority cultures, as advocated by, for example, Kymlicka, Charles Taylor, Joel Anderson, Alex Honneth and Anna Galeotti.

I argue that the first of these forms of multiculturalism is not fully compatible with liberalism, and so rule it out of consideration. I argue that there is a liberal case (with various qualifications) both for group rights and for recognising minority cultures. However, I do not think either of these forms of multiculturalism should alter the liberal position on face-covering per se.

8.2 The theory of 'maximal' toleration

In *The Liberal Archipelago* (2003), Chandran Kukathas argues for a theory of liberalism as toleration. On this view, a liberal state, as he defines it, would tolerate diversity and not seek to impose any comprehensive idea of the good.

A theory such as this would tend to militate against a burqa-ban more strongly than the liberal position on face-covering per se previously outlined. That position assumes that face-covering is voluntary. If it were imposed on unwilling individuals the liberal state would have reason to intervene. This is not the case with liberalism as toleration. Even if burqa-wearing were imposed upon women within the minority culture where it was worn, a liberal society as conceived by Kukathas should tolerate it. Kukathas expresses his idea of liberal society thus:

> A collection of communities (and so, authorities) associated under laws which recognize the freedom of individuals to associate as, and with whom, they wish. This model of a free society is one in which there may be many associations, but also in which none is 'privileged' or regarded as having especial moral significance. Thus there may, in such a society, be many authorities, all authority resting in the end on the acquiescence of subjects rather than of justice.
>
> (2003: 19)

This is a staunchly anti-perfectionist view. No ideal conception of society is proposed, just a diverse range of coexisting ones. On the other hand, it is not a Rawlsian conception either. There is no overlapping consensus on justice, only a consensus that each association tolerates the others, without interference. The metaphor Kukathas deploys is of an archipelago – a sea dotted with small islands. 'The islands in question here are different communities or, better still, jurisdictions, operating in a sea of mutual toleration' (Kukathas 2003: 22). And again:

> The liberal archipelago is a society of societies which is neither the creation nor the object of control of any single authority. It is a society in which authorities function under laws which are themselves beyond the reach of any singular power.
>
> (Kukathas 2003: 22)

Kukathas says that his conception of society should count as liberal, because it is based on toleration:

> The value which is fundamental to liberalism is toleration. A society or a community is a liberal one if, or to the extent that, it is tolerant. What it tolerates as liberal society is dissent or difference.
>
> (2003: 23)

An endorser of Kukathas's theory would see the burqa-question in some such way as this: 'I may not like or approve of the burqa, but so what? Toleration doesn't mean anything unless it includes tolerating things you dislike or disapprove of. Nobody outside the minority culture is obliged to wear the burqa. If women within the minority culture don't like it, they are free to leave the culture and emigrate to another island on the archipelago; if they don't, it's because the costs of leaving are greater than the costs of staying. As long as it does not impose severe burdens on those outside the minority culture – and since it is restricted to that particular island of the archipelago, it won't – there is no reason for the other islands to interfere.'

For Kukathas, tolerance is the fundamental liberal value. He argues (following Kant) that it is necessary for free public reason:

> A stance of tolerance *upholds* or *honours* reason since it forswears the use of force in favour of persuasion (whether by argument or example).
>
> (Kukathas 2003: 130)

The outcome of a policy of what we might call inter-island tolerance would be, according to Kukathas, something more than a mere modus vivendi; it would be a form of 'moral commons' (2003: 132). By this he means that, owing to the necessity of interaction between the islands (brought about by trade, intermarriage, professional relationships or other factors), norms inevitably emerge about how citizens from different islands relate to each other, which eventually lead to a 'public realm': a realm within which unofficially agreed rules govern interactions – rules which will be the result of compromises between the islands, rather than rules which prevail on any individual island.

Such a theory has its advantages. It is certainly true that tolerance is required to make public reasoning possible; if the expression of some opinions is punishable by death, for instance, then reasoning is hobbled from the start. Then again, the theory's ambitions are modest; it seeks only to eliminate conflict between groups. That is a worthwhile aim and, plausibly, more achievable on this theory than a perfectionist one which would attempt to correct the imperfect norms of individual islands. Moreover, Kukathas's theory does not rule out change. The pan-archipelago norms might over time filter back to individual islands and have an influence. Within the public realm people are allowed to persuade and disagree, and migration between islands is always at least theoretically possible.

The question is whether this form of toleration is a truly liberal one. I argue that it is not. It would lead to a plural but not to a pluralistic society – that is, to a society of separate, parallel groups rather than a society founded on 'social heterogeneity and diversity, grounded on respect and reciprocity' (Galeotti 2002: 212). Kukathas's archipelago is similar to the Ottoman Empire millet system described by Kymlicka, where the Ottoman rulers, themselves Muslims, allowed Christians and Jews within their empire to freely practise their faith, as well as 'a more general freedom to govern themselves in purely internal matters, with their own legal codes and courts' (1995: 156). As Kymlicka notes, 'This system was generally humane, tolerant of group differences, and remarkably stable' (1995: 157). It was certainly stable, lasting from the fifteenth to the early twentieth century. But it was not a liberal society, for as Kymlicka says, 'it did not recognize any principle of *individual* freedom of conscience' (1995: 2003). No religious group tried to interfere with another, but within the groups, heresy or apostasy were not tolerated.

Similarly, in Kukathas's liberal archipelago, there is no violence or oppression *between* islands, but there is nothing to prevent violence or oppression *within* islands. Kukathas's theory has no way of dealing with that – or rather it deals with it by tolerating it. This means that individuals oppressed by their communities can seek no redress from a state which is tolerant in the way Kukathas proposes. The consequences for minorities within minorities could be unpleasant.

Kukathas acknowledges this point:

> There would in such a society be (the possibility of) communities which bring up children unschooled and illiterate; which enforce arranged marriages; which deny conventional medical care to their members (including children); and which inflict cruel and 'unusual' punishment. … Yet, if this is what toleration might lead to, is it defensible?
>
> (2003: 134)

Kukathas identifies and answers several separate objections that an opponent of his form of toleration could raise. I need deal with only two here, for if I can show that his answers to these objections are not satisfactory, that is enough to defeat the claim that his conception of toleration is liberal.

8.2.1 Objection 1

> This level of toleration in effect condones the oppression of internal minorities (minorities within minority communities) and of the weakest members of such communities in particular.
>
> (Kukathas 2003: 135)

Kukathas's answer to this objection is that 'the threat of oppression is as likely to come from outside the minority community as it is from within' (2003: 135–6), and he cites a whole history of states persecuting minorities to support his claim. If the state is authorised to intervene in the practices of minority communities it may abuse this power and fabricate stories of oppression within the minority communities to justify its own oppression; again, historical precedents are not lacking.

Furthermore, *persuasion* (allowable under a policy of toleration) as a means of alleviating oppression is morally better and more efficacious than the use of force.

The last of these points can be dealt with swiftly. *If* persuasion is always more efficacious than force, then force need never be used and eschewing it makes no difference. However, it is far from clear that this is the case. The Hindu custom of *suttee* – burning widows along with their deceased husbands – was ended, under the Raj, by force. The story of how General Sir Charles James Napier helped to end it is told in his brother William's *History of Sir Charles Napier's Administration of Scinde* (1851). When a deputation of priests came to Sir Charles demanding that the practice be allowed, as it was their custom, he replied:

> Be it so. This burning of widows is your custom; prepare the funeral pile. But my nation also has a custom. When men burn women alive we hang them, and confiscate their property. My carpenters shall therefore erect gibbets on which to hang all concerned when the widow is consumed.
>
> (Napier 1851: 35)

As William Napier records, 'No suttee took place then or afterwards' (1851: 35).

It is perhaps necessary to stress that my use of this example in no way implies support for the British Imperial project. Sir Charles Napier saved a life on this occasion and in the long run the abolition of *suttee* saved multiple lives, but as commanding officer of the army which conquered Sindh he was responsible for the deaths of many thousands of Indians; and the British were not in India by invitation. No doubt, on a net balance sheet the harms caused to India by the Raj outweighed the goods. Nevertheless, ending the practice of *suttee* was a good, even though Napier's power to end it was based not on legitimate authority in India but sheer brute force. The point of the Napier case is simply to show, *contra* Kukathas, that force may prevail where persuasion does not. In such cases persuasion is evidently not more efficacious and it can hardly be more moral either, since it does not work. (And force deployed by a liberal state within its own rightful area of authority would not, of course, be vulnerable to the objection about legitimacy that can be levelled at Charles Napier.)

Kukathas's claim that the majority culture is as likely to be the oppressor as the minority culture may well be true. But the question is whether a *liberal* majority culture is more likely to be oppressive than *illiberal* minority cultures. If liberalism means, minimally, that all citizens are free and equal, as I have argued, then the liberal majority culture is very likely to be less oppressive than an illiberal minority culture.

Of course, states do not always live up to their principles. A state might claim to follow liberal principles while busily oppressing its citizens. But this objection can be levelled at *any* political philosophy, including Kukathas's own philosophy of group toleration. A state might claim to be tolerant of minority cultures while busily oppressing them. That in itself is no objection to Kukathas's theory. He is proposing an ideal state, yet to be achieved. Just so, proponents of a liberal state which protects the rights of members of minority cultures are proposing an ideal state, which has as yet been only partially or imperfectly achieved.

8.2.2 Objection 2

The second objection to his position which Kukathas addresses is: Why not have a *minimal* level of toleration, stopping short of tolerating internal tyrannies, rather than the maximal toleration proposed by Kukathas? That would serve the same purpose of making public reason possible.

It is worth noting here that the phrase 'minimal level of toleration' already makes some questionable assumptions. What Kukathas means by it is that state toleration would stop short of tolerating tyrannies internal to minorities. It is by no means clear, though, that this would make for a lower level of tolerance overall. For under it the beliefs and practices of minorities *within* groups would be tolerated, whereas under Kukathas's 'maximal' tolerance they would not.

Leaving that aside, however, Kukathas's answer to the objection is that it 'presupposes that some ultimate moral authority is both desirable and feasible' (2003: 137) – which is exactly what Kukathas disputes. In his paper, 'Reconciling Tradition and Modernity in a Liberal Society' (2010), Kukathas claims that 'there are no universal values we can safely say are universal and not in fact particular norms masquerading as universal' (2010: 9).

It is certainly true that *some* values are local norms. But to claim that *all* values are merely local norms leads us all the way to moral relativism. As has frequently been pointed out, moral relativism is self-defeating. Anyone who says 'You should not judge other cultures by the moral values of your own' is caught in a contradiction. For if values are relative, *why* shouldn't I? Edward Westermarck (1932) advocated moral relativism as leading to tolerance; yet 'for the consistent relativist, tolerance can only ever be a framework-dependent virtue, while Westermarck, and others, seem to recommend it as a universal desideratum' (Baghariam and Carter 2017).

This is not to say that relativism *never* makes sense. Things such as table manners are relative to culture; eating like a Tudor today would be extremely rude, but it was not rude in 1540. Still, it is both desirable and feasible to establish some bottom-line universal moral claims, based on the fact that there are universal truths about what is good for human beings and what is not. As Brian Barry puts it:

> It is better to be alive than dead. It is better to be free than to be a slave. It is better to be healthy than sick. It is better to be adequately nourished than malnourished. It is better to drink pure water than contaminated water. It is better to have effective sanitation than to live over a sewer. It is better to be well educated than to be illiterate and ignorant. It is better to be able to practise the form of worship prescribed by your religion than to be prevented from doing so. It is better to be able to speak freely and be able to join social and political organisations of your choice than to fear that, if your activities attract the disfavour of the regime, you face arbitrary arrest, torture or 'disappearance' at the hands of bodies organised or connived at by the state.
>
> (2001: 285)

It is true, as Barry says, that sometimes people deny others the right to these goods. But nobody wants to deny them for themselves. They are transcultural goods, although they are not distributed equally across cultures. But a liberal is, precisely, someone who thinks that rights to them *ought to be* distributed equally. As Barry says:

> The defining feature of a liberal is, I suggest, that it is someone who holds that there are certain rights against oppression, exploitation and injury to which every single human being is entitled to lay claim, and appeals to 'cultural diversity' and pluralism under no circumstances trump the value of these basic liberal rights.
>
> (2001: 132–3)

I think, therefore, that it is both desirable and feasible for there to be an ultimate moral authority, as long as it confines itself to these basic liberal rights and does not interfere in matters that genuinely are relative to culture. What Kukathas calls 'minimal' toleration, but what I should call a form of toleration that protects basic individual rights, is the form appropriate to a liberal society. I do not agree, therefore, that Kukathas's form of group toleration qualifies as a form of liberal multiculturalism; therefore it has no impact on the question of whether a *liberal* state should ban the burqa.

8.3 Group rights

8.3.1 Group-differentiated rights

In this section I consider a second kind of multicultural theory: that which advocates accommodation, in the form of special provision or exemptions from laws, for minority cultural groups within society. The case for such special provision or exemptions is based on a theory of what Will Kymlicka terms 'group-differentiated rights' (1995: 26). They are group-differentiated because one is entitled to them in virtue of membership of a cultural group. Non-members of the group are not so entitled. This theory does not make as strong claims for what is due to cultural minorities as does the theory of maximal toleration, or the theory of the politics of recognition (see Section 8.4). Kymlicka's version of group-related rights, and its close relatives, could be termed *weak multiculturalism*. It is described as such by Sarah Song (2007), though for slightly different reasons (see Section 8.3.4).

I shall outline and broadly defend Kymlicka's position, as well as more recent versions of it by other theorists, but will stress the limits of such a theory rather more than Kymlicka or his followers do. My position will be that at least some degree of cultural accommodation is in principle compatible with liberalism, two conditions being met: (1) that special provision or exemptions for a cultural group do not impose unreasonable burdens on the rest of society; and (2) that special provision or exemptions for a cultural group do not override, or cause the overriding of the rights of its individual members.

This position could in theory make some difference to the liberal position on voluntary face-covering per se. It might lead to a more accommodationist line on exemptions. Demands for exemptions from the requirement to temporarily uncover the face would be more strongly backed. However, this depends on whether burqa-wearing meets the two conditions given above: not imposing unreasonable burdens on the rest of society, and not overriding or causing the overriding of the rights of individual women within the group. I suggest that burqa-wearing may be more problematic on both those counts than some other cultural practices for which exemption could be claimed, and conclude that accepting the liberal case for accommodationism does not commit one to modifying the liberal position on voluntary face-covering per se.

8.3.2 Group-specific rights

The theory developed by Kymlicka in *Multicultural Citizenship* considers three types of group-specific rights: (1) *Self-government rights* (1995: 27), which would apply to native minorities of countries settled or colonised by larger populations; (2) *Polyethnic rights* (1995: 30) which would apply to minority immigrant populations; and (3) *Special Representation Rights* (1995: 31), which concern quotas within legislatures and so on for minority ethnic groups, either native or immigrant.

It is only the second of these which concerns us here. Polyethnic rights include 'exemptions from laws and practices that disadvantage [cultural groups], given their religious practices (Kymlicka 1995: 31). Kymlicka cites exemptions from animal slaughtering legislation, and also notes that 'Muslim girls in France have sought exemption from school dress-codes so they can wear the *chador*' (1995: 31).

Kymlicka argues that group-differentiated rights ought not to be opposed to the rights of individuals. Individual rights impose a limit, for the liberal, to the extent of group-differentiated rights: 'Liberals can only endorse minority rights in so far as they are consistent with respect for the freedom or autonomy of individuals' (Kymlicka 1995: 75). In many cases, however, Kymlicka argues that rights for minority groups pull with, not against rights for individuals: 'minority rights are not only consistent with individual freedom but can actually promote it' (1995: 75) because 'freedom is intimately linked with or dependent on culture' (1995: 75). Culture is defined by Kymlicka as 'societal culture', 'whose practices and institutions cover the full range of human activities, encompassing both public and private life' (1995: 75). The claim is that culture should matter to liberals because

> freedom involves making choices amongst various options, and our societal culture not only provides these options, but makes them meaningful to us.
> (Kymlicka 1995: 83)

Kymlicka goes on to quote Ronald Dworkin's *A Matter of Principle* (1985) and agrees with him that

> the availability of meaningful options depends on access to a societal culture, and on understanding the history and language of that culture – its 'shared vocabulary of tradition and convention'
> (Dworkin [1985: 228, 231], in Kymlicka 1995: 83)

There is an opposing liberal position (Barry 2011) that the state need not make any special provision to ensure the rights of minority group, because their rights are already taken care of by liberalism's universal commitment to equal rights and freedoms for all citizens: minority groups would already have their right to worship and to associate as they wished protected. Kymlicka characterises this position as a policy of 'benign neglect' of minority cultures (1995: 107). However, Kymlicka argues, correctly in my view, that such a position is 'not only mistaken, but actually incoherent' (1995: 108), because governments cannot avoid making decisions on such matters as public holidays and official languages, which inevitably promote some cultural identities at the expense of others. The need for group-differentiated rights thus proceeds from the liberal commitment to equal rights for all citizens; differential treatment for minority groups might be required to redress the inequality produced by promoting the majority cultural identity at the expense of other cultures.

However, this form of multiculturalism does not commit the liberal state to granting all and any minority groups' demands for differential treatment. The question in the case of any particular demand for special treatment or exemption from a law by a minority cultural group is, first, whether the practice for which exemption or provision is demanded is likely to cause unreasonable burdens to those outside the cultural group; and second, whether the practice actually does promote or is at least compatible with the individual rights of the group members.

Kymlicka is clear that not all demands for group rights should be granted:

Liberal principles impose two fundamental limitations on minority rights. First, a liberal conception of minority rights will not justify (except under extreme circumstances) 'internal restrictions' – that is, the demand by a minority culture to restrict the basic civil or political liberties of its own members.

(1995: 152)

And:

> External protections are legitimate only insofar as they promote equality between groups, by rectifying disadvantages or vulnerabilities suffered by the members of a particular group.
>
> (Kymlicka 1995: 152)

To sum up, 'a liberal view requires *freedom within* the minority group, and *equality between* the minority and majority groups' (Kymlicka 1995: 152).

This view is thus more attentive to the rights of individuals within minority groups than is Kukathas's 'maximal' tolerance. It seems entirely in line with liberal principles, and any special treatment for minority groups consistent with it ought to be unexceptionable to a liberal, wherever they are on the spectrum from political liberalism to perfectionist liberalism. The question is whether it justifies making the liberal position on voluntary face-covering per se more lenient; that is, whether it would legitimise exemptions for burqa-wearers in situations where the uncovering of the face would normally be required.

The answer will turn on the two conditions stated earlier: (1) that special provision or exemptions for a cultural group do not impose unreasonable burdens on the rest of society; (2) that special provision or exemptions for a cultural group do not override, or cause the overriding of the rights of its individual members.

8.3.3 Developments of the group-specific rights approach

This section considers developments of Kymlicka's theory, by Sarah Song (2007) and Jocelyn Maclure (2011). I argue that these developments are useful in laying down procedural rules for how to apply accommodationism but that neither leads to a significant departure from the liberal position on voluntary face-covering per se.

Song (2007) attempts to distance herself from Kymlicka's position, which she describes as 'weak multiculturalism', for a slightly different reason than the one given by me (Section 8.1). In Song's view, Kymlicka's multiculturalism is weak because he sees culture as one primary good among others (2007: 22). Song takes issue with him here, because she claims that not everyone values culture as a primary good, or values it equally: 'we need to be open to the possibility that cultural membership may be differently valued by different members' (2007: 29). This is not a serious objection to Kymlicka's position, however. It is the case with all primary goods that they may be differently valued by people. Song also stresses how cultures are not monolithic or fixed but are 'internally contested, interactive, and loose-jointed' (2007: 32). No doubt this is true, but there is no reason to think Kymlicka would disagree. Granted that cultures are contested, interactive and loose-jointed, one still wants to say: *to the extent that it makes sense to talk of cultures as coherent entities at all*, then we can ask whether particular practices of a culture should be accommodated.

Despite her efforts to distance herself from Kymlicka, Song argues for the Kymlickian position of '*rights-respecting accommodationism*' (2007: 9). Like Kymlicka, she argues that justice may require accommodation for cultural minorities, but that it should be limited by 'the protection of the basic rights of individual members of minority groups' (Song 2007: 9). This is the same limitation as Kymlicka's own rule that accommodations must not permit 'internal restrictions' (1995: 152).

Song advocates what she calls a 'deliberative approach' (2007: 9) to questions involving potential conflict between group rights and the rights of individuals within those groups (cf. Khader 2011). The deliberative approach involves looking at the question in its context and weighing up all the factors before coming to a decision:

> My approach does not suggest global answers to particular cultural dilemmas, such as the issue of veiling among Muslim girls …What is constant is a commitment to protecting the basic rights of women and girls, but what such a commitment requires with respect to the practice of veiling … will depend on context and what individuals at the center of these controversies are themselves saying.
>
> (Song 2007: 12)

This approach does not represent a significant departure from Kymlickian multiculturalism, and there is no reason to think that Kymlicka would wish to dissent from it. It is, however, a useful reminder that such questions are complex and their contexts both particular and dynamic. A cultural accommodation for burqa-wearing might be justified in one context or at one time, and not justified in another context or at another time.

A more recent application of Kymlicka's form of multiculturalism is developed by Jocelyn Maclure (2011). Maclure's aim is 'to present, and seek to defend, the legal obligation to accommodate, under certain circumstances, minority religious beliefs or practices' (2011: 262).

Although Maclure's focus is on religious beliefs and practices, his argument applies to cultural practices generally. Maclure's argument for accommodation stems from Kymlicka's point that in a culturally diverse society, governments, and public institutions, cannot avoid making decisions on matters of public policy which will have differential impacts on different cultures (Kymlicka 1995: 108). Thus although the purpose of rules on, say, school uniform, may not be discriminatory in their purpose, they may very well be discriminatory in their effect. Therefore, under certain circumstances, accommodation is necessary to correct 'indirect and involuntary discrimination' (Maclure 2011: 267), such as a school ban on headgear which would impact more harshly on male Sikhs, who would not be allowed to wear turbans, than on others.

It is true, as Brian Barry points out, that *all* laws have unequal impact and this is no evidence that they are unfair:

> If we consider virtually any law, we shall find that it is much more burdensome to some people than to others. Speed limits inhibit only those who like to drive fast. Laws prohibiting drunk driving have no impact on teetotallers. Only smokers are stopped by prohibitions on smoking in public places. Only those who want to own a handgun are affected by a ban on them, and so *ad infinitum.*
>
> (Barry 2011: 34)

However, in most cases the unequal impact is intentional: laws against speeding are *supposed* to impact on those who wish to drive fast, not on those who do not. Maclure's concern is with those laws or rules where the unequal impact is an *unintended* side-effect. In such cases an exemption would not run counter to the reason why the law was formulated.

Unintended adverse impact does not of itself justify exemption from a rule, however. It must also be shown that the costs of exemption are acceptable to others. An exemption from wearing a school cap and an exemption allowing a burqa to be worn in class raise different questions. The school cap exemption is easier to justify. It is hard to see how not wearing a cap but complying with the rest of the uniform code would impose unreasonable burdens on other pupils or on teachers.

An exemption to allow a pupil to cover her face in class, however, is much more likely to impose unreasonable burdens on the school community, creating problems of identification, communication and security. Within a school context it is unlikely that an exemption allowing Wahhabist Muslim girls to cover their faces would be justified. In some other contexts, where identification alone was at issue, and alternative means of identification available, perhaps an exemption would be justified. (This is assuming, of course, that burqa-wearing does not lead to the overriding of rights of individual women within the community, a question explored in Chapter 11).

Maclure identifies two problems that could result from a policy of accommodation: Proliferation and Instrumentalization (2011: 270).

'Proliferation' refers to the consequences of being unable to distinguish between mere preferences and what Maclure calls, citing Taylor, 'strong evaluations' (2011: 268) – that is, meaning-giving beliefs which are central to one's identity. Because rules can be onerous and people tend to want as many exemptions as they can get, the temptation is to represent mere preferences as strong evaluations, resulting in a proliferation of demands for exemptions.

'Instrumentalization' refers to the risk that people will exploit accommodationism to get other things, such as extra holidays. Or steak and Harvey's Bristol Cream sherry every Friday night – as the Church of the New Song, created by inmates of the US Federal Prison system in the 1970s, claimed was their religious requirement (Hamilton 2014: 205). This seems to be not so much a separate problem from proliferation as a particular case of it. Instrumentalization would be a leading *cause* of proliferation.

The proliferation problem raises the possibility of a slippery slope. However, Maclure argues that there are ways to block the slope: tribunals could assess the sincerity of claims for accommodation, and moreover, accommodation claims must still meet the requirement of reasonableness (2011: 273). One would need to look at the effects on others of granting the claim, and also the burdens it places on the institution which is asked to accommodate:

> Accommodation claims must be reasonable because exemptions, compensations, or adaptation measures modify, to varying degrees, the prevailing terms of social cooperation. The obligation to accommodate is meant to redress an injustice by correcting indirect discrimination; logically, it should not do so by creating new situations of unfairness. Yet, for an accommodation claim to be turned down, it must be shown that its deleterious effects are real and significant.
>
> (Maclure 2011: 274)

Maclure's argument is useful in that, as well as justifying a liberal policy of exemptions in principle, it also identifies crucial restrictions on that policy. Because of those restrictions, Maclure's argument makes little difference to the liberal position on voluntary face-covering per se. That position already grants the right to cover the face habitually, and would only require burqa-removal in situations where identification, communication or security were at issue.

Exemptions in these cases would be likely to have real, significant, deleterious effects precisely because of the nature of those situations: for impairing or compromising identification, communication or security is generally likely to be deleterious.

Maclure's argument, like Kymlicka's which it follows, therefore tends to support the liberal position on habitual voluntary face-covering per se, rather than modifying it. However, the Kymlickian position would be likely to extend cultural exemptions in other areas which do not involve face-covering.

8.3.4 Case study: Aishah Azmi

Let us consider how a theory of group rights with the built-in protections against adverse impact on others advocated by Kymlicka and Maclure would play out in a specific case. I choose the case of Aishah Azmi, who in September 2011 was suspended from her position as a teacher at Headfield Church of England School in Dewsbury, Yorkshire, for refusing to remove her niqab in the classroom, previously referred to in Chapter 1 (Wainwright 2006). Ms Azmi claimed unfair discrimination and took her employers to a tribunal, but lost the case. The school's decision not to allow her to teach unless she uncovered her face was upheld. Direct discrimination was ruled not to have occurred because Ms Azmi was subject to the same rule that would have debarred a teacher from covering their face for non-religious reasons; and indirect discrimination was also ruled not to have occurred, because covering her face interfered with the performance of her duties. Wearing the niqab hindered trust and communication between her and the children she was teaching – a conclusion reached after the school had monitored her teaching with her face covered for an agreed period, and listened to the views of the children in her class (see the report of the Tribunal Judgement, delivered on 30 March 2007, in the case of *Azmi v. Kirklees Metropolitan Borough Council* (http://www.bailii.org/uk/cases/UKEAT/2007/0009_07_3003.html)).

It ought to be no surprise that covering the face hinders communication, given the crucial role the face plays in human interaction (see Chapter 3). Teaching with one's face covered – especially to children of primary school age, who are more reliant on encouraging looks and smiles, more easily made shy or scared, and less equipped to deal with unfamiliar situations than older, more self-sufficient students – imposes a burden that is both unreasonable and unnecessary.

In this particular case, then, the first condition is not met, and we do not even need to investigate the second condition. However, there may be other cases where face-covering does not impose an unreasonable burden – for example, if uncovering is required merely to establish identity, when other means of identification are available. In such cases, the first condition would be met. However, the second condition – whether the practice of burqa-wearing as a whole overrides or causes the overriding of the rights of the individual – also needs to be met for an exemption to be justified. That is not a simple question, and will be explored in more detail in Chapter 11, where the issue of coercion is considered.

Pending that exploration, we can say that *if* the practice of burqa-wearing can be shown not to override or cause the overriding of the rights of individual women, then exemptions from requirements to uncover the face would be legitimate provided they did not impose unreasonable burdens on the rest of society. Therefore, in a few cases the position of weak multiculturalism might justify exemptions from a rule requiring the face to be shown.

Given, however, that exemptions could only be justified where alternative means of communication or identification were available and equally efficacious, one is inclined to doubt whether the rule in such cases would be necessary at all. Practically speaking, the position of weak multiculturalism would be almost indistinguishable from the liberal position on voluntary face-covering per se.

8.4 The politics of recognition

New life was breathed into multicultural theory by the 'politics of recognition', first advocated by Charles Taylor, and more recently in somewhat different forms by Joel Anderson, Axel Honneth and by Anna Galeotti.

The politics of recognition is fundamentally different from Kukathas's theory of maximal tolerance. In Kukathas's theory, the essential is that the practices of cultural groups be *permitted*. Kukathas states:

> Toleration, in the sense in which it is being used here, is an undemanding virtue, since it requires little more than indifference to those who are, or that which is, tolerated. It may, on occasion, require a measure of forbearance, but it does not require respect or empathy or admiration or even much concern for others. It certainly does not require taking the tolerated individual or groups seriously; and it is perfectly consistent with a contempt for everything for which they stand, as well as with an unwillingness to engage them in rational dialogue, or even to understand them.
>
> (2003: 130)

The politics of recognition, on the other hand, requires a good deal more than indifference to those who are tolerated. It requires that they be recognised: that is, that a positive attitude of respect be shown towards them, in virtue of who they are both as individuals and as members of a culture. Clearly, this is more demanding than Kukathas's maximal toleration.

In his essay 'The Politics of Recognition' in the book *Multiculturalism* (Taylor 1994) Taylor makes the following claim: 'A number of strands in contemporary politics turn on the need for, sometimes the demand, for *recognition*' (1994: 25). He argues that

> our identity is partly shaped by recognition or its absence, often by the *mis*recognition of others, and so a person or group of people can suffer real damage, real distortion, if the people or society around them mirror back to them a confining or demeaning or contemptible picture of themselves.
>
> (Taylor 1994: 25)

Taylor's thesis is that guaranteeing equal rights for all citizens is not sufficient to address this problem of misrecognition. In addition, and potentially conflictingly, there is a need for a 'politics of difference' (Taylor 1994: 38) which requires us to recognise 'the unique identity of this individual or group' (1994: 38).

Recognition entails not merely acknowledgement of identity but endorsement and respect. Furthermore, this may be demanded not merely for current members of the group in question, but future members too. Some recognition-demands aim to 'maintain and cherish distinctness, not just now but forever' (Taylor 1994: 40). In Taylor's own example of the francophone community of Quebec, what is demanded is not merely that the state recognises the right of the Quebecois to speak French, but that it takes steps to ensure that their descendants will do so too. To achieve this, it was not sufficient for the state to set up francophone schools; it was also deemed necessary to pass a law preventing francophones from sending their children to anglophone schools (Taylor 1994).

8.5 Two more versions of the politics of recognition

More recent versions of the politics of recognition, such as those advanced by Anna Galeotti (2002) and Joel Anderson and Axel Honneth (2005), make more ambitious claims for the role of recognition. In Galeotti's formulation, recognition of minority groups is to replace the classical liberal form of tolerance – where the state permits non-harmful cultural practices but is neutral towards them.

Instead, for Galeotti, tolerance demands official recognition of minority cultural practices. For Anderson and Honneth, recognition forms part of their theory of personal autonomy. They take the liberal perfectionist view that autonomy is an essential good which liberal states should seek to promote, and by combining this with a commitment to the politics of recognition, arrive at a 'recognitional theory of autonomy'. It will be seen, then, that Galeotti places more emphasis on recognition of groups while Anderson and Honneth place more emphasis on recognition of individuals. The two approaches are not necessarily incompatible, but Anderson and Honneth's theory does appear to suggest possible limitations on the group recognition required by Galeotti. I first outline each theory in turn, before turning to a discussion of the limits of recognition.

8.5.1 Toleration as recognition

In her book *Toleration as Recognition* (2002) Galeotti begins by noting that the traditional liberal idea of tolerance as non-interference with (non-harmful) individual choices has not prevented controversy erupting over a number of issues in contemporary liberal states. She cites, for example, 'the wearing of the Islamic headscarf in public schools, the admission of gays into the army and regulations concerning speech that incites violence or hatred' (2002: 4).

In Galeotti's view, 'what gives rise to most genuine contemporary issues of toleration are, in fact, differences between groups rather than between individuals' (2002: 5). Such cases, Galeotti claims, do not involve *choice*. These cases are not about moral disagreement, but instead about 'asymmetries in social standing, status, respect and public recognition' (2002: 5).

In a nutshell, 'what is really at stake in contemporary issues of toleration is equal respect and social standing for minority groups, rather than equal liberties for individuals' (2002: 6). What toleration as recognition means is that we do not ignore differences, but publicly recognise them. This makes minority groups feel included within the polity. Public recognition can be grouped into six categories:

1. Claims for public toleration of social differences…
2. Claims for limiting toleration of practices and forms of speech that are seen as offensive to the dignity of members of newly-included groups, and which thus damage their collective image and public presence…
3. Claims for revising public conventions that are based on a majority culture, and which exclude minority members from certain activities…

4. Claims for special policies aimed at providing minority members with more opportunities and resources…
5. Claims for special support for minority cultures in order to prevent their being swamped by the majority culture…
6. Claims for collective rights to group autonomy and collective liberty.

(2002: 197)

Galeotti acknowledges that some of these claims might be difficult to uphold in particular cases: for example, the second one potentially clashes against freedom of expression, while some readjustments under the third one might be too burdensome to carry out. Her contention is not that all recognitional claims must be upheld. The aim is 'an undertaking to question and revise those conventions which are based on what the majority considers to be the norms, so as to take into account the views of minorities' (2002: 202). But each claim must be taken on its own terms and not all will be granted; it is the *consideration* of the claim which does the important work here.

Toleration as recognition, Galeotti says, leads to an inclusive and *pluralistic* society. This is in stark contrast to the *plural* society of minimally interacting 'islands' of Kukathas's liberal archipelago, where tolerance means 'hands-off' rather than recognition.

It is not a foregone conclusion that Galeotti's toleration as recognition would justify burqa-wearing in all circumstances. But it would ensure that any claims for exemptions from particular restrictions from face-covering be considered with due attention and respect.

8.5.2 Recognition as the ground of personal autonomy

Joel Anderson and Alex Honneth emphasise a different role for recognition, more focused on the individual within society. In their essay 'Autonomy, Vulnerability, Recognition and Justice' (2005), they offer a conception of personal autonomy in terms of 'mutual recognition' (2005: 127). They embrace the idea of relational autonomy, summarised in the claim:

> Autonomy is a capacity that exists only in the context of social relations that support it and only in conjunction with the internal sense of being autonomous.
>
> (2005: 129, quoting Jennifer Nedelsky)

From this claim they develop their recognitional theory. The key idea is that autonomy can only be achieved in socially supportive conditions. Anderson and Honneth consider a helpless baby's journey to adult autonomy, with all the support it requires along the way (2005: 130). When one becomes an adult, the support of others becomes less direct, more complex and diffuse, but does not cease to be necessary. Therefore, 'one's autonomy is *vulnerable to disruptions in one's relationship to others*' (Anderson and Honneth 2005: 130). The competencies that comprise autonomy depend on attitudes to oneself (self-trust, self-respect, self-esteem) and these, in turn, are dependent on the sustaining attitudes of others (Anderson and Honneth 2005: 131). One's relationship to oneself is not a matter of solitary reflection, but the 'result of an ongoing *intersubjective* process' (Anderson and Honneth 2005: 131).

Liberal states are already supposed to put in place conditions which will help citizens achieve personal autonomy, by providing the '*material and institutional circumstances of autonomy*' (Anderson and Honneth 2005: 129) – that is to say, welfare, education, shelter, help for the disabled, religious tolerance and so on. Anderson and Honneth support such provisions but argue that by themselves they are not sufficient to guarantee autonomy. The state must also protect or assist the necessary socially supportive conditions for autonomy. The implication is that in a culturally diverse society this will necessarily include multicultural policies.

Such a theory could justify a more accommodationist position on burqa-wearing than the liberal position on voluntary face-covering per se. In order for the individual to develop the personal autonomy prized by Anderson and Honneth, their culture would have to be recognised. Thus Anderson and Honneth's theory would suggest a similar approach to accommodation to Galeotti's, although the routes by which they reached this approach differ. Policy might be more accommodating in three ways.

8.5.3 Three types of accommodation

1. Demands for exemptions from the requirement to temporarily uncover the face would be more strongly backed, for the need for recognition of one's cultural practices would supply a sound reason for exemption. We might expect, then, that exemptions from the requirement to temporarily remove the burqa in institutions would be granted more frequently under Anderson and Honneth's approach, as under Galeotti's. Claims 1 and 3 of Galeotti's categories of recognitional claims, Section 8.5.1, would have particular force here.

2. The obligation to recognise burqa-wearing would be something to set against any possible harms, such as a rise in masked crime. The threshold at which burqa-wearing was judged to have reached an unacceptably harmful level would therefore be likely to be raised.
3. A liberal state which subscribed to the politics of recognition would refrain from public disapproval or criticism of burqa-wearing; and liberal individuals who took the politics of recognition seriously would also be careful not to voice disapproval (and would school themselves not to feel it). Claim 2 of Galeotti's categories of recognitional claims, Section 8.5.1, would apply here.

8.6 Limits of the politics of recognition

Neither Galeotti nor Anderson and Honneth argue that the politics of recognition mean that any and all claims by minority groups, or individuals qua members of minority groups, are to be granted. However, neither theory has much to say about where the limits should be drawn. In this section my aim is to consider what kind of claims should *not* be recognised.

8.6.1 Harmful practices

I start from the position that cultural claims, like religious claims, can be *disaggregated,* to employ Laborde's useful term (see Chapter 2). That is to say, although one may take a respectful, recognitional stance in general towards minority groups, specific practices are to be evaluated individually and not all necessarily qualify for recognition. Harmful practices, for example, are likely candidates for failing to merit recognition. FGM, or clitoridectomy, is a clear example of a practice which ought not to be tolerated even in Kukathas's attenuated sense of 'toleration', let alone the recognitional sense of Galeotti. Interestingly, Galeotti herself brings up clitoridectomy as a contested practice several times, and does say that it should not be recognised, but she does so with great circumspection. Although the word 'clitoridectomy' appears five times in her index, only one of those references makes it clear that recognition should not extend to such a practice, and even then a careful reading is required to discern her view. It is worth quoting in full and indeed necessary to quote in full, as the point is made so periphrastically:

> I do not deny that cultural differences may sometimes pose problems of ethical and legal incompatibility (the typical example being clitoridectomy), nor that fundamentalism is widespread among Islamic immigrants and may nurture terrorism (as has happened in France); yet I hold that, as a rule, neither incompatibility nor political self-defence are sufficient justification for stopping public toleration of differences, with some clear exceptions (such as the two just mentioned).
>
> (Galeotti 2002: 86)

Although clitoridectomy is an 'exception' to the general rule of public recognition of cultural differences, Galeotti spends no words explaining why it is an exception, and does not explicitly condemn the practice. An attendant risk, perhaps, of the politics of recognition is a lack of forthrightness in ruling out cultural practices that do not deserve recognition. This is not a flaw in the theory itself but a psychological reluctance of its proponents to emphasise things that should *not* be recognised rather than things that *should* be, from a fear that stressing the exceptions might undermine the well-founded claims (and in the passage quoted above that is the line Galeotti seems to take). However, such reluctance is not justified. Having clear limits does not make recognition any less valuable.

In the case of the burqa, the point to decide is whether it counts as a harmful practice. If so, that would be a prima facie reason for not affording it recognition (and therefore, in Galeotti's terms, not tolerating it). I do not think a case that it is harmful has been made. But this is discussed in detail in Chapter 11.

8.6.2 Divided cultures

Cultures are not monoliths. Galeotti herself notes that cultures 'are not only subject to continual changes and influence from others … but are also internally segmented and divided' (2002: 208). When cultures are divided, it is no easy matter for the liberal state to rule on which of the contested beliefs or practices are to be recognised. Moreover, focusing on cultural groups risks failing to recognise the claims of dissident or reforming individuals within the group.

By preventing francophone citizens from having their children educated in English, as Charles Taylor advocates (1994), the state prioritises group rights over individual rights. This could have the effect both of stultifying the ambitions of individuals and also preventing the community itself from ever changing. There is a danger generally of allowing the politics of recognition to restrict the autonomy of individual members of cultural groups.

The point is made by K. Anthony Appiah, who argues that Taylor's ideal in which people are respected for their identity – respected *as* black, or *as* gay and so on – should not be an endpoint:

> I think we need to go on to the next necessary step, which is to ask whether the identities constructed in this way are ones we – I speak here as someone who counts in America as a gay black man – can be happy with in the long run.
>
> (1994: 162)

The politics of recognition tends to impose a script and 'proper ways' of living up to one's identity: thus 'there will be expectations to be met, demands to be made' (Appiah 1994: 162). Therefore recognition could require that

> one's skin color, one's sexual body, should be acknowledged politically in ways that make it hard for those who want to treat their skin and sexual body as personal dimensions of the self.
>
> (Appiah 1994: 163)

The politics of recognition must therefore be kept within bounds or it could squash the personal autonomy of individuals who choose not to conform to the norms of their cultural group.

A further point is that the politics of recognition could have a similar such squashing effect on future generations as well. Provisions demanded now by spokespeople for cultural groups (who often are among the most traditionalist of their group) are to shape the lives of those as yet unborn, and put a brake on future modernising movements.

8.6.3 The rights-protecting requirement and the autonomy-protecting requirement

Consistency with liberal principles therefore requires a limitation on policies of recognition which are designed to perpetuate cultural practices. The practices must not be such as to as to infringe upon the fundamental liberal rights of the individual. We can call this the Rights-Protecting Requirement.

There is a further limitation. If the practices are such as to restrict the personal autonomy of some members of the cultural group, that is reason for a liberal state's declining to perpetuate them. Liberals at any point on the PL-Perfectionist spectrum would have reservations about a policy which severely limited or impaired the personal autonomy of some group members.

Such practices ought not to be tolerated. We can call this the Autonomy-Protecting Requirement.

Perhaps the particular policy discussed by Taylor, of preserving francophone communities by making francophone schooling compulsory for them, survives both requirements. Fundamental rights such as the right to free speech or to due process or religious freedom are not affected, so the Rights-Protecting Requirement would seem to be satisfied. Speaking French rather than English does not impair autonomy, so the Autonomy-Protecting Requirement also seems to be satisfied. The communal gains in preserving the language of the Quebecois (including its songs, poetry, stories and so on) might be thought enough to outweigh the relatively small restriction of denying francophone children an anglophone education. After all there are plenty of other opportunities to learn English.

Still, there is room for debate here. Appiah does not agree that compulsory francophone education for French-speaking children in Quebec would satisfy the Autonomy-Protecting Requirement: 'I think (and Taylor, I gather, does not) that the desire of some Quebecois to require people who are "ethnically" francophone to educate their children in French steps over a boundary' (Appiah 1994: 163).

Note that the factors a liberal state should consider in deciding this case do not depend on the claims of the politics of recognition. They are the reason the claim was made, but not the reason one should accede to it. The decisive questions for the liberal are not whether the cultural practice is important, nor how endangered it is. The decisive questions are whether the practice satisfies the Rights-Protecting Requirement and the Autonomy-Protecting Requirement.

All such demands for the protection of cultural practices must pass these tests. Suppose a demand were made by a conservative Islamic group that schools be set up where all girls were to wear the burqa, appealing to the politics of recognition: *This practice is important to our culture and deserves to be recognised; without recognition the survival of the practice is not guaranteed.*

I do not think that this demand would pass the Rights-Protecting Requirement and the Autonomy-Protecting Requirement. But the point is that it would have to pass them if the policy demanded were to be implemented by a liberal state. Neither the importance of the tradition nor its endangerment supply a sufficient reason for perpetuating it.

Taylor acknowledges this to some extent. He argues, effectively, for what one might call a two-tier form of liberalism, in which fundamental individual rights ('rights to life, liberty, due process, free speech, free practice of religion and so on'

(Taylor 1994: 59) form the bottom tier, while a second tier allows for 'privileges and immunities that are important' as well (1994: 59). The rights of the bottom tier are indefeasible, while the second tier relates to important privileges or immunities that could in principle be restricted or revoked, although one would need a compelling reason for doing so (1994: 59).

8.6.4 A potential problem

There remains, however, a potential problem. What if the cultural group affected does not accept the reason for revoking or restricting their privileges or immunities? What if the cultural group accepts neither the Rights-Protecting Requirement nor the Autonomy-Protecting Requirement? What if, in short, they do not accept liberal principles? As Taylor points out, in Islam there is no tradition of a separation between church and state, for example (1994: 62). Liberalism is not culturally neutral. It is a Western tradition, historically an outgrowth of Christianity (Siedentorp 2015). In a multicultural society there may be

> substantial numbers of people who are citizens and also belong to the culture that calls into question our philosophical boundaries. The challenge is to deal with their sense of marginalization without compromising our basic political principles.
>
> (Taylor 1994: 63)

When this kind of clash occurs liberalism must defend its values. Taylor cites the Rushdie affair as a case in point and condemns the fatwa against him: 'There will be variations when it comes to applying the schedule of rights, but not where incitement to assassination is concerned' (1994: 62). In 2011, writing with Jocelyn Maclure, he states:

> Except in flagrant cases of defamation or incitement to hatred, the state cannot restrict some people's freedom of expression on the pretext that ideas or representations have the effect of profaning what, for others, is considered sacred.
>
> (2011: 108)

They go on to add: 'We would certainly not like to live in a society where Salman Rushdie or Richard Dawkins would be censored' (2011: 109).

Yet this defence is immediately followed by 'With that said, just because we have the right to do x does not mean that doing x is wise or desirable'

(2011: 109). The suggestion seems to be that writers and artists should self-censor, or at least think very, very carefully before not self-censoring. Freedom of expression must be balanced, in Taylor and Maclure's view, by 'an ethics of concern for the other' (2011: 109). This highlights a potential tension between liberal values and the politics of recognition. The requirement of recognising the values and beliefs of other cultural groups makes it tricky to be full-blooded about defending liberal values. To defend liberal values in cases like the Rushdie affair means asserting the primacy of free expression over the protection of religious sensibilities. To do so necessarily implies that liberal values are superior to other values. But the politics of recognition seems to require, or at least nudge us in the direction of recognising all cultures as of equal value. As Taylor says, with explicit demands for cultural recognition, 'the presumption seems to be of equal worth [of all cultures]' (1994: 66). That is surely right: no one demands recognition for their culture on the basis that it is of lesser value than the dominant one.

Yet the demand is problematic. It is not true that all cultures are of equal value. It would be a most remarkable fact if they were. Let us first note that even to make the claim that all cultures are of equal value implies some kind of universal standard against which they could be judged and found to be equal. A claim of equal value is not a claim of incommensurability. But let us grant that there is such a standard and we are reasonably clear about what it is. A dilemma then presents itself.

8.6.5 The synchronic/diachronic fork

Is the claim of equal cultural value *diachronic*? If that is the case, then all cultures throughout history have been of equal value. There is no such thing as progress. A culture cannot improve. If it did it would be of greater value than it was before, which is what is denied. Neither could there be such a thing as decadence. A culture cannot deteriorate. If it did it would be of less value than it was before, which is also denied.

If one rejects this view, then the claim of equal cultural value must be *synchronic*. That means that all the cultures in the world at this moment are of equal value. It was not always thus, but right now it is. That seems an extraordinary coincidence. Moreover, it is by its nature an ephemeral state of affairs. Unless we are able to freeze this moment somehow, then as different cultures develop their value will diverge again so that some are of greater value than others, as was formerly the case.

8.6.6 A recommended attitude

Taylor agrees that the presumption of equal value for all cultures is impossible to grant. However, he says there is *something* true in the presumption; if it is not true that all cultures have *equal* value, they do at least all have value:

> As a presumption, the claim is that all human cultures that have animated whole societies over some considerable stretches of time have something important to say to all human beings.
>
> (Taylor 1994: 66)

Taylor refers to this as 'a starting hypothesis with which we ought to approach the study of any other cultures' (1994: 66–7).

He sums up by saying:

> Just as all must have equal civil rights, and equal voting rights, regardless of race or culture, so all should enjoy the presumption that their traditional culture has value.
>
> (Taylor 1994: 68)

What Taylor is recommending here is an *attitude*. It is a reasonable, humane attitude, and has expediency in its favour. A multicultural society in which this attitude prevails is likely to function more smoothly than one in which it does not. But in the end it seems to come down to little more than decency and good manners. When it comes to deciding actual policies – should a conservative Islamic group set up schools where the girls have to wear burqas? – the decision cannot be made on the basis that all cultures have value. That should inform the spirit in which the question is investigated, and the tone in which the debate is conducted and the manner in which the decision is announced. But it should not influence the policy itself, which is to be decided in line with liberal principles. The tests are whether the privilege or immunity demanded satisfies (1) the Rights-Protecting Requirement and (2) the Autonomy-Protecting Requirement.

To sum up, Charles Taylor's argument for a politics of recognition offers reasons why provision could be made by a liberal state to facilitate or preserve certain cultural practices, as long as they do not offend against liberal principles; it persuasively suggests an appropriate tone in which public debate about questions should be conducted. But I do not see that it offers reason to modify in essentials the Liberal Position on voluntary face-covering per se.

8.6.7 Limits of state power

Anderson and Honneth (2005) make the valid argument that if liberal states value autonomy, and if autonomy requires socially supportive conditions, then liberal states should foster or provide socially supportive conditions.

However, the implication that this must result in recognitional multicultural policies – that is, policies that provide recognition for cultural groups within society – does not necessarily carry through. I agree that liberal states ought to provide socially supportive conditions to facilitate the possibility of personal autonomy, but the recognitional policies adumbrated by Anderson and Honneth may in some cases be outside the legitimate sphere of the liberal state.

First, the three attitudes identified by Anderson and Honneth as underpinning the competencies necessary for autonomy – self-respect, self-trust and self-esteem – are not necessarily attitudes that the state can do a great deal about. Self-respect – characterised by Anderson and Honneth as 'the ability to stand up in public without shame' (a view they attribute to Amartya Sen) and as 'the ability to assert claims' (attributed to Joel Feinberg) (2005: 132) – is perhaps the most amenable to protection by the state. The state can at least block interference with standing up in public and with the assertion of claims. But let us examine how this would translate into practice in relation to burqa-wearing. The state would protect the right of burqa-wearing individuals, and those who support them, to stand and assert their claims in favour of public face-covering for those women who choose it. To be even-handed, however, the state should also protect the right of those who wish to stand up and offer a critique of public face-covering for women. Both parties to the debate are thus enabled to preserve self-respect. But this says nothing about how any particular question relating to burqa-wearing should be decided. If the question is, for example, whether temporary facial uncovering should be required of a witness in a court of law, then allowing each side to assert their claims without shame does not of itself settle the question.

Anderson and Honneth add that the state should actively support self-respect (2005: 133). The state could attempt to do this through education policy, by emphasising the importance of self-respect through the national curriculum, in citizenship classes and other lessons. However, in cases where the minority culture itself does not support equal respect for all its members, the state would find itself actually in opposition to the minority culture. In any case it is not obvious that the state would be able to achieve a great deal through education policy. It seems unlikely that a citizenship class once a week could override the whole tradition of values and beliefs in which a young person has been brought up. If your citizenship teacher tells you that girls are as worthy of respect as boys, and every member of your extended family informs you otherwise, the citizenship teacher's words may not carry much weight.

Self-trust seems even less amenable to influence from the state. 'Self-trust' is described by Anderson and Honneth as 'basic self-confidence' (2005: 133), and also as the ability to trust one's feelings, impulses and desires (2005: 134). This is linked very closely with trust in one's relationships, especially intimate ones: Anderson and Honneth point out that those who have been raped or physically abused find it much more difficult to trust their emotions. A state concerned with protecting and fostering autonomy must have firm laws against rape and physical abuse. Liberal states already have those. Perhaps they should be more strongly enforced. But other than punishing and deterring such outrages it is hard to see how the state could do much to secure trusting intimate relationships among its citizens. It cannot police relationships to prevent emotional cruelty, sarcasm, contempt, indifference, lack of warmth or lack of respect. The state cannot enforce trusting relationships. Trust by its nature cannot be enforced. Perhaps the most the state can do, apart from punishing violence, is to provide safety-nets and escape routes for victims when trusting relationships break down: fair divorce laws, women's refuges and a benefit system that makes separation possible.

Again, though, such policies would not necessarily be multicultural. In cases where violence or cruelty occurs within a minority culture and with its sanction, the state would find itself working in opposition to the minority culture.

'Self-esteem' is not defined by Anderson and Honneth, but seems to mean a self-image or identity that one feels proud of, or at least satisfied with, and which gives one the ability to be a fully functioning agent in society. This seems the least amenable to protection by the state of all. Self-esteem, Anderson and Honneth rightly point out, can be impaired by negative or insulting comments, and conclude that

> a conception of social justice that is seriously committed to protecting the autonomy of individuals must include a protection against threats of denigration.
> (2005: 137)

Some limited protection is possible and already available in certain areas: there is a law against incitement to racial hatred, and where racist comments fall short of incitement they are de facto prohibited in any public institution or forum and would trigger calls for the resignation of any public figure or official who made them; there are equal opportunities laws restricting what can be said in job advertisements, so that women and ethnic or cultural groups are not unfairly excluded; we have laws against libel, which operate if a personal denigratory statement is made publicly and cannot be proved true.

But the liberal state cannot and should not go very much further than that. If the state were to attempt to prohibit *all* denigratory remarks (and Anderson and Honneth's interpretation of what counts as a denigratory remark is extremely wide: they cite 'stay-at-home dad' as an example of a negative term (2005: 136)), the consequence would be a totalitarian policing of private utterances which would take away more autonomy than it secured.

This is not to argue that, since it is impossible for the state to guarantee self-respect, self-trust and self-esteem in all its citizens, it should not even try to do anything. Half a loaf is better than no bread, and where the state can help and protect those attitudes (subject to not eroding freedoms which are themselves necessary for autonomy, like freedom of speech) it should do so.

But I wish to re-emphasise that such policies may not be multicultural in nature. Much of Anderson and Honneth's discussion appears to suppose that threats to the attitudes necessary for the competencies which underpin personal autonomy are likely to come from outside one's culture or community. They employ the all-embracing word 'society' rather than speaking of communities and subcultures within a society, and often blame 'society' for failures to secure autonomy for its citizens: 'society's *recognitional infrastructure* can leave the autonomy of individuals unacceptably vulnerable' (2005: 142). By all means let us blame society when it is society's fault. Sometimes, however, it is not society as a whole which is to blame, but minority cultural groups within it.

8.6.8 The need for recognition may be at odds with multicultural policies

A clear example of this emerges from Catriona Mackenzie's paper, 'Relational Autonomy, Normative Authority and Perfectionism' (2008), which compares the cases of two women, Mrs B and Mrs H. Mackenzie's aim is to argue for a 'weak substantive' view of personal autonomy, halfway between Christman and Anderson's (2005) and Oshana's (2006), and in doing so she makes use of Anderson and Honneth's theory that recognition from others is essential for autonomy. What I focus on here, however, is a point which emerges, perhaps inadvertently, by the way: the fact that policies to ensure the recognition necessary for autonomy may militate *against* multicultural policies.

Mackenzie considers first the case of Mrs B – a quadriplegic who brought a suit against the hospital for keeping her alive against her will. In a legal judgement Dame Butler-Sloss found in her favour and the ventilator was switched off. Mackenzie supports this decision, which she says was made according to the principle of respect for autonomy, and approvingly quotes Butler-Sloss quoting Kim Atkins:

> Respect for autonomy is an acknowledgement of the limitations of our knowledge of other people and a willingness to incorporate that understanding into our worldviews.
>
> (Mackenzie 2008: 515–16)

Mrs B is an ideal model for endorsement accounts of autonomy such as Christman and Anderson's: she has reflected long and hard on her situation and has deeply considered reasons for her choice.

Mackenzie contrasts this textbook endorsement case with the case of Mrs H. Mrs H has cancer, and has lost her hair, one leg and husband (who left her because her disability was burdensome and an embarrassment to him). She tells hospital staff she wants no further treatment but wishes to be left to die (though the hospital could keep her alive in the medium-term). Mrs H poses a problem for endorsement accounts: she genuinely wants what she says she wants, but her view is a result of 'oppressive social relationships that undermine her ability to flourish' (2008: 518). There are norms of traditional femininity in her culture that she no longer satisfies. This seems a clear, indeed an extreme case of what Khader termed an IAP – an Inappropriate Adaptive Preference (Khader 2011).

It is not at all clear that society as a whole is at fault in the case of Mrs H. It is the minority culture to which Mrs H belongs that is to blame: a culture in which women are not granted equal respect with men and are judged on a narrow notion of femininity and wifely/motherly capabilities, and in which men's responsibilities to their wives are taken less seriously than women's responsibilities to their husbands.

Mackenzie does not specify which minority culture Mrs H belongs to or say very much about its oppressive social relationships. But there is a description in Zarghuna Kargar's book *Dear Zari* (2012) of a similar case which occurred in Afghanistan in the 1980s. A young wife and mother, Wazma, loses her leg in a Russian rocket attack. After this her husband Waheed (who previously had been loving and affectionate towards her) leaves her, taking their child away, and marries another woman. Kargar interviews Wazma:

> What if the rocket attack had taken Waheed's leg instead of hers? Wazma smiled and replied that she would have stayed and looked after him. She would never have left him. She said she knows she was cast out because she is a woman.
>
> (2012: 158–9)

Nor is this an isolated case:

> Wazma is not alone. Hundreds of women in Afghanistan suffer like this. According to the United Nations, the decades of war that have plagued Afghanistan – the rocket attacks, landmines and bombs – have left more than a million people disabled … It is not unusual to find a man like Waheed with a heart made of stone, as Wazma puts it; a man who would reject his wife because she had become disabled. However, there are many women – young and old – who are married to disabled men and take care of all their needs. It is easier for a disabled man to find a wife because the woman has no say in the marriage, but it is almost impossible for a disabled woman to find a man who will accept her.
>
> (Kargar 2012: 159)

This is a culture which actively wants women to have less autonomy than men, or indeed none at all. Mackenzie's answer to Mrs H's problem implicitly recognises this. 'Society' is presented as the *solution* to the problem, not the cause of it.

Following Anderson and Honneth, Mackenzie states that autonomy 'can only be developed and sustained intersubjectively' (2008: 526). But no such intersubjective support is available to Mrs H from her husband or community – as cruelly evinced by her husband's desertion of her. She lacks self-trust, self-respect and self-esteem because her culture (not society at large) refuses to accord her those qualities.

How, then, could Mrs H's autonomy be respected? Mackenzie argues that 'we' (i.e. the hospital team and any liberal-minded sympathisers who reject Mrs H's culture's values) must treat her as a human being with her own needs and values, try to understand her perspective and try to change her attitudes towards herself (2008: 528). Once this change has been effected she would qualify as autonomous. She might then decide she no longer wanted to die; or, if she still wanted to end her life it would be the same kind of autonomous decision as that made by Mrs B, and should be respected. This approach is both relational and grounded in the agent's first-person perspective.

What Mackenzie is suggesting in effect is that the prevailing liberal culture of our society should step in to supply the deficiencies in Mrs H's minority culture. Her minority culture does not grant disabled women the social-relational conditions necessary for autonomy. Those conditions must therefore be supplied, in the first place by health professionals, and more generally by the institutions (the education system, media and laws) of a liberal state.

The implication, whether intended by Mackenzie or not, is that the liberal state has a duty to rescue people from minority cultures which are socially oppressive towards their members – to provide an alternative infrastructure in which intersubjective support and recognition are provided. Many cultures, particularly those with strongly conservative religious views, are particularly oppressive towards women, but women are not the only victims: homosexuals or persons of lower caste or those who are socially disgraced in some way are also likely to be denied intersubjective support and recognition.

This is no easy task for liberal states. In cases like Mrs H's, where the oppressed person is already being cared for by hospital staff, at least the means are on hand to provide the necessary personal support (although altering her attitudes to make her autonomous will still be far from easy). But in the presumably far more frequent cases where the oppressed person is not in the care of a state institution, it is hard to see what sort of rescue operation could be mounted. Would such people even identify themselves as oppressed, if the oppression had successfully destroyed their self-respect, self-trust and self-esteem? And even if they did, could the state actively intervene, remove them from their community, provide them with a new place to live, a new social network, and a team of professionals to de-programme them? Not only would this be logistically and economically impracticable, but the attempt would also arouse bitter resentment and opposition from the communities at the state's poaching their members in this way.

What the state could do is to prohibit, and enforce the prohibition of, cultural practices which in general impair the self-respect, self-trust and self-esteem of individuals and groups within communities: for example, forced marriages, polygamous marriages, unequal divorce customs, FGM, threats or violence against apostates.

At the same time, given the socio-relational character of autonomy, the liberal state needs to protect religious and cultural practices which give the individual a sense of belonging, and within which their most meaningful relationships occur. There is therefore a tension between (1) protecting and supporting the social infrastructures within subcultures which make autonomy possible and

(2) suppressing customs which undermine the self-respect, self-trust and self-esteem of individuals and groups within those subcultures. Thus there is a need for the kind of sensitive, deliberative intervention recommended by Serene Khader (2011).

Burqa-wearing is a prime site for this tension. On the one hand, the liberal state should protect burqa-wearing to the extent that it is a social practice which, by giving wearers a sense of belonging, makes personal autonomy possible; on the other hand, if it is a practice which impairs the self-respect, self-trust and self-esteem of women then the liberal state would have a prima facie duty to prohibit it. Which of these alternatives is true is an empirical question, and the answer is not necessarily a static one. But it turns on whether the practice is coerced. A burqa worn under coercion would not produce a sense of belonging or make personal autonomy possible. The issue of coercion is discussed in Chapter 11.

8.6.9 The liberal position on face-covering per se is compatible with a recognitional view of autonomy

At this point, we can state that, even if one takes a position towards the liberal perfectionist end of the spectrum and a recognitional view of autonomy, there is still no reason to move away from the liberal position on voluntary face-covering per se. To restate the three areas where movement might be considered:

1. Demands for exemptions from the requirement to temporarily uncover the face should not gain extra force from a recognitional approach. Those requesting such an exemption would have a right to be heard and to assert their claim. But so would those who disagreed. The liberal state's obligation to safeguard self-respect extends to granting a fair and respectful hearing to public assertion of claims, not to granting the claims themselves.
2. If burqa-wearing turned out to have harmful side effects on others, such as a rise in masked crime, the politics of recognition ought not to affect the level at which the harms were judged unacceptable. In such circumstances, the state could make clear that the only reason for a ban was to protect citizens from harm. There is no reason why such a ban should impair the self-respect, self-trust or self-esteem of those supported the practice. It could and should be made evident that it was not the cultural practice itself that necessitated the ban, but its abuse. To make that clearer the state would continue to allow burqa-wearing at private or ceremonial events.

3. A liberal state which subscribed to the politics of recognition need not refrain from allowing public disapproval or criticism of burqa-wearing, as long as this was balanced by the right to speak up and defend the practice. If the liberal state were to prohibit criticism of burqa-wearing (or any other cultural practice) it would offend against its own principle of free expression. The essential proviso is that such criticism should not be permitted to be defamatory or intimidatory towards individuals or groups.

9

Gender and the burqa

The argument

In Chapter 3 it was argued that the liberal position on voluntary habitual face-covering per se should be to allow it, except in individual cases where security, identification or communication were at issue, when temporary uncovering could justifiably be required. However, that position takes no account of the gender asymmetry of burqa-wearing. The burqa is a face-covering for women, not for men. The question addressed in this chapter is whether consideration of that gender asymmetry should cause liberals to modify the basic position on face-covering *per se*. The gender asymmetry of burqa-wearing could lead to injustice against women, where gender-symmetrical face-covering would not. If that were the case, there could be justification for a ban, or other means of discouraging or preventing burqa-wearing.

I shall argue, following Susan Moller Okin, that certain practices of some minority cultures may be at odds with liberal principles, and in those cases the liberal state is justified in preventing or discouraging them.

I shall examine Clare Chambers's argument that cultural practices, even if apparently freely chosen, are unjust when the choice is (1) socially constructed and (2) the result is disadvantageous to the chooser. I accept her argument in principle but stress that both her conditions are matters of degree, and in neither her chosen example of breast enhancement surgery nor in the case of burqa-wearing would those degrees be likely to reach levels high enough to warrant a ban.

So I shall conclude that Chambers's argument would not justify a burqa-ban as far as justice towards the burqa-wearer herself goes. The question of the injustice towards individuals *other than the burqa-wearer herself* is the subject of Chapters 10 and 11.

9.1 A defence of liberal feminism

My argument takes as a given the principle that women and men have the same rights and freedoms and are equally entitled to justice, and assumes that this principle can and should be realised within the framework of liberal institutions: that is to say, the kind of liberal feminism embraced by Okin, Chambers and Nussbaum. I do not therefore consider radical or Marxist varieties of feminism, which would oppose liberal institutions as instantiations of patriarchy or bourgeois hegemony.

I also do not consider Islamic feminism as such. To be clear, I do not of course mean that Muslims cannot be feminists. But they are either liberal feminists, in which case there is no need to consider their view separately; or they are not, in which case they are outside the scope of my consideration. One might put it that there is a fork between 'weak' Islamic feminism and 'strong' Islamic feminism, and neither prong of the fork is eligible to be considered under the question of whether a *liberal* state should ban the burqa.

By weak Islamic feminism I mean a feminism in agreement with the principle tenets of Western liberal feminism – that all male and female citizens are, or should be, free and equal, that women labour under unfair disadvantages that should be removed and that this can be achieved under liberal institutions – but which happens to be espoused and practised by Muslims. This can be considered on the same terms as liberal feminism per se. It is not an alternative to liberal feminism but a form of it, and need not be considered separately.

On the other prong of the fork, strong Islamic feminism, any rights claimed for women or girls must be consistent with the position on women's and girls' rights, relative to men's, laid down in authoritative Islamic texts – the Qu'ran and the Hadith. By strong Islamic feminism I mean the position that is characterised by Amal Treacher as follows:

> Muslim feminists, in contrast to secular feminists, demand women's place and rights within an Islamic framework. They argue that Islam has delivered women from being perceived and treated as commodities. Within this account, Western women are exploited as cheap labour, oppressed as sex objects, and robbed of their femininity. Unlike Western women, Muslim women do not have the double burden of equality – work and home – which has been counterproductive. Further, Western feminism has not produced true liberation for women *as* women; rather, it has forced them to become like men.
>
> (2003: 64)

The requirement for the Islamic framework imposes a limitation on this kind of feminism. Only equality demands which are consistent with Islam, or some interpretation of it, can be admitted. Liberal feminism does not have this restriction, or any corresponding to it.

Strong Islamic feminism is similar to radical feminism in its essentialism. Like many forms of radical feminism it assumes that there are differences in the essential natures of men and women, and consequently what is good for men is not necessarily good for women (hence the reference to 'women's place and rights', as though it is taken for granted that they will be different from men's). By contrast the liberal feminist position does not depend on assumptions about the essential natures of men or women. Nor is it committed to denying any such differences. It is to the liberal way of thinking irrelevant whether men or women in general are likely to have some particular quality, faculty or disposition. For a liberal, an individual of either sex has the same right to develop and pursue whatever skills or ambitions they may have, regardless of whether they are unusual for their sex in having those skills or ambitions. As John Stuart Mill put it:

> Even if [a presumption of fitness] be well grounded in a majority of cases, which it is very likely not to be, there will be a minority of exceptional cases in which it does not hold; and in those it is both an injustice to the individual, and a detriment to society, to place barriers in the way of their using their faculties for their own benefit and for that of others.
>
> ([1869] 2008: 22–3)

The possibility might be raised that there could be a middle, or mixed position between weak and strong Islamic feminism. Anna Kemp, in her book *Voices and Veils: Feminism and Islam in French Women's Writing and Activism* (2010) ascribes a more Islam-conscious identity to her account of what I have termed weak Islamic feminism, as resisting 'both patriarchal Muslim traditions and nativist feminist caricatures of Islam as inherently patriarchal' (113–14).

Yet this is not genuinely a middle position. It is not a defining tenet of Western liberal feminism that it must depict Islam as inherently patriarchal. The key point on which feminists agree, Muslim or not, is that patriarchy, Muslim or not, should be resisted. Kemp is perhaps understandably concerned that Western feminists operate a double standard, condemning patriarchal Muslim practices more harshly than patriarchal Western ones. But that concern duly noted, the kind of feminism she describes is no different from weak Islamic feminism: that is, liberal feminism which happens to be espoused and practised by Muslims.

Indeed, any kind of middle or mixed position would be vulnerable to the fork outlined above. For any *elements* of that position which could be characterised as strong Islamic feminism would be outside the scope of my consideration here; while elements of weak Islamic feminism, being subsumed under liberal feminism, need not be considered separately.

The liberal principle that all citizens are free and equal already contains a commitment to feminism, in that 'citizens' comprehends both women and men. The assumption is that both women and men value the same rights and freedoms and should have them to the same extent. Historically, perhaps, liberals have not been sufficiently alert to the fact that they do not actually get them to the same extent (with the honourable exception of John Stuart Mill). Liberal feminists would no doubt want to point out that in the past and in contemporary societies, it has tended to be women who chiefly suffer from inequality or lack of freedom. For this reason it might be a good strategy to focus on the experiences of women and to pass laws or enact policies that benefit women specifically. Marilyn Friedman, for instance, argues in her essay 'Autonomy and Male Dominance' that we should prioritise female autonomy over male autonomy

> under conditions of male dominance, female autonomy is more *valuable* than male autonomy because it better promotes social realisation of the moral equality of all persons. Because it is more valuable, we all have good reason to advance women's autonomy whenever possible while at the same time restraining male aggression.
> (2005: 169)

Nevertheless, that would be a temporary prioritisation, designed to bring about equality; once equality was achieved then there would be no need to prioritise either sex.

9.2 'Is multiculturalism bad for women?'

Susan Moller Okin's essay 'Is Multiculturalism Bad for Women?' clearly sets out the possible and indeed likely conflict between liberal feminism and multiculturalism. She states that those opposed to oppression 'have been too quick to assume that feminism and multiculturalism are both good things which are easily reconciled' (Okin 1999: 10). Instead, Okin argues that there is considerable likelihood of tension between them – more precisely, between feminism and a multicultural commitment to group rights for minority cultures.

(1999: 10)

Okin's argument is straightforward. Many cultures do not respect the liberal norm of gender equality. Granting them group rights thus risks allowing oppression of women to continue. As Okin puts it,

> Suppose ... that a culture endorses and facilitates the control of men over women in various ways (even if informally, in the private sphere of domestic life). Suppose, too, that there are fairly clear disparities in power between the sexes, such that the more powerful, male members are those who are generally in a position to determine and articulate the group's beliefs, practices and interests. Under such conditions, group rights are potentially, and in many cases actually, antifeminist.

(1999: 12)

Okin offers the example of the French government's permissive policy in the 1980s towards the polygamy practised by many Arab and African immigrants (1999: 9–10). Polygamy was allowed for these immigrants (though not for other French citizens) because it was part of their culture, resulting in some 200,000 polygamous families living in Paris alone. A cultural practice was thus protected (for a while, until the French government reversed its policy); but the result was not good for the women concerned. According to Okin, reporters discovered that

> the women affected by polygamy regarded it as an inescapable and barely tolerable institution in their African countries of origin, and an unbearable imposition in the French context.

(1999: 10)

Okin points out that proponents of group rights, while alert to inequalities between groups, can be blind to inequalities within them. But 'those who make liberal arguments for the rights of groups must take special care to look at inequalities within groups' (1999: 23). Okin agrees with Kymlicka that group rights are not justified if they enable groups to oppress their own members, but she argues that such oppression, particularly of women and girls, is more widespread than Kymlicka acknowledges (Okin 1999: 21).

Okin's prescription is that group rights should not be granted unless the individual rights of all group members have been given equal weight:

> Unless women – and, more specifically, young women (since older women are often co-opted into reinforcing gender inequality) – are fully represented in negotiations about group rights, their interests may be harmed rather than promoted by the granting of such rights.
>
> (1999: 24)

Okin does not go into detail about the actual mechanism by which women should be represented in such negotiations. Practical questions present themselves. Who presides over negotiations? Who chooses the representatives? What balance between men and women, young and old, should there be? In the event of flat-out disagreement how is the issue to be decided? A vote could instantiate a tyranny of the majority, but without a vote how are competing interests to be weighed?

Okin leaves these practical questions alone because they are in a sense beside the point. Her actual prescription is of less importance than the purpose for which it was conceived. Her purpose is that the granting of group rights should not harm the interests of women. The means by which this is achieved is secondary. If indeed negotiations did not lead to women's interests being protected against harmful group rights, then negotiations, or that particular type of negotiations, would be the wrong way to go about it. Another mechanism would have to be found.

It is important to note that Okin's whole line of argument depends on the claim that Western liberal societies are, in general, better for women to live in than many of the traditional cultures from which minority immigrant groups originate. If Okin were asking this question from Saudi Arabia or Afghanistan then the answer would be, 'No, multiculturalism is not bad for women, women need more of it.' Okin is clear that she is speaking from within a Western liberal tradition, which is *better* in terms of women's rights and the quality of women's lives than many other cultures. As she puts it:

> While virtually all of the world's cultures have distinctly patriarchal pasts, some – mostly, though by no means exclusively, Western liberal cultures – have departed further from them than others. Western cultures, of course, still practice many forms of sex discrimination … [examples follow] … But women in more liberal cultures are, at the same time, legally guaranteed many of the

same freedoms and opportunities as men. In addition, most families in such cultures ... do not communicate to their daughters that they are of less value than boys, that their lives are to be confined to domesticity and service to men and children, and that their sexuality is of value only in marriage, in the service of men, and for reproductive ends. This situation... is quite different from that of many other women in the world's other cultures, including many of those from which immigrants to Europe and North America come.

(1999: 16–17)

My view is that Okin is correct in this claim. Certainly *some* non-Western cultural practices, such as forced marriage, polygamy or FGM, impact harshly on women and should not be tolerated by a liberal state. The question is whether the considerations Okin raises imply that a liberal state should be less permissive towards the burqa. Before turning to that question, though, I discuss and answer some objections to her argument.

9.3 Two objections to Okin

9.3.1 Azizah Y. al-Hibri's response

I have chosen Azizah Y. al-Hibri's essay written in reply to Okin, 'Is Western Patriarchal Feminism Good for Third World/Minority Women?', for two reasons. First, I see it as representative of a common and in my view ineffective approach towards arguments about multiculturalism: that is, to cast doubt on an arguer's credentials, authority or agenda rather than take on the premises or validity of their argument. And second, al-Hibri's objection brings out an important feature of Okin's argument: namely, that Okin's criticism does not depend on identifying culture with religion. It makes no difference whether any particular cultural practice which is oppressive to women is religiously motivated. The important point is that it oppresses them.

Al-Hibri makes a threefold objection to Okin. First, she charges Okin with having 'stereotypical views of the "Other"'; second, with making 'a conflation of different belief systems'; and third, with being in 'conflict with American constitutional principles' (1999: 41). As we shall see, none of these objections, even if well-founded, seriously damages Okin's argument.

Al-Hibri's first charge is based on the claim that Okin's characterisation of individual cultures and religions as more patriarchal than Western societies is erroneous, being based on a sketchy, outsider's understanding. Al-Hibri states:

> Her understanding of other cultures/religions is derived from secondary sources outside these cultures/religions. As a result, she makes simple but significant errors in assessing other belief systems.
>
> (1999: 42)

By way of example, al-Hibri points out that the stories of the creation of Eve and the fall of Adam in the Qur'an are not the same as the Biblical creation story, though Okin assumes that they are. In the Qur'anic version of the story, al-Hibri says, Eve was not created from Adam's rib but as his equal, and Adam and Eve were tempted, and succumbed, simultaneously.

Okin therefore made a factual error. But this in no way implies the stance that al-Hibri attributes to her:

> It is ... the example *par excellence* of Okin speaking in her dominant voice about the *inessential Other*. So inessential is this Other that, even when included in the discussion, it is rendered remarkably indistinguishable and voiceless.
>
> (1999: 42)

Okin's argument could easily be revised to include a more accurate account of the Qur'anic creation myth, or indeed to omit it, and would be undamaged by such a revision. It remains the case that *to the extent* that Western cultures are less patriarchal than non-Western ones, multicultural policies in Western societies can have bad results for women. Al-Hibri might simply deny that it is true that Western societies are less patriarchal in any way at all, but it is hard to see what objection she could make to Okin's example of polygamy in France, which is a non-Western tradition, practised by Muslims, and which has Qur'anic support. According to sura 4 verse 3:

> If you fear that you will not act justly towards the orphans, marry such women as seem good to you, two, three, four; but if you fear you will not be equitable, then only one, or what your right hands own.
>
> (*Koran*, trans. Arberry 2008)

This verse justifies the marrying of up to four women who do not have living parents, with two conditions: (1) if a man fears he will not be able to treat his wives equally then he should stick to one wife; (2) but that limitation does not apply to slave women ('what your right hands own'), of whom a man can presumably marry as many as he likes without worrying about equal treatment.

Al-Hibri and other Muslims who do not endorse polygamy might question the above interpretation of that verse, and indeed other interpretations are possible (see Sardar 2015: 306). They would argue that polygamy is more of a cultural tradition than a religious one. This brings us to the second of al-Hibri's charges: that Okin conflates culture and religion, treating them as interchangeable and objecting to what is bad for women in both. Al-Hibri's own position is that they are distinct, and that it is *culture* which endorses practices which are bad for women, not religion (at least not when the religion is Islam). The confusion has occurred, she says, because Muslim countries are permitted to retain local customs if they are judged to be consistent with Islamic revelation:

> As a result of this principle, many countries retained local customs that we find controversial, and that have been erroneously viewed in the West, and sometimes locally, as Islamic.
>
> (1999: 43)

Al-Hibri does not say whether it is erroneous to view *all* the practices found to be controversial as Islamic. But let us say for the sake of argument that that is what she means, and let us also say for the sake of argument that she is right. This still leaves Okin's argument undamaged. Even if Okin has incorrectly identified some practices as religious when she should have identified them as purely cultural, this does not touch her claim that multicultural policies can be bad for women. If a policy of allowing burqa-wearing turned out to have bad effects for women, then the effects are bad regardless of whether the origins of that tradition are cultural or religious. Okin (in my view plausibly) does diagnose the origins of many practices that oppress women as religious. But her position does not depend on that diagnosis.

Finally, let us turn to al-Hibri's third charge against Okin, that her position 'conflicts with American principles that we value greatly, such as the separation of church and state and the freedom of belief' (1999: 44); she points out that 'in [the USA], people are entitled to their religious beliefs whether secular feminists approve of these beliefs or not' (1999: 44).

But nowhere has Okin said that people are not entitled to their religious *beliefs*. She objects to certain specified religious (and/or cultural) *practices* which involve gender inequalities: for example, 'child marriage, forced marriage, divorce systems biased against women, polygamy, and clitoridectomy' (Okin 1999: 17).

Freedom of belief cannot extend to a free pass for practices which are both harmful and unjust. No defender of religious freedom, al-Hibri or Okin or anyone else, advocates that. In fact unlimited freedom of religious practice leads to self-contradiction (suppose the case of granting unlimited religious freedom to a sect who saw it as their duty to extirpate all other religions).

9.3.2 Bikhu Parek's response to Okin

A more sophisticated critique is offered by Bikhu Parekh. Parekh agrees with Okin's substantive conclusions; in particular that 'respect for cultures can never be unconditional and condone acts of inhumanity and oppression' (1999: 70). He agrees with her opposition to FGM and to forced marriage. However, he is less happy with her 'wider theoretical framework' (1999: 71). As Parekh sees it, Okin's framework is that 'the fundamentals of liberalism' are universal values and other cultures must adopt them. He first disputes whether there is any agreement on what the fundamentals of liberalism are, even within liberalism. This accusation seems answerable. The specific value of gender equality with which Okin is concerned is surely a fundamental liberal value, as are freedom of expression, freedom of association, freedom of worship and the principle that, whatever the given rights and freedoms are, they should be apportioned equally.

However, Parekh makes that point almost as a kind of feint before he gets to his real objections: granted that agreement can be secured on liberal fundamentals, three problems arise: (1) Okin offers no reason why non-liberals should accept these fundamentals; (2) requiring minority liberal cultures to conform to the value of gender of equality implies that they conform to *all* liberal values; and, lastly, (3) he charges Okin with presenting an oversimplified picture of gender equality, given that in some cultures women are accorded different rights, powers and respect at different times of their lives.

Although this is a more searching critique than al-Hibri's, Parekh's points also seem answerable on Okin's terms. Okin is explicit that modern liberal societies treat women citizens better than do non-liberal societies. The reason for this fact is that women are treated as the equals of men in liberal societies. At any rate that is the ideal and it is more closely attained in liberal societies than in non-liberal ones. This is an empirical claim which Okin supports with copious examples of mistreatment of women and girls in non-Western societies, such as FGM, forced marriage and polygamy (Okin 1999).

Even if one were not satisfied by Okin's examples (perhaps she is cherry-picking) the question could be explored by more rigorous collection and statistical analysis of data about how women fare in different societies – their life expectancy; educational attainments; chances of being the victim of violence, rape or murder; comparative survival rates for girl babies and so on. Steven Pinker in *The Better Angels of Our Nature* cites data from the World Health Organisation and the United Development Fund for Women which show that serious domestic violence against women is far more common 'outside Western Europe and the Anglosphere', and that 'laws on violence against women also show a lag from the legal reforms of Western democracies' (2011: 497–8).

Even without hard data, one can get a sense of one's existing impression of whether women's lives go better in liberal societies than non-liberal ones by posing a simple Veil-of-Ignorance-style thought experiment. If one did not know whether one would be embodied as a male or female citizen in society and one had the power to choose what kind of society to become embodied in, would one choose a liberal or a non-liberal society? The answer is clearly that one would choose a liberal society.

These considerations seem to offer grounds for the claim that liberal cultures, most of which happen to be Western, are better for women to live in (which is not to say that they are perfect).

Here is where Parekh's next point comes in. If all cultures are to accept gender equality, are they also to accept other liberal fundamentals such as free speech, autonomy, individualism and so forth? Okin's answer to this question would seem to be a straightforward yes. That is to say, all cultures in a liberal society must accept those principles to the extent of allowing others to embrace them. No individual is under an obligation to be autonomous or to speak their mind, but they have no right to prevent members of their own or other cultures from exercising those rights or to punish them for doing so. This neither undermines Okin's argument about gender equality nor supports Parekh's claim that such a requirement 'shows scant respect for [minority cultures'] identity' (1999: 72). Cultural identity may be respected in a wide variety of ways and does not depend on being allowed to punish fellow members of one's culture for being autonomous or plain-speaking.

Parekh's third point is that Okin misses the subtlety of gender relations in other cultures. No doubt her account could be refined, made more complex and detailed, to take into account how women in various cultures are treated at different stages of their lives, and how other factors such as class, wealth and birth cut across the gender divide. Those would be interesting areas for a social anthropologist to research. But such refinements would not shake Okin's normative principle of the equality of the sexes. Parekh indeed agrees with Okin on that principle, but he does not agree that such a principle should translate to a claim that women 'should be equally autonomous, free to challenge their social roles, unconstrained by the subtle controls of patriarchal cultures, and so on' (1999: 72). His reason is that such a view would be 'unlikely to command universal consent' (1999: 72). Perhaps not, but one does not refute a view merely by refusing to consent to it. The argument attributed to Okin seems sound: if men and women have equal rights, and if men have the right to be autonomous and to challenge their social roles, then women also have that right.

Parekh might reply that having *equal* rights need not mean having the *same* rights. For example, men and women might have an equal right to use a swimming pool, but not at the same times. That reply suggests that it would be in line with a principle of gender equality if women were denied the same right to autonomy as men but granted some other right of equal value and significance instead (which was denied to men). The problem with this response is that it could not satisfy women who objected: 'I don't want that right; I want the right to autonomy.' This is not on all fours with saying 'I don't want to go swimming on Wednesday; I want to go swimming on Thursday.' In the latter case the actual experience is the same whichever day one goes swimming. But in the case of autonomy (or any other right that men enjoy), it makes a real difference if one is offered something else.

Parekh then makes a fourth point in response to Okin which is not so much an objection to her position as an invitation to look beyond it. If, instead of treating liberalism as hegemonic, liberal theorists place liberal values within a multicultural framework as one culture in dialogue with others, then 'different cultures can cooperatively explore their differences and create a rich and lively community based on their respective insights' (Parekh 1999: 74–5).

Yet it is not necessary for liberals to abandon a commitment to the universalism of liberal values in order to achieve this. Liberals believe that liberal values are good for everyone and capable of being accepted and appreciated by everyone. If they ceased to believe this they would cease to be liberals. A liberal state worthy of the name must protect the fundamental liberal rights and freedoms in law. This does not in any way prevent cultures exploring their differences and creating a rich and lively community.

9.4 Could voluntary burqa-wearing be unjust?

9.4.1 The burqa and freedom of choice

The examples that Okin discusses all seem clear cases where multiculturalism has bad results for women. Polygamy, FGM, divorce laws which grant women lesser rights than men, and child or forced marriage are all bad for women. They are illegal in most liberal states, with good reason, and a liberal state should not grant cultural exemptions for them. The case of the burqa, however, not discussed by Okin, is a little different.

Habitual face-covering is not illegal in most liberal states, including the United Kingdom, the United States, Canada, Australia and most of Europe. France, Belgium, the Netherlands and Bulgaria, who do ban it, are exceptions. Moreover, habitually covering one's face might seem, *if freely chosen*, not harmful in the obvious and permanent ways that the examples discussed by Okin are. I emphasise 'if freely chosen' because forcing someone to habitually cover their face in public against their will seems a real case of harm (see Chapters 3 and 11). But when it is a person's free choice the case appears, at least on first inspection, to be different. Liberals are generally wary of overriding free choice when no harm to others is in question, and though I have argued for a Liberal Paternalist Principle, under which paternalist intervention by the state is justified when the restriction of liberty is small and the harm prevented is great, I have also argued that banning the burqa would not be justified under that principle (see Chapter 5).

There are of course clear reasons for a liberal feminist to *disapprove* of burqa-wearing. It is a practice followed only by women, not by men; it restricts women from entering the public sphere; and it suggests ownership of women by male relatives or husbands, since they are the only males in whose presence a woman may unveil. Moreover, the burqa is associated with cultures where women often are oppressed in various ways (forced marriages, unequal divorce laws, etc.) and might be disapproved of on the grounds that even if not oppressive in itself it symbolises oppression. However, liberals do not believe that disapproving of things is a sufficient reason for banning them. Allowing things one disapproves of might indeed be called a defining feature of liberalism.

Still, liberals do believe that practices which are *unjust* are candidates for being banned. If burqa-wearing turned out to be unjust then the liberal position on voluntary face-covering per se would be inadequate to deal with it. A less tolerant approach could be called for: either a ban or, if that was not practicable, more subtle forms of discouragement.

The standard liberal position would be that, as long as wearing the burqa was freely chosen, it could not be unjust. Clare Chambers, however, in her book *Sex, Culture and Justice* (2008), challenges this view. While accepting liberal normative values of equality and autonomy, she argues that personal choice alone is not sufficient to guarantee the justice of a practice. Traditional liberalism, with its commitment to individual freedom of choice, tends to neglect the way choices are socially constructed. Chambers's aim is to 'combine a liberal feminist commitment to universal values with an awareness of the ways that culture structures our identities and relationships' (2008: 5).

9.4.2 Foucault's conception of power

Chambers grounds her theory on a Foucauldian conception of power. She accepts Foucault's contention that

> first, power currently operates more significantly through creation than repression and second, that power is more effective the less it focuses on crude repressive mechanisms.
>
> (2008: 22)

How to interpret this? Let us characterise 'power' as meaning that the power-wielder(s) can *make* others do things they would *not* choose to do otherwise; and can *stop* others doing things they *would* choose to do otherwise. Foucault is saying, first, that the power-wielder can achieve this by making the other – the acted-upon – complicit: rather than force them to do things or not to do things, the power-wielder gets them to *want* to do, or not to do those things. In other words, rather than override their choices, the power-wielder influences the choices from the start; sets the frame within which choices can be made. That is what power being 'creative' means. As Chambers puts it:

> Power is not a repressive force coming from outside the individual, constraining her actions, but a creative force manifested in the individual's everyday life.
>
> (2008: 23)

The second point is that this sort of power is more effective than forcing people to do things against their will, for the obvious reason that when people are coerced they are almost certain to resent it, and rebel or take revenge if ever an opportunity presents itself. As Elias Canetti put it in *Crowds and Power*, every command that is backed by power, if obeyed, leaves behind it a 'sting', which is lodged in the person who obeyed the command forever:

> There is no man who does not turn against a command imposed on him from outside; in this case everyone speaks of pressure and reserves the right to vengeance or rebellion.
>
> (1992: 354–5)

The more sophisticated forms of power that Foucault identifies do not cause secret opposition or resentment in this way. They co-opt the acted-upon, making them a willing accomplice. Chambers notes that this type of creative power affects the body: the way we move, hold ourselves, our gait, the actions we perform, as well as clothing and appearance norms (2008: 25). This is of particular relevance to feminism:

> Different social norms, different ideas about how men and women ought to behave, shape us physically. It is because women's bodies are shaped by the result of human, social factors that it is most appropriate to think of them as shaped by power.
>
> (Chambers 2008: 25)

Women do not, for the most part, follow these appearance norms grudgingly. Great care, time and effort, to say nothing of money, are enthusiastically expended on make-up, clothing, shoes, depilation, beauty products, cosmetic surgery and so on. Men, too, follow appearance norms, but as Chambers points out:

> The problem with disciplinary appearance norms is not just that they are different for men and women, and not just that they are more exacting and expensive (in both time and money) for women, but that their effect is to cast women as inferior.
>
> (2008: 29)

Such norms are disabling (high heels make women less active and mobile, for example), they invite contempt from men, and anyway the norms demanded are, for most women, impossible to achieve (Chambers 2008: 29).

All this is achieved without any coercion whatsoever. One might compare it to Sunstein and Thaler's idea of libertarian paternalism (2003), where people are nudged towards beneficial choices. For example, as mentioned in Chapter 5, Sunstein and Thaler suggest putting fruit before sugary desserts in cafeteria lines, customers being more likely to choose the healthy option if they encounter it first. This is a case of a subtle and invisible operation of power, getting agents to choose a particular option without their being aware that they are being nudged to do so.

But that is different from Foucault's conception of power in two key ways. First, there is an identifiable agent behind this exercise of power: the organisation that runs the cafeteria, or their advisers, purposefully chose to set things up this way. This contrasts with the Foucauldian conception of power, where ubiquitous, inherited power structures are already in place, without any agent or agents needing to be consciously responsible for them. Second, in the Sunstein and Thaler case the intention is beneficent. The cafeteria line is set up that way for the customers' own good. Moreover, the good is presumed to be a universal one. No power imbalance is involved in deciding that *those* particular customers need a healthy diet. The assumption is that everybody benefits from a healthy diet, and the same choice-frame should be in place whoever visits the cafeteria. The Sunstein and Thaler form of paternalist power thus seems much less objectionable than the Foucauldian form; if objectionable at all.

9.4.3 Objections to Foucault's conception of power

The difficulty with Foucault's characterisation of power is that there seems no way to resist it, since it is ubiquitous and inevitable. Foucault's thesis is that the traditional, brutal, physical methods of punishment which were formerly used by the state to discipline citizens (he begins his book *Discipline and Punish* (1995) with a graphic description of the public torture and execution of a regicide, Damiens, in 1757) have given way to less visible, more pervasive and more efficient forms of power: 'traditional, ritual, costly, violent forms of power … soon fell into disuse and were superseded by a subtle, calculated technology of subjection' (Foucault 1995: 221). These methods of subjection characterise the modern state and are to be found in all fields: in the military, in education, in medicine, in business, in the police, the judiciary and, in short, in every kind of institution. This is not a top-down form of power, but one that permeates every hierarchical level, using such methods as 'time-tables, collective training, exercises, total and detailed surveillance' (Foucault 1995: 220). To these methods should be added the threat of punishment – but with such efficient disciplinary methods it needs to be invoked rarely, and there is no call for the spectacular public punishment of earlier times.

But if power is all-pervasive it appears to be irresistible. Moreover, there seems to be far less *reason* to resist it than in former days. The story that Foucault tells could reasonably be recast as a tale of progress. Another way to put his story is that state power has become more humane, less oppressive, easier to live under, more respectful of the individual, allowing greater freedom in daily life, removing the need to live in fear of violent, cruel punishment and early death. Which story is closer to the truth? A Veil-of-Ignorance-style thought experiment suggests the answer: given the choice between living under the subtle, invisible forms of power practised by modern states and the brutally wielded power of the eighteenth-century French monarchy, a sane chooser would opt for the former.

That is a side issue, however. Granted that modern state power is preferable to the state power of the *ancien régime*, there might still be reasons for resisting modern state power. But what are they? Foucault offers no norms by which we could judge some exercises of power to be better than others. When Foucault does discuss norms it is in the context of their role as instruments of power:

> The power of the Norm appears throughout the disciplines ... The Normal is established as a principle of coercion in teaching with the introduction of a standardized education and the establishment of the *écoles normales* (teachers' training colleges); it is established in the effort to organize a national medical profession and a hospital system capable of operating general norms of health; it is established in the standardization of industrial produces and processes ... normalization becomes one of the great instruments of power at the end of the classical age.
>
> (1995: 184)

Norms are thus characterised by Foucault as *inside* the system of power, an integral part of its workings. In Foucault's reading, they give one no place to stand outside the system from which to judge it.

Nancy Fraser has given a critique of Foucault along these lines in her book *Unruly Practices*. Foucault, she says,

> claims to suspend [the question of normative] justification in his study of knowledge/power regimes. He says he does not take up the question of whether or not the various constraint-laden practices, institutions, procedures, and apparatuses he studies are legitimate or not.
>
> (1989: 21)

This bracketing of the normative, Fraser argues, causes problems for Foucault. The language he uses when describing and analysing power – 'domination', 'subjection', 'subjugation' – does not sound neutral. Perhaps it is: but then one might question the purpose of his project. Is it merely descriptive? Or perhaps Foucault is only bracketing off *liberal* norms – that is, norms based on ideas of rights and legitimacy – and has some other kind of norms in mind from which power could be critiqued. But Fraser sees no sign of this:

> I find no clues in Foucault's writings as to what his alternative norms might be. I see no hints as to how to concretely interpret 'domination', subjugation', 'subjection' and so forth in some completely new 'postliberal' fashion.
>
> (1989: 29)

Summing up, Fraser says:

> Foucault seems to vacillate between two equally inadequate stances. On the one hand, he adopts a concept of power that permits him no condemnation of any objectionable features of modern societies. But at the same time, and on the other hand, his rhetoric betrays the conviction that modern societies are utterly without redeeming features. Clearly, what Foucault needs, and needs desperately, are normative criteria for distinguishing acceptable from unacceptable forms of power.
>
> (1989: 33)

Defenders of Foucault might challenge this analysis and argue that he does furnish both possibility and reasons for resistance to certain forms of power over others. That argument is outside the scope of this book. But whether or not Fraser is right about Foucault's failure to supply norms that would justify resistance to power, she is certainly right that without such norms resistance would be irrational if not impossible. To point out that a choice is socially constructed is not in itself an objection, if *all* choices are socially constructed. If social construction is all there is we cannot be emancipated from it. Emancipation requires a normative theory – an idea of a better life we can be emancipated *into*. As Chambers puts it:

> The problem is not how to free individuals from social construction *tout court*, but rather how to free them from *unjust* social construction. As such, it is crucial to develop a normative theory of which sorts of social construction are just and which are not.
>
> (2008: 79)

The theory Chambers develops depends on the liberal norms of freedom and equality.

9.4.4 Chambers's two conditions for a normative theory of just and unjust social construction

The question, then, is how to distinguish between just and unjust forms of social construction. Chambers offers two conditions, both of which must be present, for a socially constructed choice, or set of choices, to count as unjust. The conditions are *disadvantage* and *influence*:

> Together, they express the idea that if an individual is encouraged to make choices that disadvantage her, then the ensuing inequality is unjust.
>
> (Chambers 2008: 118)

Although the formulation is different, this is very close to Serene Khader's conception of the Inappropriate Adaptive Preference or IAP (Khader 2011; see Chapter 7). The key difference is that Khader focuses on loss of autonomy where Chambers focuses on injustice. However, both types of objection to a socially constructed choice or preference would be based on similar grounds, and whether the objection should be upheld would depend on the same considerations.

Chambers argues that the presence of both the social influence and the disadvantage factors would justify the intervention of a liberal state. Chambers suggests and discusses three main types of intervention: an equality tribunal, to which complainants could have recourse to remove disadvantageous consequences of choices; state-sponsored information or education campaigns to make people more aware of the consequences of choices; and finally, state proscription of choices which have disadvantageous consequences (2008).

In combination the two factors are *necessary* conditions for identifying a choice as unjust. If someone is influenced to do something that is either neutral or positively advantageous there can be no injustice in that. Conversely, if someone does disadvantage themselves but nobody else has influenced them to do so, there is no one against whom a charge of injustice could be pressed.

But are they *sufficient* conditions for a choice to count as unjust? This is a question which Chambers does not address in much detail. The answer must depend on the severity of the disadvantage and the irresistibility of the influence. Those towards the political liberal end of the liberal spectrum would want those conditions to be stringently interpreted. They would not want it to be easy for personal choices to be labelled unjust and thus susceptible to state interference. Even those towards the perfectionist end of the spectrum will be reluctant to intervene on every choice that is a tiny bit the result of influence and a tiny bit disadvantageous. Going too far down this road would leave behind anything recognisable as liberalism. Let us look more closely at the problems of applying the two conditions, starting with disadvantage.

9.4.5 Disadvantage

The idea of *disadvantage* is a normative one. It relies on shared values about what counts as a disadvantage. It is universalist. That in itself is no problem for liberalism, which is a universalist creed. As Chambers herself notes, the liberal value of equality already entails universalism:

> It is in the nature of liberal equality that it cannot be denied to people on the basis of characteristics such as gender, race, or culture.
>
> (2008: 97)

It is true that liberalism has particular origins. It originated in Christian Europe, more particularly in Protestant Europe, and it is interesting to note that the countries in which it grew, such as Great Britain, Germany and later the United States, were 'late marriage societies', which have always tended to grant more status and rights to women than early marriage societies (Flanders 2015). But particular origins do not preclude universal application. As Chambers says, 'Liberalism is particular in origin and universal in application' (2008: 114). (The same might be said of science, incidentally.) So it is not a problem in principle that disadvantage invokes universal values. The problems arise when we attempt to secure agreement on what those values are.

Jonathan Wolff and Avner De-Shalit in their book *Disadvantage* argue that disadvantage is to be understood in terms of a lack of well-being, where well-being is understood in a pluralist form. Following the capabilities approach of Sen and Nussbaum (discussed in Chapter 7), they identify fourteen areas or dimensions of flourishing – that is, the list of ten categories developed by Nussbaum (previously listed in Chapter 4) plus four more of their own. The extra categories are the following:

11. Complete independence (ability to do as you wish without dependence on others)
12. Doing good to others
13. Living in a law-abiding fashion
14. Understanding the law

(Wolff and De-Shalit 2007: 190–1)

This list seems to offer a comprehensive account of the most important dimensions of flourishing (I should stress that by 'comprehensive' I do not mean that they imply a comprehensive form of liberalism; several of the dimensions could be satisfied in many different ways). I also agree with Wolff and De-Shalit that a lack or shortfall in one or more of the dimensions would be an indicator of disadvantage. This looks like a good model to help us apply Chambers's condition of disadvantage.

Given agreement on that, however, we must still ask what would count as disadvantage severe enough to warrant state intervention (assuming the presence of the other condition, social influence). Disadvantage is not an all-or-nothing quality, but a gradable one. Minor disadvantage might not suffice to make a socially influenced choice unjust, or unjust enough to worry about; but then there is room for disagreement about what counts as minor. Chambers offers a sliding scale to help make judgements about this:

> The greater the difference [between those making the socially-influenced choice and those not making it] in disadvantage, and the more enduring and less reversible that disadvantage, the more we should worry.
>
> (2008: 121)

That is helpful in at least providing a field for controversy. But it leaves wide open the possibility that two reasonable people, while agreeing on Chambers's conditions for disadvantage, would disagree about their application, because they disagreed on the extent of the differential. Before questioning Chambers's *application* of the principles, however, we must look at the other condition, social influence.

9.4.6 Social influence

I do not dispute Chambers's contention that our choices are socially constructed. Neither do I dispute her key point that many of the socially constructed choices made by women are disadvantageous to them, compared to the socially constructed choices made by men. In particular I agree that both FGM and cosmetic surgery such as breast implants are (disadvantageous) socially constructed choices.

However, although in the case of disadvantage Chambers offered a scale to measure, in a general way, the severity of disadvantage (i.e. the differential between those disadvantaged and those not, and the enduringness and irreversibility of the disadvantage), she offers no such scale for measuring social influence – or not explicitly, at any rate. The fact is, however, that some kinds of social influence are more resistible than others. In a pluralistic liberal democracy there are countless competing currents of social influence. But some groups are more receptive to choosing, rejecting or blending different currents of influence than others. Chambers herself notes that

> some cultural and religious groups are worse than liberal societies in emphasizing differently advantageous norms of behaviour for different people within the group, often but not always based on gender ... We also need to recognize that individual members of such groups will find it harder to choose to take advantage of the liberal framework of rights that formally applies to them than [Brian] Barry implies.
>
> (2008: 127–8)

The Social Influence condition, therefore, requires a scale to gauge its severity, corresponding to the one Chambers offered for the Disadvantage condition.

I propose: 'The less open to competing currents the chooser is, and the more difficult it is for her to conceive of resistance to the influence of her social or cultural group, the more we should worry.'

Like Chambers's criteria for deciding on the seriousness of disadvantages, this offers a sliding scale based on two variables, in this case the openness of the culture to outside influence, and the possibility of resistance to norms within it. Also like Chambers's disadvantage criteria, it identifies the level of concern called for ('the more we should worry) without specifying what remedial action should be taken. That is a separate question, to be decided according to the practical politics of the situation.

9.4.7 Chambers's application: FGM

Chambers's application of her two conditions leads her to the conclusion that the two practices of FGM and cosmetic surgery for women are equally banworthy. Let us look at FGM first. This is the less controversial of Chambers's proposals. Most liberals would agree that FGM should be banned. It is a clear case of harm against the individual. The harm is not usually chosen by the individual. It is usually inflicted by force. It is most often practised on young girls who are not old enough to give meaningful consent anyway.

However, suppose these elements were removed, and that FGM was performed 'only on women above a certain age who gave their consent and who were given information about the risks involved and the particularity of the custom' (Chambers 2008: 177). Chambers would still wish to ban it as unjust, under her two conditions of Disadvantage and Social Influence.

There is no doubt that the practice falls foul of the Disadvantage condition. Those who undergo it suffer loss of both bodily health and bodily integrity (items 2 and 3 of the Nussbaum Capabilities list) and there may well be emotional damage too (item 5).

Equally there is no doubt that the practice is socially influenced. It is a product of cultures in which women's sexual pleasure must be curtailed to reduce the chance of sexual infidelity (see Dorkenoo in Chambers 2008: 34), and in which women are expected to have undergone FGM in order to be accepted as a part of the community, and men are unwilling to marry an unmutilated woman (see Chambers 2008: 179; and Mackie in Chambers 2008: 194). Moreover, these are cultures in which tradition is particularly strong, and dissent is not respected as it is in Western liberal cultures.

Chambers's theory thus provides sound reasons to ban FGM.

9.4.8 Chambers's application: Breast implants

Chambers argues that cosmetic breast implants are banworthy for the same reasons and to the same extent as FGM, because

> nobody (in this case, women) should have to harm themselves (by undergoing breast surgery or FGM) in order to receive benefits (such as a successful career, a sense of self-worth, or the ability to be married) that, for other members of society (in this case women) do not carry similarly harmful requirements.
>
> (2008: 197)

However, I am not convinced that her case is persuasive.

She points out that the practice is or can be disadvantageous. The surgery is risky and can have harmful side effects. That is no doubt true. But breast implants carry health *risks* rather than the certainty of impairment which FGM carries. Moreover, improvements in techniques could make breast implants safer, as well as more reversible. It is not irrevocable, as FGM is.

The desire for breast implants is also the result of social influence, promising enhanced career prospects or greater attractiveness. But here I would argue that the influence is less concerted, less intense and more resistible. Breast implants occur in a culture where their merits and demerits are freely debated, and where there are strong countervailing currents of opinion which can be encountered in magazines, television programmes, radio phone-ins, the internet, social media and at the more intellectual end of things books like Chambers's. Moreover, there is no shortage of examples of successful women in a variety of fields whose success is not founded on having had breast implants. This contrasts very strongly with the closed cultures where FGM is the norm. I do not think therefore that breast implants are as banworthy as FGM, and more evidence would be needed of the severity of the disadvantage they cause and the strength of the social influence that encourages them to make a persuasive case that breast implants are banworthy at all.

Whether the banning of a practice is justified on liberal paternalist grounds, using Chambers's criteria, depends on two things: how severe the disadvantage

9.5 Is burqa-wearing unjust to women?

9.5.1 The burqa and social influence

Finally, let us test the practice of burqa-wearing against Chambers's two conditions. I shall take Social Influence first, for the nature of the social influence is necessary to explain the nature of the disadvantage.

Thus far, much of my discussion of burqa-wearing has treated it, in classically liberal fashion, as the choice of an individual. And of course it is possible for a strong-minded and autonomous individual to choose to cover up as a purely personal choice, perhaps to make a political statement, possibly in the teeth of disapproval from her own family. But such a choice is posterior to, and dependent on, burqa-wearing as an *institution*. It is not typically or primarily an individual choice, but an adherence to a rule or ideal about how women should comport themselves in public.

9.5.2 Genealogy of the burqa

It is worth considering at this point the genealogy of the burqa, to show the extent to which it is a socially influenced practice. As Chambers says, following Foucault,

> genealogy contributes to an understanding of how social and cultural practices limit individual autonomy, constraining our options, our self-understanding and our preferences.
>
> (2008: 38)

A genealogical account reveals that the burqa is not the product of a liberal society or of a society in which women were considered to be the equals of men. Face-veiling for women is in fact a pre-Islamic custom. According to Leila Ahmed (1992), the ancient Assyrians prescribed veiling for upper-class women while prostitutes and slave women were forbidden to veil (and subject to savage punishments if they veiled illegally). Ahmed says, citing Gerda Lerner, that use of the veil classified women according to their sexual activity and signalled to men which women were under male protection and which were fair game.

(Ahmed 1992: 15)

The significance of the veil in its early days, then, was to signal that those who wore it were the property of powerful men. They were untouchable not in virtue of their own rights but in virtue of the rights of the man who owned them. There was no choice for women about whether to wear it or not. The matter was determined by social coercion (influence is too weak a word).

Women under the protection of men continued to wear the veil under Islam. In some respects, the spread of Islam improved the condition of women. It did at least give them some rights which were backed by the authority of a sacred text. As Ahmed states, however:

In establishment Islamic thought, women, like minorities, are defined as different from, and in their legal rights lesser than, Muslim men. Unlike non-Muslim men, who might join the master-class by converting, women's differences and inferiority within this system are immutable.

(1992: 7)

Wearing of the veil by women is a visible symbol of difference; and of inferiority, for it signifies that the woman wearing it is under the protection of a man and her person is to be respected for that reason only.

In more recent times, unveiling for women in Islam came to be seen as a sign of liberation. There was a movement in the nineteenth century for Islam to modernise and become more like Western cultures. As mentioned earlier (Chapter 7), in 1899, the Egyptian Qassim Amin published *Tahrir Al-Mara* (The Liberation of Women) which advocated, among other things such as reform in education, polygamy and divorce laws, that women must unveil.

The need for a general social and cultural transformation is the central thesis of the book, and it is within this thesis that the arguments regarding women are embedded: changing customs regarding women and changing their costume, abolishing the veil in particular, were key, in the author's thesis, to bringing about the desired social transformation.

(Ahmed 1992: 145)

However, Ahmed argues that Amin had, at the least, a mixed agenda. In Ahmed's view, Amin was convinced of the superiority of Western civilisation, and so

> his assault on the veil represented not reasoned reflection and analysis but rather the internalization and replication of the colonialist perspective.
>
> (1992: 160)

Ahmed here equates being convinced of the superiority of Western civilisation with a colonialist perspective. But they are not the same thing. It is possible to be convinced of the superiority of Western civilisation in certain respects (such as the role, status and rights of women) without supporting colonialism. But even supposing that Ahmed is right and Amin was a closet colonialist, that does not invalidate the case he makes for reform. That rests upon the reasons he gives, not his (putative) agenda. Amin argued that the veil as worn in nineteenth-century Egypt was a socially imposed form of oppression of women, and Ahmed gives no reasons to suggest that he was wrong about that.

Throughout much of the twentieth century, removal of the burqa was widely seen as linked with modernity, progress and the liberation of women. In his drive to create a modern, secular state in Turkey, Kemal Ataturk popularised Western dress, and while he never banned the burqa, burqa-wearing declined precipitously. Burqas were also cast aside in Egypt, Afghanistan and other Muslim countries. Without exploring in detail the reasons for this change, we can be clear on one point: such a sweeping change was not the chance aggregation of millions of unrelated free choices. It was a social change brought about by social influence. It ceased to be shameful for a woman to be seen in public seen with her face uncovered; it ceased to be seen as meritorious for her to cover up. Women responded to new expectations of how they should present themselves in public.

In the second half of the twentieth century, burqa-wearing began to return in Islamic countries, such as Afghanistan, Egypt, Iran, Pakistan and Saudi Arabia. This coincided with a much larger rise in hijab-wearing. The motivations may have been a rise in anti-Western sentiment, and a desire to display allegiance to political Islam. It is clear at any rate that such a mass change in behaviour has to be the result of social influence. A recent Pew Research Poll (2014) conducted for Michigan University, which surveyed a number of Muslim countries, found that 74 per cent of respondents in Saudi Arabia thought it most appropriate for a woman to wear either burqa or niqab in public. That was by far the highest figure, but it was still as high as 35 per cent in Pakistan, 12 per cent in Iraq and 10 per cent in Egypt. Further inferential evidence that the rise in burqa-wearing across the Muslim world was the result of social pressure on women comes from another question asked in the survey: 'Should women be able to choose their own clothing?' Only 14 per cent of people in Egypt agreed that they should, 22 per cent in Pakistan, 27 per cent in Iraq and 47 per cent in Saudi Arabia. Even in Turkey, barely half (52%) thought women should be free to choose their own clothing (Pew Research Poll 2014).

Of course those are figures from countries with overwhelmingly Muslim populations, which seem, at this moment in history, to be moving in the direction of conservative rather than liberal interpretations of that faith. Perhaps the social pressure is less strong in polyethnic secular states like Great Britain. Figures are hard to come by for how many women wear the burqa or niqab in Britain and it is impossible to say whether the percentage of Muslim women wearing them matches the percentage in their country of origin. Nevertheless, to whatever extent burqas *are* worn by women in Britain and other polyethnic states, this is likely to be the result of social influence in their families' or communities' countries of origin.

9.5.3 Cultural affirmation

The importance of cultural affirmation reinforces the hypothesis that burqa-wearing is the result of social influence. Human beings are powerfully inclined to seek cultural affirmation, and very few women would choose to cover their face if the practice was frowned on by their communities. This point is made persuasively by Laurence Thomas in his essay, 'Evil and the Norms of Society' (2012). He states that the need for affirmation by others is an intrinsic part of human nature:

> Proper human development is inextricably tied to being affirmed by others. From the parent-child relationship to the formation of ties of friendship and romance, human beings seek affirmation. It is also the case that our sense of self, from appearance to abilities, is tied to the ongoing affirmation that we receive from others – not just our friends and loved ones, but people in general. At a basic level, human beings can be said to have a thirst for affirmation.
>
> (2012: 92)

Thomas goes on to provide a specific example relevant to the topic here:

> For example, a Muslim woman may not particularly like wearing the hijab. However, she may do so on occasion because it affords her a standing that she would not otherwise have among various members of the Muslim community.
>
> (2012: 94)

Against this background, it is implausible that a widespread habit of face-covering by women could be anything other than the result of a social norm (or of coercion, but as Thomas points out, coercion itself would have to have its origin in a social norm: see 2012: 92). Burqa-wearing, then, meets the first of Chambers's conditions. It is the result of social influence.

9.5.4 The burqa and disadvantage

Since the condition of influence appears to be met in the case of the burqa, we must ask if the condition of disadvantage is also met. If so, then on Chambers's argument burqa-wearing is unjust. It would not necessarily follow that a ban would be the most efficacious way of responding to the injustice. But it might be.

In considering whether, or to what extent, burqa-wearing brings disadvantages I focus only on disadvantage to the wearer, following the approach that Chambers takes. She is concerned to intervene on behalf of individuals who make socially influenced and personally disadvantageous choices. The disadvantage burqa-wearing might cause to others is a different and, for the liberal, less controversial question. I consider this question in detail in the next two chapters, on the effect of the burqa on others in the forms of offence and harm. Here I follow Chambers's line in focusing on injustice suffered by the individual chooser.

That the burqa disadvantages the wearer in relation to men in a variety of ways seems uncontroversial. (At least it is uncontroversial if one accepts liberal norms of equality and liberty, as Chambers does and as I do.) The disadvantages could be itemised as follows: (1) the burqa conveys a symbolic message that the wearer is not equal to men, (2) the burqa restricts social intercourse, (3) it is an impediment to career and public life and (4) it renders many pleasurable physical activities extremely difficult or impossible.

That list may not be exhaustive but covers all the most important points. At the risk of being over-obvious let me briefly spell out why each is a disadvantage.

1. The first of the disadvantages stems from the very fact of burqa-wearing being socially influenced. It is influenced by the norms of a culture in

which women are not considered to be equal to men. The symbolic message of the burqa is that its wearer is under the protection of a man. She is not respected in the same way that a man would be respected, as a person in her own right. She is respected as the property of a husband or male relative who will defend her honour (and perhaps more importantly his own) against the predations of other men. It is true that this is not the only symbolic message that the burqa carries. It might also be a political statement, rejecting Western values and proclaiming adherence to political Islam. But that does not cancel out the older and more fundamental meaning. It is the older and more fundamental meaning which disadvantages the wearer, by assigning her subordinate status to men, who do not wear burqas.

2. That the burqa restricts social intercourse should not come as a surprise. It is designed to do so. It does not make all social intercourse impossible. Burqa-wearers can still communicate freely in private with husband and family. But it severely restricts social intercourse outside the family. Facial communication is impaired. Burqa-wearers are unable to smile at people or even give an eyebrow flash of recognition. They are themselves harder to recognise than non-burqa-wearers. Not only does the burqa impede communication in this way but it renders communication less likely to be attempted, operating as a barrier between the wearer and others. For a highly social species such as ourselves this must count as a disadvantage, especially in comparison to men, who do not wear burqas.

3. Wearing a burqa restricts career options and public life. Any career which involved communicating with the public, and/or presenting a trustworthy face – doctor, teacher, police officer, barrister, manager, newsreader, lecturer, actor, singer, performer, TV presenter and so on – would be highly problematic. Political office would also be, practically speaking, impossible: a mayoral or parliamentary candidate who only ever appeared in public with their face covered would stand zero chance of getting elected (or of being selected for candidacy in the first place). It probably is not a coincidence that the careers from which a burqa-wearer would be effectively debarred tend to be high-status, high-paid jobs. Men are not debarred from them because men do not wear burqas.

4. Wearing a burqa makes certain sports and pastimes hard if not impossible to pursue. Athletics, playing tennis or football, water-ski-ing, cross-country running, disco-dancing and so on are not realistic options. One might want to point out that high heels or tight skirts would also make

playing tennis difficult. But high heels and tight skirts can be replaced by more suitable clothing. The point about the burqa is that it is worn all the time in public. It should be noted here that it is not the face-covering aspect of the burqa that is the main problem, however, but the bulkiness of the whole garment. A chador which left the face uncovered would cause the same problems. Although the burqa does cause this particular disadvantage, then, it is not unique in doing so. Nevertheless, not being able to follow physical recreational pursuits is a disadvantage, and one from which men do not suffer, because men do not wear burqas (or chadors).

The burqa, then, to some extent satisfies both of Chambers's conditions. But the question is whether the disadvantage is *severe* enough, and the social influence *irresistible* enough, to justify a ban.

I would argue that a burqa-ban would not currently be justified in a polyethnic liberal state such as Great Britain on the grounds of Social Influence and Disadvantage to the wearer. It may be justified on other grounds, to be explored in Chapters 10 and 11. But whether the banning of an unjust custom, in Chambers's terms, is justified depends on two empirical factors: how strong the social influence is, and how severe the disadvantage. Let us take the two factors separately.

1. Although burqa-wearing is undoubtedly the result of social influence, that influence is one current of influence among many for Muslims in contemporary Britain and other liberal societies. The majority of Muslim women do not wear it. A Muslim woman who chose not to wear it might find herself lacking affirmation in her immediate community but not in the wider Muslim community as a whole. Many Muslims have argued publicly and vociferously against it (such as Yasmin Alibhai-Brown: see *Refusing the Veil*, 2014). The social influence that pushes (some) Muslim women to wear it may be strong, but is not irresistible.
2. The disadvantages outlined above are real, but none is irrevocable. Burqa-wearing is different from FGM, which is irreversible (at least given current medical knowledge and technology). A disadvantage which can be removed at any time – provided the individual is able to resist the social influence responsible for it, and as argued that ought not to be impossible in this case – does not seem severe enough to warrant a ban.

9.5.5 Instead of a ban

This is not to argue that burqa-wearing is just on Chambers's terms after all. It may be unjust, but not unjust enough to justify a state ban. Any injustice would be removable by other means. Liberal feminists might disapprove of it. They might seek to end it. But since burqa-wearing, unlike FGM, is *revocable*, then in true liberal style feminists can seek to end it by persuasion, argument and example rather than legislation.

This approach has an important advantage over a state ban. What feminists oppose in cases of practices which are unjust to women is not just the disadvantage. It is the social influence too. A state ban would only address the disadvantage. But feminists want to address the social influence as well. They do not just want women to stop disadvantaging themselves; they want women to stop *wanting* to disadvantage themselves. Opposing burqa-wearing through persuasion, argument and example combats both the social influence *and* the disadvantage.

10

The effect of the burqa on others: Offence

The argument

This chapter represents a departure from the line the argument has followed thus far. Instead of considering the effects of burqa-wearing upon the wearer, I now consider the effects of burqa-wearing on others. First, I summarise the argument to this point, to consolidate and emphasise the conclusion that the liberal position on voluntary habitual face-covering per se would not justify a burqa-ban on grounds of the effect on the wearer herself.

I then begin to examine how burqa-wearing might impact upon others, starting with the question of *offence* (Chapter 11 will consider *harm* to others). I consider Joel Feinberg's offence principle, that if a practice causes severe, prolonged and unavoidable offence to the senses or sensibilities, there would be liberal grounds for banning it. I accept the argument in principle, and consider four ways in which the burqa might be thought offensive. I argue that none of them is severe enough to justify a ban. The liberal response to voluntary habitual face-covering per se need not be modified yet.

10.1 Summary of argument to this point

Thus far I have considered the question of whether a liberal state would be justified in banning the burqa assuming that all burqa-wearers in Western states wear the burqa through personal choice. No doubt social influence is in part responsible for that choice, as it would be for any choice. But I have assumed that such influence is not irresistible. Burqa-wearing in liberal states, I have assumed, is not coerced, and any individual woman who chose not to wear the burqa would not be punished with violence, ostracism or other sanctions. Moreover, burqa-wearers in liberal states live within a culture where the possibility of women, including Muslim women, not wearing burqas is very easy to see. No woman in a liberal state should have reason to feel that there is no option but to wear a burqa. Additionally, I have assumed that the choice to wear one, once made, is easily revocable. I have assumed that it is as easy to doff the burqa as to don it.

On this model it is not possible for a liberal to justify banning the burqa for the sake of the burqa-wearers. They are exercising the free choice which liberals value. It is true that the burqa disadvantages the wearer in a number of ways. It is also true that I have argued for a Liberal Paternalist Principle (see Chapter 5), which would justify state restriction of liberty on paternalist grounds when the restriction is small and the benefit, or harm avoided, great. However, such a principle would not seem to justify a ban on voluntary burqa-wearing, since the restriction of liberty would be considerable, and disadvantages incurred by burqa-wearing are neither permanent nor irrevocable. (It seems that anyone who did argue for a burqa-ban on paternalist grounds would also be committed to arguing for the abolition of convents and monasteries: a *reductio* that few liberals would be willing to embrace.)

I have argued that, assuming burqa-wearing to be voluntary, the liberal position on burqa-wearing should be the same as the liberal position on habitual face-covering per se. That is, it should not be banned, although temporary removal could legitimately be required for reasons of security or identification. The only foreseeable circumstances in which a ban on voluntary burqa-wearing could be justified would be if malefactors took advantage of the disguise afforded by the burqa and used it to commit crimes and escape undetected, in sufficient numbers as to present a real increase in risk to the public. Under this slightly unlikely scenario (a small number of robberies have been committed under cover of the burqa in Britain, but they remain few and far between) a liberal state might be justified in banning the burqa; but then the ban would not be because the state objected to burqa-wearing as such, but rather to abuses of burqa-wearing which harmed or endangered citizens.

Thus far I have concentrated on the effects of voluntary burqa-wearing upon the wearer herself. Apart from the scenario of the burqa being used by imposters as a criminal disguise I have not considered its effect on others. I now turn to consider how the practice of burqa-wearing might impact on others, starting with the possibility of its causing offence.

10.2 Feinberg's offence principle

As argued in Chapter Four, liberals must support some version of a harm principle: a principle by which it is sometimes legitimate to restrict the liberty of individuals in order to prevent harm to others. Joel Feinberg argues that liberals also need a principle which would justify state action to limit *offence* to others. He states that for a liberal state it is a good reason in support of a prohibition that it will (probably) prevent serious offence (Feinberg 1985: 1).

Note that this claim is modest in two ways: preventing offence is a good reason for banning a practice, but not an overriding reason. Other, opposing reasons may prevail over it. Moreover the offence has to be *serious;* one cannot demand that the state intervene to protect one from trivial annoyances. Feinberg also adds, using italics to emphasise the point, *'offense is surely a less serious thing than harm'* (1985: 2). Therefore it is to be tackled by less severe sanctions. Tackling offence may not always best be done by the criminal law – perhaps milder methods of discouragement, such as 'individual suits for injunctions', or court orders issued by police or revoking of licences, will meet the needs of the case; and if the criminal justice system is needed it should impose fines, or short prison sentences of days, for crimes of offence (1985: 3).

What, then, does Feinberg mean by offence? He compares the feelings caused by offence to feelings caused by nuisance, such as barking dogs, loud music or nasty smells. He dramatises what he means by a thought-experiment, 'A ride on the bus', in which an unfortunate passenger, whom you are asked to think of as yourself, is subjected to a nightmarish catalogue of six different types of offence:

> A. Affronts to the senses ... B. Disgust and revulsion ... C. Shock to moral, religious or patriotic sensibilities ... D. Shame, embarrassment including vicarious embarrassment) and anxiety ... E. Annoyance, boredom, frustration ... F. Fear, resentment, humiliation, anger.
>
> (Feinberg 1985: 10–13)

Each type of offence is illustrated by a selection of outlandish behaviours – for example, a man who sits next to you and deliberately scrapes his fingernails on a slate, refusing to desist when asked to do so (affront to the senses); a group of passengers who eat a picnic of live insects and pickled sex organs of animals, making themselves vomit and then starting again on the food, as well as eating each other's vomit (disgust and revulsion); another group who pile on board with a coffin and proceed to abuse the corpse and hit its face with hammers (shock to moral/religious sensibilities); a passenger who has oral sex with a dog (shame, embarrassment); a couple who conduct an animated and inane conversation loudly enough to distract you from your thoughts (annoyance, boredom, frustration); and a passenger who plays with a realistic model hand grenade and knife while laughing maniacally (fear, resentment, humiliation, anger).

There is no escape from the bus. You have an unmissable appointment and there is no other way to get to it.

The thought experiment is effective because rather than relying on abstract argument it forces one to feel, viscerally, just how intolerable it would be to endure such relentlessly offensive acts. One would surely feel justified in demanding that these awful people be removed from the bus forthwith. I therefore accept the necessity of Feinberg's offence principle.

Feinberg also mixes in some trivial offences with the more serious ones; as well as the corpse-abusers and vomit-eaters there is a passenger with a horrible shirt of 'violently clashing orange and crimson', offensive to one's aesthetic sensibilities. That is irritating, but there is no need to throw *him* off the bus. This illustrates that the offence needs to be serious before the liberal state would be justified in intervening.

Between the trivial and the serious there is a large amount of disputable ground, however. Having an offence principle may encourage people to claim offence simply because they disapprove of some practice and want to see it banned. And indeed Feinberg says his principle is as 'dangerous as it is necessary' (1980: 74) and needs to be hedged about with qualifications.

One qualification Feinberg suggests is that what is viewed as immoral conduct (e.g. sexually immoral) should not be banned on the offence principle, if conducted *in private*. The invasion of liberty would be too great. However, if it is blatantly displayed there might be grounds for banning it:

> Some conduct may be so offensive as to amount to a kind of 'psychic aggression', in which case, the private harm principle would allow its suppression on the same grounds as that of physical assault.
>
> (Feinberg 1980: 76)

Another qualification Feinberg offers to his offence principle is that the offence must satisfy a '*standard of universality*' (1980: 88). Feinberg imagines a mixed-race couple walking hand-in-hand through the streets of Jackson, Mississippi. No doubt this would offend many of the passers-by in that still very conservative and segregated state. But Feinberg would not want to ban mixed-race couples appearing in public. He suggests the following limitation of the principle:

> For 'offense' (repugnance, embarrassment, shame etc) to be sufficient to warrant coercion, it should be the reaction that could reasonably be expected from almost any person taken at random, taking the nation as a whole, and not because the individual belongs to some faction, clique or party.
>
> (Feinberg 1980: 88)

But now another problem looms. If we accept this qualification, then there is no guaranteed protection against 'abusive, mocking, insulting behaviour or speech attacking specific sub-groups of the population – especially ethnic, racial, or religious groups' (1980: 88). If a majority of the nation do not mind such abusive behaviour towards minorities, 'our amended offense principle will not justify the criminal proscription of such speech or conduct' (1980: 88).

Feinberg's response is to patch up his principle 'in an *ad hoc* fashion':

> For that special class of offensive behavior ... that consists in the flaunting of abusive, mocking or insulting behaviour of a sort bound to alarm, anger, or irritate those whom it insults, I would allow the offense principle to apply, even though the behaviour would *not* offend the whole population.
>
> (1980: 88–9)

This solution in its turn raises difficult questions. Can we be sure it will not apply to the interracial couple in Jackson? Who is to say whether their intent is to anger and irritate and alarm rather than make a statement of principle? Conversely, who is to say that those who mock or insult a religion are not also making a statement of principle?

Ad hoc responses have the inbuilt weakness that they focus on eliminating a particular anomaly without bringing in the underlying principle in virtue of which the anomaly is objected to. In this case, Feinberg's *ad hoc* response seems to be based on the fact that he himself does not hold racist views and is opposed to racism. I would suggest that if called on to defend his ad hoc exceptions Feinberg might reply that they rely on another principle, that persons should not be discriminated against by reason of their race. The two principles could then operate side by side, and in case of conflict between them the Non-Discrimination-by-Race Principle would trump the offence principle.

All of which shows that the application of the offence principle requires careful thought, but not by any means that we do not require one. I agree with Feinberg that we do need such a principle, to protect us against serious, sustained, persistent and intrusive offence, and I agree, too, that its use must be hedged about with qualifications. I turn now to the question of whether the offence principle could justify banning the burqa.

10.3 The burqa and offence

10.3.1 Four types of offence

Burqa-wearing could cause offence by its symbolism: the values or messages it presents to the world. There are at least four ways in which its symbolism might be offensive. I shall examine them one by one.

10.3.2 The burqa and misogyny

Historically the burqa is associated with the oppression of women. Its asymmetry – women wear it, men do not – marks women out as different. It makes women non-individuated and denies them a place in public life. Moreover, the fact that it is men – husbands, fathers, brothers – who control when women wear the burqa (she may remove it in the presence of an authorised man, or in his house, when no other unauthorised men are present) implies systematic male dominance, if not ownership. This is so even if the burqa-wearer herself denies that this is the case. She may say, 'My burqa does not carry those meanings for me; I wear it to submit to Allah, not to men.' She may be sincere in this protestation. But other people cannot be prevented from drawing their own conclusions and interpreting its symbolism for themselves. One could not, for example, wear a tee-shirt with a swastika on it and expect people to interpret it as a Buddhist symbol of good fortune and prosperity. For many the burqa symbolises misogyny, masculine control, a distrust and fear of women's sexuality and a double standard which disfavours women. Given other misogynistic features of cultures where the burqa originated – such as FGM, forced marriage, honour killings – those symbolic meanings seem well-founded. Such meanings are offensive to anybody with feminist principles or sensibilities.

10.3.3 The burqa and political Islam

Symbols change their significance over time and under new conditions. Increasingly, wearing the burqa in Western liberal states has acquired an additional meaning: a statement of a rejection of Western liberal values, such as tolerance, free speech, secularism (and one might also add commercialism, selfishness, hedonism, sexual promiscuity) in favour of a return to traditional Islamic values. It could signify a deliberate refusal to adopt the host country's way of life, and a commitment to political Islam. Such meanings could be offensive to those who cherish liberal values.

10.3.4 The burqa and its implied view of men

Historically the burqa was worn as a protection against sexual predation by men. Today its symbolism still suggests that if female beauty were not hidden from sight passing men might be unable to control their lust. As Yasmin Alibhai-Brown puts it:

> Veils cast all men as animalistic creatures with no control over their carnal natures, who are programmed to fall uninvited on bosoms and lips, and have their way with any passing female.
>
> (2014: 95)

Many would find this characterisation of male sexuality offensive.

10.3.5 The bad taste objection

Another way in which voluntary burqa-wearing could cause offence is on the grounds of bad taste. By this I mean that choosing to wear the burqa shows insensitivity towards the plight of the many women throughout the world who are forced to wear it. There is no doubt that such coercion is common in many countries, and is enforced by frightening violence. Phyllis Chesler, writing in the *Middle East Quarterly*, notes:

> The Taliban, for example, flogged women on the street if their burqas showed too much ankle while Islamist vigilantes poured acid on the faces of Afghan and Pakistani schoolgirls who were not sufficiently covered.
>
> (2010: 39)

In such a context it seems peculiarly tasteless to wear a burqa through choice – like dressing up as a concentration camp inmate to go to a fancy dress party. It may also awaken unwelcome memories in others; as Chesler says,

> Many Westerners, including Muslims, ex-Muslims, and Christians, Jews and Hindus who have fled Muslim lands, may feel haunted or followed when they see burqas on Western streets.
>
> (2010: 44–5)

Here, then, is another way in which the burqa could cause offence.

10.3.6 Offence caused by the burqa is not serious enough to warrant a ban

Although the burqa could cause offence in any or all of the ways described above, it is not the kind of high-impact, unavoidable and sustained offence that Feinberg argues makes an Offence Principle necessary. The kinds of offence the burqa may cause are merely communications of symbolic messages which some people may not like. But that is free speech. That is what liberals are committed to defending.

As Russell Blackford puts it:

> Wearing a burqa may cause offense. Indeed, nobody has to react with approval when a burqa is worn in public, but the practice causes no significant harms to others. Nor does it cause the sort of high-impact offense to a captive audience that might reasonably justify bans on some kind of images, odors, noises and so on, in certain public spaces. Indeed, wearing a burqa can be interpreted, quite plausibly, as an exercise of free speech, since it communicates something of the wearer's religious and moral commitments.
>
> (2012: 135)

Therefore, although I accept Feinberg's offence principle for the kinds of extreme cases he describes, burqa-wearing should not be banned under it, because the offence is not so intolerable, unavoidable, intrusive or persistent as to meet his criterion of *serious* offence. In the context of the antics of the passengers on that bus, indeed, a burqa-clad woman boarding would probably come as something as a relief.

11

The effect of the burqa on others: Harm

The argument

In this chapter I explore whether the prevention of harm to others could justify a liberal state's banning of the burqa. I consider three possible cases of harm. First, I examine the French justification for its 2010 burqa-ban, to safeguard the requirement of *vivre ensemble* (living together).

Second, I examine more closely the previously discussed scenario of the burqa being used as a criminal disguise. This would cause harm to others and could therefore offer a justification for a ban.

Third, suppose it to be the case that significant numbers of women are coerced into wearing the burqa. Coerced public face-covering would be a serious harm to the individual. I argue that if this is occurring or if it were to occur, then a ban could be justified; but only if there were no other way of preventing the coercion that was at least equally efficacious.

In such cases of harm, the liberal response to habitual voluntary face-covering per se would not be adequate. Whether they really are occurring is an empirical question.

11.1 A difference of approach from Nussbaum

I adopt a somewhat different approach from that taken by Martha Nussbaum in *The New Religious Intolerance* (2012). Her argument against a burqa-ban centres on the empirical question of whether wearing of the burqa does in fact cause harm to non-wearers in those European states that have banned it. She argues that it does not and therefore a ban is unjustified. However, even granting that she is right about that, her case rests on a snapshot of the practice of burqa-wearing in particular European countries in the year 2012. But cultural practices are not static. They are dynamic. In the twenty-first century they are more dynamic than ever before. Changes in populations brought about by migration and by birth rate, as well as the greater exposure to ideas and images facilitated by the internet, mean that a cultural practice can grow and evolve quite rapidly, producing unexpected consequences. To argue that burqa-wearing is harmless to others in Europe in 2012 is not to argue that it will and always must remain so. I am therefore more interested in the question of whether, *if* it were to cause harm, at what point a liberal state should take action against it, and whether a ban would be the best means of doing so.

11.2 The burqa and harm

11.2.1 The role of the harm principle

It seems clear, as argued in Chapter 4, that liberals must subscribe to some form of the harm principle. Without such a principle, the liberty of one individual could destroy the liberty of another, which rather removes the point of liberalism. Mill's classic formulation, however, is too strict. Mill states that 'the *only* purpose for which power can be rightfully exercised over any member of a civilized community, against his will, is to prevent harm to others' (2000: 13; my italics). Mill rules out any other purpose for restricting people's actions, but I have already argued for a Liberal Paternalist Principle as supplying an additional legitimate purpose, and accepted Feinberg's argument that serious offence to others could also supply a legitimate reason for state restriction of liberty. Let us then employ the version formulated by Feinberg:

> It is always a good reason in support of penal legislation that it would probably be effective in preventing (eliminating, reducing) harm to persons other than the actor (the one prohibited from acting) *and* there is probably no other means that is equally effective at no greater cost to other values.
>
> (1985: 26)

11.2.2 Elaborating the harm principle

We should note first that Feinberg's harm principle does not entail that all or any harms require penal legislation for their elimination or reduction. That harm is caused or is at risk of being caused is a good reason for legislation but not an overriding one. The cost of prohibiting an activity in terms of loss of liberty or unwanted side effects might offer a stronger reason *against* the legislation where the harm is slight or unlikely. In short, harm by itself does not supply a sufficient reason for penal legislation. Nor does it supply a necessary reason; evidence of harm is *a* good reason but not necessarily the only one. As explained above, both Feinberg's Offence Principle and my Liberal Paternalist Principle supply alternative justifications for state intervention.

Feinberg points out that his harm principle could legitimise penal legislation against more than harm caused to specific individuals; it would also be legitimate to prohibit actions that cause 'the unreasonable risk of such harm, or harm to important public institutions and practices' (1985: 11). Examples of harm against a specific individual would be murder or rape; an example of conduct that risked harm would be reckless driving; an example of public harm is tax evasion.

11.2.3 The problem of defining harm

Those examples are uncontroversial. But other cases might be less clear-cut, and indeed a standard objection to the harm principle is the difficulty of defining harm. B. Jennings, in an essay entitled 'Beyond the Harm Principle', argues that the concept of harm is slippery and can be manipulated to suit the purposes of the lawmaker (1996: 220). Jennings states:

> The harm principle ought to give us a bright line to know when individual autonomy can be overridden. The line is not really so bright, however, because people don't always know harm when they see it, or else see it too readily when it is not reasonably there.
>
> (1996: 224–5)

It is certainly true that harm cannot be defined with mathematical precision as long as we are talking about human beings as the objects of it. Harm to, say, trees can be defined uncontroversially. But then the tree does not have an opinion about whether it has been harmed or not. Human beings can and do have differing views about what counts as harm.

However, we can formulate a definition of harm that takes this into account, as Feinberg does: 'A person is harmed when someone invades (blocks or thwarts) one of his interests' (1980: 45). This definition does not depend on all persons' interests being the same. There is room for difference. My interest is, at least to a certain extent, what I take it to be.

This taking-it-to-be must however be situated within normative limits. Interests are not identical with preferences. In the case of Chloe Jennings-White (considered in Chapter 4), an able-bodied woman who wishes to undergo an operation to render her a paraplegic, she is (I have argued) mistaken about what her interests are. She thinks it is in her interests to be paralysed, but that is because she suffers from an extreme case of Body Integrity Disorder. Preventing her from carrying out her preference is not blocking her interests. It is serving them.

Still, the normative limits can be quite wide. They need to be universal: that is, based on an idea of what is good for all human beings. We can rule out serious, permanent and irrevocable damage to one's body as being in somebody's interests. But this still leaves a great deal ruled in. Within the normative limits there is considerable room for differing about interests. It may be in one person's interests to worship in the Church of the Seventh-Day Adventists, and in another person's interests to play football every Sunday, and in either case they would be harmed by having that interest blocked.

We are still not out of the woods. An appeal to interest is not a sufficiently clear guide for legislative decisions. For interests may compete. We will need supplementary principles to help weigh competing interests.

Feinberg offers three indices to measure the weight of interests: (1) their importance to the welfare of the possessor (their 'vitality' in the possessor's general scheme of interests), (2) the degree to which they are reinforced by other interests, private and public and (3) their moral quality (controversially) (1980: 32).

Feinberg's first index includes very basic conditions for welfare – health, vigour, emotional stability, minimal level of wealth, and 'the ability to engage normally in social intercourse' (1980: 32). These are all said to be 'standard interests'; that is, they apply to everyone.

Feinberg's second index, the degree to which interests are reinforced by other interests (e.g. preventing me from driving might also prevent me from working) also rests on the notion of standard interests. Index 3 does not rest on the notion of standard interests, and for that reason would be harder to deploy in a debate about weighing interests. I therefore leave it out of account. But indices 1 and 2 alone are enough to give us a basis for debating rationally whether someone is harmed by someone else's conduct.

This does not mean of course that such questions will always be easy to settle. Both 'harm' and 'interest' have fuzzy edges. But we should note that harm is an everyday term that we all understand: we at least have enough general agreement about what harm is to be able to argue about it. Indeed, its value as a principle for limiting criminal laws depends on this everyday usage; as Nina Persak says:

> It is important to realise, that the notion of 'harm', as represented in the criminal law, ought to be an extra-legal term, or at least a term outside the black-letter criminal law. If it were – a positive law-term – then the harm principle could not perform its main limiting function, because once a criminal legal norm has been established, the harm (in the later sense) would necessarily be assumed. In other words, the harm would necessarily always be present in the prohibited conduct (thus giving the impression it satisfies the requirement of the harm principle) by way of being the positive law. Like the saying, 'The law has to be obeyed because the law says so', the thing would be entirely circular.
>
> (2006: 63)

All this is not to argue that there can never be grey areas when we try to decide whether the consequences of an act are harmful. But it is to argue that there are clear cases. I shall examine three clear cases where burqa-wearing could bring about harm: that is, where the uncontroversial interests of others besides the voluntary burqa-wearer are uncontroversially invaded, thwarted or blocked. The first is the violation of the rights and freedoms of others in a liberal state (the *vivre ensemble* defence of a ban). The second is the wearing of the burqa as a disguise to facilitate criminal activities. The third is where voluntary burqa-wearing makes possible coerced burqa-wearing.

11.3 The *vivre ensemble* defence

11.3.1 The French republican tradition

As noted in Chapter 2, although French republicanism has important liberal elements (such as the equal rights and duties of all citizens), it is better characterised as a form of communitarianism. It imposes duties on its citizens which are owed not primarily to other individuals but to a republican conception of the common good. This conception depends on a social theory which, in the previously quoted words of Peter Baehr and Daniel Gordon

> can be seen as a specific inflection of democratic thought that we call the elongation of the political into the sociable. The concept of citizenship is the starting point. Citizenship in modern democratic regimes enshrines the idea of politico-legal equality ... Full-face coverings such as the burqa and niqab

raise the issue of whether democratic 'solidarity' is related to citizens being visible to one another. If I can see your face but you cannot see mine, is this a politically equal encounter? That a degree of mutual visibility is a prerequisite of political equality is strongly implied by Western democratic/republican metaphors: enlightenment, openness, transparency, illumination, recognition, legibility, disclosure, accountability, publicity and, not least, public.

(Baehr and Gordon 2013: 257)

Baehr and Gordon argue that in France the political has an essential *social* dimension. Citizenship means more than participation in political processes such as voting. It also entails accepting duties of reciprocity towards others and public civility, in other words the kind of obligations stressed by communitarians. The 'living together' defence is based on these obligations.

11.3.2 *Vivre ensemble* part one: Public order

The *vivre ensemble* requirement falls into two parts. The first is the protection of the public from harm by securing public order. However, as stated in Chapter 2, the ECHR did not consider the public order requirement as a justification for the ban and left unanswered whether in this case it was a legitimate justification or not. My own view is that this would certainly be a sound liberal justification for a ban *if* there were evidence that face-covering threatened harm to citizens by, for example, facilitating crime or terrorism. That is an empirical question. I deal in detail with the issue of direct harm to others by breaches of public order in Section 11.4, but to anticipate, I do not believe there is evidence that burqa-wearing has led to increases in crime or terrorism or other public order offences in France or other Western liberal states.

11.3.3 *Vivre ensemble* part two: Protection of rights and freedoms of others

The second part of the *vivre emsemble* defence – 'protection of the rights and freedoms of others' – was considered and upheld by the ECHR. It is worth restating their decision here:

The Court takes into account the respondent State's point that the face plays an important role in social interaction. It can understand the view that individuals who are present in places open to all may not wish to see practices or attitudes developing there which would fundamentally call into question the possibility of open interpersonal relationships, which, by virtue of an established consensus, forms an indispensable element of community life within the society in question. The Court is therefore able to accept that the barrier raised against others by a veil concealing the face is perceived by the respondent State as breaching the right of others to live in a space of socialisation which makes living together easier.

(ECHR Judgement in the case of *S.A.R. v. France* 2014, Application 43835/11, paragraph 122)

The question is whether this counts as a specifically liberal reason. On the whole this seems a defence likelier to appeal to a communitarian than to a liberal. Communitarians such as Amitai Etzioni stress that the common good should, at least in some cases, override the personal choices of the individual. Etzioni argues that usually the common good is taken care of by informal social forces. But 'if these forces slacken, the government must step in' (Etzioni 2004: 2). Whether Etzioni himself would support a burqa-ban is a moot point. He sees the burqa as an extreme, almost pathological expression of privacy:

One can see strong mandated and expected privacy in other eras and cultures, most readily in extreme and offensive forms, in societies in which rights are not respected and virtuous privacy is strenuously and even violently enforced. For instance, those Islamic societies that strictly follow the *sharia* (Islamic law) require women to conceal their hair, skin and the contours of their body – a dress code embodied in extreme form by the *burqa*.

(Etzioni 2004: 32)

Perhaps if the extreme privacy of burqa-wearing were shown to threaten the common good of an open society such as France, Etzioni would see merit in a ban. But it is not the case that communitarian thinking *commits* one to a ban. Etzioni states that 'a good society provides a careful balance between social order and liberty' (2004: 55) and it is not a foregone conclusion that social order would always win. However, what one can say is that *if* a burqa-ban is upheld solely for the sake of living together/social order, then that is more of a communitarian reason than a liberal one. So the justification accepted by the ECHR turns out to be the least purely liberal of the three justifications advanced.

A more liberal view, with greater emphasis on the freedom of the individual, would note that many things are needed for people to live together, to form interpersonal relationships, and for strangers to meet in the public sphere and perform transactions together with ease and trust: politeness, smiles, good manners, handshakes, expressions of thanks, concealment of true feelings, a common language and so on. But these requirements would lose much of their value if legally enforced. Since liberals generally value personal autonomy, they would incline to the view that it is up to the individual how open they are to others in the public sphere: individuals must be legally allowed to be shy, private, uncommunicative, even rude and misanthropic in their daily dealings with others or, indeed, to reject society altogether for the life of a hermit.

There is also the issue of free speech, which is of greater importance to liberals (at any point along the PL-Perfectionist spectrum) than it is to communitarians. Lori Watson and Christie Hartley make the point that the burqa is not just a garment but a means of expression:

> One reason for such proposals [if banning burqas] is that the burka can be thought to express the sentiment that women should be invisible in public places. Even if this is true, under most conditions, banning the burka in public places would be an unacceptable violation of freedom of expression.
>
> (Watson and Hartley 2018: 159)

Obviously, liberals would not accept the message that women should be invisible in public. But as Watson and Hartley point out, 'the equal status of women as citizens … can be addressed by other social policy' (2018: 159) rather than by suppressing the opposing view.

On balance, then, I contend that the *vivre ensemble* defence fails as a *liberal* defence of a ban, insofar as it prioritises duty to the republic above individual freedoms. However, the fact that the burqa could be adopted as a criminal disguise to facilitate public order offences which directly harm individuals still needs to be considered.

11.4 The burqa as criminal disguise

11.4.1 Crime and terrorism

As was argued in Chapter 3, the face is the primary means by which human beings identify one another. Long before burqa-wearing was a phenomenon in Western countries, people engaging in planned criminal activities often covered their faces (with scarves, masks, balaclavas, tights, etc.) to enable them to escape the scene without being identified. Institutions where criminal attacks were more than ordinarily likely, such as banks, adopted a policy of requiring customers and visitors not to cover their faces, insisting on the removal of motorcycle helmets, for example.

This being so, one can see why the emergence of a group of people who habitually cover their faces in public might give rise to concerns over public security. Nor would those concerns be irrational; the higher the number of people whose faces were covered, the higher the possibility that one or some of them could have nefarious intent. It is, after all, easier to commit a crime and escape undetected if one's face is covered. It would not be only, or even mainly, regular burqa-wearers themselves who would fall under suspicion. An opportunist could imitate the burqa-wearers to commit a crime and get away with it and uncover after the deed. A relevant feature of the burqa, as compared to other forms of face-covering, is that people are generally reluctant to challenge burqa-wearers. Wearing the burqa is viewed by many as a religious obligation, and most of us have some sensitivity about appearing to question or challenge religious obligations. The burqa-wearer is unapproachable in a way that a mask-wearer, or a motorcyclist who refused to remove their helmet, would not be. Those of nefarious intent could take advantage of this fact. In 2013, for example, a group of burqa-clad robbers (neither Muslims nor women) conducted a smash-and-grab raid on Selfridges, Oxford Street, London (BBC News website 2014); although they were later apprehended.

Such occurrences, however, remain few and far between. There is no evidence so far that the rise in burqa-wearing in the United Kingdom has contributed to an overall rise in crime. Whether it ever will do so is an empirical question. The reasonable position seems to be that *if* burqa-wearing led to an increase in masked crime, then the liberal state would have a prima facie case for banning it in order to protect its citizens, while regretting the loss of liberty this entailed. Whether that case was compelling would depend on just how serious the crime-rise was. It is simply a question of the numbers. The larger the number of such crimes, the stronger the case for a ban. So far, though, the numbers do not seem to be high enough to even begin to put together such a case, as far as the United Kingdom is concerned at any rate.

As well as common-or-garden crime for personal gain, the burqa has also been linked with terrorism. Nussbaum puts this view (with which she strongly disagrees, at least in a North American or European context) as follows: 'We are living in an era of terrorism and in the war against terror it is legitimate to suspect women wearing the burqa' (2012: 107).

Some countries have indeed taken action against burqa-wearing on these grounds. For example, Chad banned the full-face veil in 2015, following a bombing attack by burqa-wearing Boko Haram militants, in which twenty people were killed; Congo Brazzaville also banned the full-face veil in 2015 'to counter terrorism' (BBC News website 2015b); Cameroon banned it later the same year following two suicide bomb attacks by burqa-wearers (BBC News website 2015a).

Nussbaum accepts that '[in] the Middle East it might possibly be a clever strategy for a terrorist to don a *burqa*' (2012: 107) and would presumably concede the same for areas of Africa where there is an appreciable Muslim population of the burqa-wearing persuasion. However, she argues that it would be a stupid strategy for a terrorist to wear a burqa in North America or Europe as this would be more likely to attract attention than escape it (2012: 107).

I am not sure that this is true. A burqa-clad person boarding a bus in, say, East London would attract no attention whatsoever. Again, though, it is an empirical question whether a burqa would be an effective disguise in North America or Europe, and we need spend no time trying to settle it here. We can simply say that *if* no or hardly any terrorists in those countries ever adopt such camouflage, then we agree with Nussbaum that a ban is unnecessary; and *if* in future it were to turn out that they do, then a ban could become necessary.

11.4.2 Nussbaum and ethical consistency

There is, though, another point on which I take issue with Nussbaum. She takes the view that burqa-wearing raises no more problems than other types of face-covering, and ethical consistency requires that if we are not suspicious of other types of face-covering, then we should not be suspicious of burqas either. Here is how she puts her case:

> It gets very cold in Chicago – as, indeed, in many parts of Europe. Along the streets we walk, hats pulled down over ears and brows, scarves wound tightly around noses and mouths. No problem of either transparency or security is thought to exist, nor are we forbidden to enter public buildings so insulated … Moreover, many beloved and trusted professionals cover their faces all year round: surgeons, dentists, (American) football players, skiers and skaters … In general, what inspires fear and mistrust in Europe, and, to some extent, in the United States, is not covering per se, but Muslim covering.
>
> (Nussbaum 2012: 106–7)

This section of the book is almost identical to a piece Nussbaum wrote for the *New York Times*'s Opinionator column in 2010, but there is one perhaps significant change. In the original piece she said that it was 'clearly' Muslim face-covering which inspired fear and distrust, and she has now removed that word and replaced it with the phrase 'in general'. That is a slight concession, but the charge in substance still stands. The only factor she is able to find to account for the difference between reactions to the kind of everyday face-coverings she describes, and to the burqa, is fear and mistrust of Muslims.

But there are other relevant factors, which she does not consider. An obvious one is that hats, scarves, surgeons' masks and so on are removed when the occasion requires: we would think it objectionable if someone persisted in wearing a scarf wound around their face, or a surgeon's mask, in a bank, a classroom or a court of law, for example. A burqa is worn *all the time* in public, and, because it is thought of as a religious symbol, people are aware that asking for its removal might cause offence. Having a different reaction to the burqa than to a scarf wound around the face on a cold day is no evidence of a double standard, but of a consistent standard. I applaud Nussbaum's principle of seeking consistency. But it seems to undermine her case here.

I do not, in any case, think it helpful in general to impugn the motivations or agenda of persons arguing either for or against a burqa-ban. There is always a chance that one might be wrong about the motivations or agenda, and even if one is right, one still has to answer the arguments advanced, so it is better to stick to those.

But to end this section, I should say that on the current weight of evidence I agree with Nussbaum that there is not yet any justification for banning the burqa on the grounds of security. There are insufficient instances of burqa-related crime or terrorism in the West to justify a general ban at this point. In certain settings, such as airports, international borders, law courts, banks and so on, the wearer might legitimately be obliged to temporarily remove it. That would seem to take care of security problems without recourse to a blanket ban.

11.5 Coercion and the burqa

11.5.1 What is coercion?

I take wearing a burqa under coerced conditions to be a clear case of harm. It is also a much likelier harm than the harm of burqa as criminal disguise considered in section 11.4.

But what is coercion? There has been considerable philosophical debate about whether coercion is a wrong in itself. There are three main positions:

1. coercion is always wrong by definition;
2. coercion is *prima facie* wrong but may be justified in some circumstances (as in state coercion in punishing criminals);
3. Coercion is morally neutral, and wrongful only when the circumstances of a particular case make it wrongful.

(Anderson 2017)

For the purposes of my argument here, however, I can leave it open whether coercion in general is always or prima facie wrongful. I need show only that it is wrong in the particular case of forcing women to cover their faces habitually in public all the time.

But what counts as coercion? Robert Nozick gives the following characterisation of coercion (which he attributes to Hart and Honoré):

person P coerces person Q if and only if

P threatens to do something if Q does A (and Q knows he's making this threat).

This threat renders Q's doing A substantially less eligible as a course of conduct than not doing A.

P makes this threat in order to get Q not to do A, intending that Q realize he's been threatened by A.

Q does not do A.

P's words or deeds are part of Q's reason for not doing A.

(1969: 441)

Coercion therefore entails threatening a person with consequences they will not like if they carry out a course of action that the threatener wishes to prevent. (The model works equally well for compulsion as for prevention: coercion entails threatening a person with consequences they will not like if they do not carry out a course of action that the threatener wishes.) It is worth noting the parenthetical condition '(and Q knows he's making this threat)'. The threat could not operate successfully without Q's knowledge of it. If Q did what P wanted while unaware of what would happen if they did not do so, this would not be a *result* of the threat, and therefore Q's action would not be coerced.

Nozick's formulation also entails that coercion must be successful if it is to count as coercion (see Nozick's fourth condition, 'P does not do A'). Presumably, coercion that did not succeed – in the case where Q ignored or defied the threat – could count only as attempted coercion.

Nozick distinguishes between threats and offers:

> Offers of inducements, incentives, rewards, bribes, consideration, remuneration, recompense, payment do not normally constitute threats, and the person who accepts them is not normally coerced.
>
> (1969: 447)

The crucial difference between a threat and an offer is that a threat, if carried out, makes the recipient worse off than before, while an offer, if carried out, makes one better off. Whether an overture is a threat or offer depends on what the baseline conditions are – that is, what the normal state of affairs is, before the overture is made. Threats project a *worsening* of normal conditions; offers project an *improvement* of normal conditions. Nozick considers the case of a slave who is told: 'If you do A, I won't beat you tomorrow', when normally the slave is beaten daily (1969: 450). Against those baseline conditions, the overture might be counted as an offer. But then one wants to object that the true baseline condition is a free society where there are no slaves, and beating people for no reason is outlawed. It is coercion in the context of such a baseline in the first place that has placed the slave in the position where a one-day cessation of their daily beating appears as an offer.

Anderson considers the question of 'throffers', that is to say overtures where doing what is demanded is rewarded by the carrying out of an offer, and not doing it is punished by the carrying out of a threat:

> Some have discussed 'throffers', which are proposals that make one better off than normal under one conditional, worse off than normal under the alternative conditional. On the above analysis, throffers will be included among the threats because the conditional containing the less-preferred consequent makes one worse off than one normally would be.
>
> (Anderson 2017)

Throffers therefore need not be distinguished from threats, except in the sense that they may be more likely to succeed.

One final point is that threats need not be explicit. They may be implied. As Anderson puts it: 'If one's powers and wishes are well enough known through past demonstrations, one may even be able to avoid making many overt threats while still getting one's way' (2017). Nevertheless, for coercion to occur, as argued above, Q must be aware of the implied threat. Coercion relies on a power imbalance *that both parties know about*. As Gideon Yaffe explains:

> The key to the explanation for the freedom-undermining force of coercion is that, as a general rule, coercers don't merely produce, but also track, the compliance of their victims. ... [T]he coercer is rarely attached to the particular nasty consequence that he threatens; with some limits, he is ready to bring about whatever consequences would serve to bring the victim around to compliance.
>
> (Yaffe 2003)

Coercion therefore relies on the coercer having dominance over the coercee, and the ability to make or imply whatever threats are deemed necessary to produce the desired behaviour.

11.5.2 When burqa-wearing is coerced

With regard to the burqa, then, I stipulate that coerced burqa-wearing should satisfy the following conditions:

1. The husband, father or brother, or other person in position of power threatens a woman with hard treatment if she does not wear the burqa in public all the time (and she knows she is being threatened).
2. The hard treatment includes but is not limited to physical violence (other possibilities are withholding food, ostracism or social shaming).
3. The hard treatment would make the woman's baseline position worse.
4. The baseline position is freedom from violence, starving, ostracism or social shaming.
5. The woman wears the burqa in order to avoid the hard treatment.

11.5.3 Why coerced burqa-wearing is a harm

Coerced burqa-wearing is harmful because the woman's autonomy is undermined. Suppose that it were the case that some burqa-wearing is in fact coerced – by actual violence or credible threats of violence or by ostracism and social shaming. A double harm is involved. First, the means used for coercion – physical violence or the threat of it or other forms of abuse – would themselves count as harms. Second, and more importantly, having to wear a burqa to avoid the coercive measures is itself a serious harm. As argued in Chapter 3, wearing a burqa brings severe disadvantages to the individual, cutting the wearer off from many social interactions, inhibiting the ethical responses of others towards her, rendering any position in public life difficult if not impossible, and cutting off the possibility of pursuing most professional careers, to name some of the most salient.

Such disadvantages do not count as harms when a woman freely chooses to wear the burqa, if one accepts the priority of second-order autonomy over first-order autonomy, as Nussbaum does and I do (see Chapter 6); that is to say, loss of autonomy in the conditions of one's daily life is not a harm if one has autonomously chosen those conditions, as long as that choice is revocable. If the disadvantages are freely embraced then the liberal has no more reason to object than they would have reason to object to a nun's freely choosing to immure herself in an enclosed order. However, it would be a grave harm to immure a woman in an enclosed order against her will. In the same way it would be a grave harm to force a woman into a veil against her will.

11.5.4 Harm as blocking of interests

Coerced burqa-wearing is a clear case of blocking of interests. Applying Feinberg's first two indices (see p. 210, above) for measuring the weight of interests, we see that the interests involved weigh heavily in the scale.

The first index is their importance to the welfare of the possessor, which includes such conditions as health, vigour and emotional stability. Burqa-wearing could impact negatively on health and vigour, and would be fairly certain, if coerced, to impact on emotional stability; being forced to shroud oneself against one's will day after day is not likely to be conducive to emotional well-being. Feinberg also mentions 'the ability to engage normally in social intercourse' (1980: 32), which would undeniably be affected adversely by burqa-wearing.

Feinberg's second index is the degree to which these standard interests are reinforced by other interests, private and public (1980: 32). It is clear that the interests threatened by coerced burqa-wearing are indeed reinforced by other interests. For example, the ability to engage in normal social intercourse is connected to one's interest in forming friendships, and also to one's (putative) interest in pursuing a professional career.

I conclude that coerced burqa-wearing is a serious harm, compounded of (1) the violence or other abuse which are the instruments of coercion, and (2) the long-term blocking of interests that coerced burqa-wearing entails. Let us call the first one coercive measures and second one the blocking of interests.

I hold that the second one is a more serious harm than the first, because the interests at stake are long-term, indeed life-long.

This is not to make the claim that coerced burqa-wearing is widespread in any particular liberal state at the present time. Possibly it is rare or non-existent. We need to acquire data on that before we can say whether action by the liberal state is required. Acquiring data that would show burqa-wearing to be coerced may be no easy task. I consider some possible approaches in Section 11.8. But for now let us just ask, *if* coerced burqa-wearing were taking place, what should a liberal state do about it?

11.6 Nussbaum, coercion and the burqa

11.6.1 Nussbaum's arguments against a ban on grounds of coercion

Nussbaum considers the question of coercion and the burqa and argues trenchantly that coercion offers no justification for a ban, at least in current circumstances. In this section I aim to identify some problematic areas of her argument.

She begins thus:

> A fourth argument [the previous ones being Security, Transparency and Civic Friendship, and Objectification] holds that many women wear the *burqa* because they are coerced. This is a rather implausible argument to make across the board, and it is typically made by people who have no idea of the circumstances of this or that individual woman. We should reply that of course all forms of violence and physical coercion in the home are illegal already, and laws against all forms of violence and physical coercion should be enforced much more zealously than they are. Do the arguers really believe that domestic violence is a peculiarly Muslim problem? If so they are dead wrong.
>
> (Nussbaum 2012: 122)

There seem to me to be two points at which this confident line of argument is open to question. First, Nussbaum's claim that the argument from coercion is implausible 'across the board'. I take it she means that it is implausible to assert that burqa-wearing actually is coerced 'in many cases'; the evidence is lacking, we do not know what kind of numbers are involved. This interpretation is supported by Nussbaum's follow-up statement that those who make the claim are ignorant of the circumstances of individual burqa-wearers. Nussbaum's objection seems open to a *tu quoque*, though. Is she in possession of data which show that no or very little burqa-wearing is coerced? If so, she should produce the data; but if not, then like those she criticises she is speaking from a position of ignorance.

The second point is that Nussbaum here responds to the accusation of coercion as though it were merely an accusation of violence. That is, she concentrates on the coercive measures but not on the blocking of interests which is their end. Nussbaum might respond that if you take care of the first the second will take care of itself. I lack her confidence about this. It may be harder to enforce the laws against violence than she assumes. A woman who is subject to physical abuse may well be too scared to report it. What is more, the coerced wearing of the burqa may itself conceal signs of violence which would otherwise arouse suspicion. Yasmin Alibhai-Brown writes, in a *Guardian* article:

> A fully burqaed woman once turned up at my house, a graduate, covered in cuts, burns, bruises and bites. Do we know how many wounded, veiled women walk around hidden among us?
>
> (Alibhai-Brown 2015)

This is not to make any claims about the *extent* of violence against Muslim women. Contrary to what Nussbaum appears to assume, arguing that in many cases burqa-wearing may be coerced does not commit one to any claim that violence against women is greater among Muslim families than the rest of the population.

Besides, actual physical violence is not the most important issue here. It is the credible *threat* of violence that makes for coercion. Or the threat of sustained hostility, starvation or ostracism. In such cases it is no good appealing to laws against physical violence and demanding their enforcement.

Moreover, as I have argued it is not the coercive measures themselves which are the worst harms (although they are indeed harms). The worst harm is the blocking of interests at which they aim. Suppose we take the opposite approach from Nussbaum and think about tackling the blocking of interests rather than the coercive measures? In other words, suppose we made burqa-wearing illegal, so that the blocking of interests from which coerced burqa-wearers suffered were no longer possible. Breaking this law would not, of course, be susceptible of concealment.

Coerced burqa-wearing *relies on the legality* of burqa-wearing, in two senses. There is the obvious sense that there would be no point in forcing a woman to wear a garment which she would then be obliged to remove by the authorities (and penalised for wearing). Furthermore, coerced burqa-wearing is *facilitated* by the fact that other women can be seen to be wearing burqas. A husband who wishes to make his wife cover up can say 'Why don't you wear a burqa, like Mrs X?' Note also that once a woman has been coerced into wearing a burqa she, too, can be presented as an example that non-burqa-wearing women should follow. The more Mrs X's there are, the more force this manipulative appeal has.

The issue of headscarf-wearing in French schools offers a useful parallel. Sarah Song, in her book *Justice, Gender and the Politics of Multiculturalism* (2007) describes the case. In 2003, Jacques Chirac established a commission to report on the controversy over whether Muslim girls should be allowed to wear headscarfs to school, led by Bernard Stasi. The commission recommended a ban. Patrick Weil, a member, was initially against a ban but changed his mind after hearing the evidence:

> In the last two to three years, it has become clear that in schools where some Muslim girls wear the headscarf and others do not, there is strong pressure on the latter to 'conform'. This daily pressure takes different forms, from insults to violence. In the view of the (mostly male) aggressors, these girls are 'bad Muslims', 'whores' who should follow the example of their sisters who respect Koranic prescriptions.
>
> (Weil, in Song 2007: 174)

Song goes on to state:

> The public hearings made it clear that the issue of veiling in France has become more than a matter of individual freedom to express religious belief or cultural identity; it has become, in Weil's words:
>
> 'a France-wide strategy pursued by fundamentalist groups who use public schools as their battleground'. If this is true, then a ban on headscarves may be the best way to protect the majority of Muslim girls who do not wish to wear the veil from the pressures to do so.
>
> (Song 2007: 174).

The same argument could be advanced in favour of a burqa-ban, *if* coerced burqa-wearing is occurring (note that I make no claims here about whether it is). A legal prohibition of the burqa makes coerced burqa-wearing impossible. At the same time, the reason for the coercive measures would be removed.

In other words, instead of trying to end the blocking of interests by stamping out the coercive measures, as Nussbaum wants to do, we might achieve better success in ending the coercive measures by stamping out the blocking of interests.

There is, however, a principled objection to a burqa-ban which deserves serious consideration: the objection that such a ban would be unjust to the voluntary burqa-wearers, under the *principle of fair imputation*. In Section 11.7 I consider this objection and argue that it is not insuperable.

11.7 The problem of unfair imputation

The latter two cases of possible harm considered in this chapter have something in common. For both in the case of harm caused by burqa-wearing criminals or terrorists, and in the case of harm caused by domestic tyrants who coerce women into wearing burqas, the proposed remedy of a ban impacts on the innocent. That is, women who are involved in neither crime nor coercion and who would voluntarily choose to wear the burqa are prevented from so doing. Are they not, we might say, being punished for the crimes of others?

Coerced burqa-wearing resulting from the legality of voluntary burqa-wearing is an instance of what Andrew von Hirsch calls 'remote harms' (1996: 260). A remote harm is one where the action or practice of an individual is not in itself harmful but makes possible or may ultimately lead to harm. Once the harm principle is extended to take remote harms into account, there is a possibility of limiting freedoms much more severely than a liberal might wish; as Hirsch says, 'all sorts of seemingly innocent things I (or we) may do may ultimately have deleterious consequences' (1996: 260).

Hirsch distinguishes three types of remote harm:

1. Abstract Endangerment, where there is no certainty but 'an unreasonable probability of hurting someone' (Hirsch 1996: 263). Drink-driving is an example of this type of remote harm.
2. Intervening Choices, where something is criminalised not because it is harmful in itself, but because it makes possible a choice which would be harmful. Gun-ownership is an example of this type of remote harm.
3. Accumulative Harm, where the individual action is too small in its effects to be harmful, but the aggregation of such acts would bring harm. Pollution would be an example of this type of remote harm.

The remote harms hypothetically caused by burqa-wearing seem to be a cross between types 2 and 3. Both masked crime and coercion are made possible by burqa wearing, but it takes the aggregation of lots of women wearing burqas to make either at all likely.

Hirsch argues that we do need to legislate to take account of remote harms, but that we must also take care to limit the extent of such legislation. Otherwise the application of the liberal harm principle could lead to illiberal outcomes.

Hirsch claims that 'an essential characteristic of the criminal law is that it conveys censure' (1996: 265). Therefore, 'criminalizing conduct should thus call for an explanation of why the behaviour merits the condemnation of the criminal law' (Hirsch 1996: 265). But with remote harms, 'the inference from causing harm to doing wrong is more tenuous' (Hirsch 1996: 265). Should an agent be held accountable for consequences of choices that occur a long way down the line from their act? A voluntary burqa-wearer who is told she can no longer wear the burqa in public because some other women are being forced to do so might reasonably respond that that is not her fault, and should not be made her business.

Hirsch's position is that activities ought not, in general, to be criminalised unless their consequences can be *fairly imputed* to the agent: that is, unless the agent could reasonably be expected to accept some responsibility for those consequences. (He terms such an approach to limiting criminalisation the *imputation principle*). One basis on which fair imputation could be made is that of 'co-operative obligations' (Hirsch 1996: 269). As members of the same society we have joint responsibilities to co-operate for the good of all. In such matters as speed limits, for instance, though some good drivers in modern cars may safely exceed them, if *everyone* sticks to them then accidents are reduced. So it is fair to criminalise breaches of speed limits, which break the obligation to socially co-operate for the good of everyone (Hirsch 1996: 268). The same would go for laws about accumulative harms such as littering or pollution.

That seems unexceptionable. But it is not so easy to justify a burqa-ban on the grounds of co-operative obligation. The obligation we owe each other as road-users is not strictly analogous to any putative obligation a voluntary burqa-wearer might owe to a coerced burqa-wearer. In the case of speeding, the good driver and the bad driver who exceed the speed limit are *doing the same thing*. But the voluntary burqa-wearing woman and the man who forces his wife or daughter to wear one are not doing the same thing at all. It makes sense to say to any individual driver, 'We can't allow you to speed, because then we'd have to allow others to speed (and that would be dangerous).' It does not make the same kind of sense at all to say 'We can't allow you to voluntarily wear your burqa, because then we'd have to allow others to force their wives or daughters to wear burqas.' The voluntary burqa-wearer could simply reply, 'No you wouldn't'. The man who forces a woman to wear a burqa against her will is doing something that's already illegal. Punish him, not me. (And if you can't, that is not my fault.)'

It looks as if we have a dilemma here. On the one hand, if the consequences of burqa-wearing are the harms of crime and/or coercion, the liberal state has good reasons to ban it. On the other hand, those harms cannot fairly be imputed to the voluntary burqa-wearer, so her behaviour should not be criminalised by a liberal state.

11.8 Solution to the problem of unfair imputation

There is a way out of the dilemma. The liberal state ought first to consider all conceivable means of preventing those harms which burqa-wearing facilitates, *short of a ban*. If it were possible to use other policies to target only the harmful versions of burqa-wearing, then no ban would be necessary and no unfair imputations need be made. I am not able to say what such policies might be, but with continuing advances in technology and in understanding of human psychology it is not implausible that some such might be devised.

But suppose that no such policies can be found. Suppose it really is the case that to stop burqa-related crime or coerced burqa-wearing nothing is as efficacious as a general ban. Now we are thrown back on our dilemma. But with a difference. The principle of fair imputation has done its work in obliging the liberal state to seek other options. None were found. The option of a ban is the only one left – a last resort, not a first resort.

In this case, I hold, the liberal state could be justified in enacting a general burqa-ban. And indeed Hirsch himself argues that 'important as imputation principles are, they can only serve as prima facie side-constraints that might sometimes have to be superceded [sic]' (1996: 271) – that is to say, the imputation principle could be overridden 'on grounds that the potential injuriousness is so grave and widespread as to trump ordinary concerns about imputability' (1996: 271).

I hope I have established that coerced burqa-wearing is a grave harm to the women affected. Whether it is widespread, or on the verge of becoming so, is something we do not know. But if the numbers affected were significant (in Section 11.9 I consider what that means) then a general burqa-ban would be justified.

That would be hard on the voluntary burqa-wearers. But the liberal state could and should do its best to soften the effect. In announcing the new law it could make clear the reasons for the ban and stress that the intention was not to censure burqa-wearing per se; moreover, the law could make deliberate provision for allowing occasions or venues (such as mosques) where burqa-wearing would be permitted.

11.9 What about the numbers?

In this section I consider what function the numbers serve in justifying a ban. I confine myself to the harm of coerced burqa-wearing, without considering the harm of burqa-related crime. That is because I consider coerced burqa-wearing much the more likely of the two harms. But my overall point, that the greater the numbers affected the stronger would be the justification for a ban, applies to both types of harm.

Data on how much burqa-wearing is coerced is extremely hard to come by. The very nature of the question ensures this. If women are coerced into wearing the burqa they are unlikely to reveal the fact for fear of reprisals by the coercer. Women who wear it voluntarily, of course, can say so without fear.

Two points might lead us to hypothesise that at least some coercion is occurring. The first is the history of the burqa globally: we know that it has been enforced in some countries, such as Saudi Arabia and the Taliban-controlled parts of Afghanistan. It is possible that no such coercion occurs among Western Muslims whose families originated from those areas, or who attend Saudi-funded mosques, but there is no reason to be sure of that. The second point is that the number of Muslim women who wear the burqa seems to be on the rise. This is anecdotal, as no figures seem to be available. A *Guardian* report of 2013 says that neither the Muslim Council of Great Britain nor the Muslim Women's Network UK has statistics on how many British Muslim women currently wear the burqa or niqab (Burr 2013). However, observation suggests that the number of burqa-wearing women is increasing quite rapidly. That is a phenomenon which requires explaining. Coercion could be at least part of the explanation.

Finding out whether coerced burqa-wearing actually is occurring would be a research task for social scientists. One important factor in their favour is that, on the above analysis of coercion, any women coerced into wearing the burqa would *know* that they were being coerced. So the social scientists would not be trying to ascertain facts that nobody knew. The information would be in principle accessible. Getting women to report coercion would still not be easy, but research techniques for this kind of thing do exist. It is possible to conduct field studies sampling large numbers of interviewees, using interviewers of appropriate background who have gained the trust of participants, using batteries of questions and scaled questions, with anonymity guaranteed.

As I have already emphasised, however, the data is lacking. We simply don't know. Until the social scientists can ascertain the facts (and keep on ascertaining them, since this is a dynamic, not a static situation), we can only say, hypothetically, what a liberal state should do *if* certain empirical claims turn out to be true.

Let us hypothesise that it turns out to be true that significant numbers of women are being coerced into wearing the burqa in Great Britain. Let us be more precise: let us hypothesise that half of all women who wear the burqa do so voluntarily, and the other half are coerced to do so. How should a liberal state respond? (We shall assume it has already responded to the fair imputation problem by seeking alternative policies to a ban, and finding none.)

If the liberal state bans the burqa, the interests of those who wear it voluntarily are blocked. If the liberal state does not ban the burqa, the interests of those who wear it under coercion are blocked. The numbers on either side are equal. The liberal state must make its decision, then, on the basis of which group is harmed most by the blocking of its interests. In other words it must weigh the interests involved.

I contend that being coerced to wear a burqa is a more severe blocking of interests than being prevented from wearing one. I have already indicated above how the interests blocked by being coerced into covering one's face on a daily and permanent basis would weigh according to Feinberg's first two indices, but let us reprise: health, vigour, emotional stability and 'the ability to engage the ability to engage normally in social intercourse' (1980: 32) would all be seriously, adversely affected. A burqa-clad woman is prevented even from smiling at people, which sounds rather like a curse from a fairy tale. Moreover (Feinberg's second index), those standard interests are tied to other interests such as forming friendships or pursuing a career, so those other interests are also adversely affected. A crucial point is that there do not seem to be any available alternative ways to satisfy those interests. An interest in engaging normally in social intercourse cannot be satisfied by doing something else instead.

Turning to the case of a woman who wishes to wear the burqa but is prevented from doing so by a state ban, it is clear that her interests are blocked too. She has an interest in following what she takes to be the dictates of her religion; for her the burqa is a declaration of modesty, submission and piety, which are important values for her. One might argue that being able to follow one's religion in the way one wishes is as important to standard welfare as is the ability to engage in normal social intercourse. I am not sure that I agree. But I see no way to settle that question. What seems conclusive, though, is that the woman who wishes to wear the burqa can satisfy those interests *in other ways*. She can express her religious beliefs and values by wearing modest clothes which proclaim her religious identity (there is no question here of banning the hijab), by attending mosque regularly, by praying and observing other religious obligations, by refraining from entering any sort of profession or career in public life and by being obedient and submissive to her husband if that is what she wants to do. Her interests may have been blocked, but they can find another course. In her community she will be known as a modest, submissive and pious woman. No one will think she is any less of a good Muslim for not wearing the burqa on the streets, because they will know she is not allowed to and she would if she could.

Martha Nussbaum in *Women and Human Development* (2001) provides a good example of a Muslim woman who was no longer able to express her devotion to her religion in the manner she had been accustomed to but found alternative means of doing so. Hamida Khala was a North Indian Muslim, of very conservative views, who got married at fifteen and went to Calcutta with her civil servant husband, who was older than her and of modern views. At first she kept purdah – that is, staying in women's quarters at home and allowing herself to be seen by no men, but this caused a strain as her husband wanted her to socialise with his colleagues and their wives. One evening she and her husband attended a dinner party where she sat in a separate room which was then invaded by the male guests – she felt distraught at this and with regret decided to give up purdah, since it had been broken. Her father advised her that purdah was not intrinsic to Islam and she could still live with reticence and modesty without it. Nussbaum recounts:

> After reading sacred texts on her own, she came to the conclusion that there was a way of living as a devout Muslim outside of strict purdah. She worked out her own rules of modest dress and demeanor – long-sleeved blouses, downcast eyes, no makeup or jewelry – and followed them the rest of her life, while going outside and learning how to conduct daily business and social affairs.
>
> (2001: 237)

This example demonstrates that it is possible to remain true to the values symbolised by burqa-wearing without actually wearing a burqa. But no such alternative course is open to the woman who is coerced into wearing a burqa: the things *she* values, such as free and open face-to-face communication, a range of social interactions and friendships or a career in public life, are fatally compromised if her face has to be covered at all times in public.

If the numbers involved are equal, then, I contend that the liberal state has a duty to support the women who are being coerced into burqa-wearing. And clearly, if the number of women coerced into wearing it is *greater* than the number of those who wear it voluntarily, then a fortiori the state must side with the coerced women.

What, though, if the voluntary burqa-wearers outnumber the coerced? Let us suppose there were 75 per cent voluntary burqa-wearers and 25 per cent coerced burqa-wearers. In such a case I still contend that the state should support the coerced burqa-wearers, because the blocking of their interests is that much more severe and because there is no alternative course for their interests to take.

But if the ration of voluntary to coerced burqa-wearers was 90:10? 95:5? 99:1? Here it gets difficult. As the number of women being coerced to wear the burqa gets smaller, then the justification for a ban gets weaker. A great number of voluntary burqa-wearers would be having their interests blocked and at a certain point this would outweigh the fact that the blocking of interests of the smaller number was more severe. One cannot state exactly what that point is. It is like being asked how many hairs are necessary to form a beard.

All I wish to establish here is that (1) being forced to wear a burqa is a more serious harm than being prevented from wearing one and (2) the greater the number of women being forced to wear one, the stronger is the liberal case for a ban.

11.10 Summary of the argument

To sum up: a liberal state would be justified in banning the burqa *if* it were used as a criminal or terrorist disguise to such an extent that this appreciably increased the risk of harm to citizens (this seems unlikely at present); *if* significant numbers of women were being coerced into wearing it (this seems possible or even plausible, but we do not yet have the necessary data); and *if* no other means short of a ban could be found to prevent either or both of these harms.

12

Conclusion

My answer to the question, 'Should a liberal state ban the burqa?', then, amounts to this:

> **A liberal state should not ban the burqa (though temporary removal may legitimately be required in certain institutional contexts, where security, identification or communication are at issue, and there is no alternative method of ensuring security, identification or communication that is a) equally effective and b) does not impose an unreasonable burden on the institution); with two provisos, viz. 1)** *unless* **burqa-wearing is shown to cause an unacceptable rise in masked crime or terrorism which could be countered in no other way; and 2)** *unless* **a significant number of women turn out to be wearing the burqa under coercion, and there is no equally efficacious method, other than a general ban, of preventing the coercion.**

12.1 The question of efficacy

The final condition of the final proviso – the question of efficacy – requires a little further discussion. After all, if coerced burqa-wearing were occurring, the liberal state would be committed to preventing it, but that does not mean the liberal state would be committed to a general ban. The liberal state would be committed to whatever were the most efficacious means of ending the coercion. That might indeed be a ban, if only because allowing burqa-wearing is necessary for coercion to occur. If no burqa-wearing were allowed, then no coerced burqa-wearing would be possible.

However, a general ban on burqa-wearing could lead to undesired consequences, leaving the coerced women worse off. Suppose a woman is oppressed by her husband and/or male relatives to the extent that they refuse to let her out in public if her face is uncovered. In that case she finds herself under effective house arrest. She is then *more* oppressed than before.

Such cases would, of course, prove the existence of coercion. They would prove the liberal state were right that there was a problem to be tackled. But they would suggest that a general burqa-ban might not be the best way of tackling it.

Other undesirable consequences are conceivable. Suppose that the portion of Wahhabist women who voluntarily wore the burqa resented the ban as an attack on their religion. (They would be mistaken about the motivation behind the ban, but after all, people do make mistakes.) They resolved to continue to wear it in public and accepted the fines or imprisonment that result, martyrising themselves. (Such a degree of martyrisation is after all mild in a historical context; it pales beside Cranmer's, Latimer's and Ridley's willingness to be burned alive rather than accept the truth of transubstantiation.) Moreover, other Muslim women who had not previously worn the burqa now took to doing so, in order to demonstrate support for the martyrs. The number of burqa-wearers would then actually grow; so would the number of Muslim women in prison. This would clearly not be the outcome intended or desired by the liberal state.

12.1.1 A softer approach

It is at least possible that a softer or more tactical approach would prove more efficacious in ending coerced burqa-wearing. A general ban would have justice on its side if its aim were to end the injustice of coercion, but justice is not necessarily enough. John Rawls's thoughts on tolerating the intolerant seem relevant here:

> The question of tolerating the intolerant is directly related to that of the principle of the stability of a well-ordered society regulated by the two principles [of justice]. We can see this as follows. It is from the position of equal citizenship that persons join the various religious associations, and it is from this position that they should conduct their discussion with one another. Citizens in a free society should not think one another incapable of justice unless this is necessary for the sake of equal liberty itself. If an intolerant sect appears in a well-ordered society, the others should keep in mind the inherent stability of their institutions. *The liberties of the intolerant may persuade them to a belief in freedom* [my italics]. This persuasion works on the psychological principle that those whose liberties are protected by and who benefit from a just constitution will, other things equal, acquire an allegiance to it over a period of time (§ 72). So even if an

intolerant sect should arise, provided that it is not so strong initially that it can impose its will straight away, or does not grow so rapidly that the psychological principle has no time to take hold, it will tend to lose its intolerance and accept liberty of conscience.

(1971: 219)

Rawls's point is that even though the intolerant sect would have no title to complain if their activities were suppressed, this may not be the most efficacious way of dealing with them. Rather, by embodying the virtue of tolerance, the liberal state has a chance of *converting*, rather than suppressing them.

I am reminded of Aesop's fable about the Sun and the Wind arguing about who is the more powerful; to put the matter to the test, they decide to see who can force a traveller to remove his cloak. The Wind tries first and furiously buffets the man about, trying to rip the cloak off him. But the man simply clutches his cloak tighter. Then it is the Sun's turn. The Sun beams down, warming the man until he voluntarily takes off his cloak.

The analogy is not exact, for in the case of coerced burqa-wearing it is not the women themselves who can voluntarily choose to remove their burqa, but their husbands or male relatives who must permit them to do so. Nevertheless, the gentle sun of tolerance might turn out to be the most effective way of getting those husbands and male relatives to relent – or at least it might form a crucial part of the solution.

Other approaches which a liberal state might pursue in tandem with tolerance could include nudge-style policies designed to diminish the appeal of the burqa to men who follow a conservative, patriarchal version of Islam. I am not able to specify what such policies might be, but they would need somehow to facilitate a cultural change, so that the burqa's positive associations for conservative Islam (modesty, piety, virtue) were weakened. Perhaps the idea, urged by liberal Muslims, that the burqa is un-Islamic, a pre-Islamic cultural practice rather than a contemporary religious obligation, might have some purchase here.

At the same time, the liberal state could be strict in insisting on *temporary* removal of the burqa when the situation demanded (in schools, airports, banks, law courts, etc.). In this way the burqa could come to be seen as a garment one slips on and off rather than a permanent barrier between the wearer and the world; its totemic qualities would diminish; and the task of dissuading men from forcing their wives or daughters to wear one might become easier, as the stakes would be less high.

Finally, the liberal state could also try to ensure that exit routes were in place for women in relationships where they continued to be forced to cover their faces in public. This would entail making it publicly clear that coercion need not be tolerated, and providing refuges for women in flight from such oppressive relationships.

Note that I am not recommending any particular policy. If a general ban were the most efficacious means of ending coerced burqa-wearing – supposing it to occur – then the liberal state would be justified in imposing such a ban. But if a concerted set of policies aimed at ending coercion, stopping short of a ban, were to prove more efficacious, then the liberal state should pursue those policies instead. The real goal of the liberal state is to protect the rights of all its citizens as free and equal persons, and it can be flexible about the means it uses to do so.

12.2 What comes next?

As I observed in the first chapter, the phenomenon of burqa-wearing in liberal Western states is a comparatively recent one. So far, five European states – France, Belgium, the Netherlands, Bulgaria and Denmark – have responded to the phenomenon by legal bans on habitual public face-covering. It is also banned in the Swiss canton of Ticino, and a nationwide ban is currently being debated in the Swiss parliament. As I have argued (perhaps over-exhaustively) I do not think that in the end there are good liberal reasons for such a ban. That is not to cast aspersions on the motivations of the legislators. But their response seems both excessive and premature.

Excessive because the problems that habitual public face-covering might raise – of security, identification and communication – could be dealt with by workarounds such as alternative means of establishing ID. And, as previously suggested, having regulations requiring temporary removal in specified situations. That would be less of an infringement of personal liberty and less easy to misinterpret as Islamophobic.

Premature because, as I noted in my Chapter 1, the wearing of the burqa is a dynamic situation, not a static one. The practice could subside as rapidly as it has arisen. Whether it does or not may be partly dependent on geopolitical events. But it seems to me that, to whatever extent burqa-wearing is a deliberate challenge to the ideology of western liberal states, banning it only increases the motivation for such a challenge. A sensitive approach that is both flexible and deliberative is better suited to managing cases of public face-covering.

I hope, therefore, that other liberal states will not follow the suit of France, Belgium, the Netherlands, Bulgaria, Denmark and Ticino. I hope, too, that in time France and the others will reconsider, rescind their burqa-bans and substitute for them more flexible and sympathetic policies for dealing with face-covering. It is interesting to note that in the Netherlands the burqa-ban (even though only partial) is already proving hard to implement as police officers are reluctant to enforce it (Boffey 2019).

I began by noting that the burqa posed a challenge for liberalism. I believe I have demonstrated that to be true. But I hope I have also demonstrated that liberalism is equal to the challenge. It is a rich, living, thriving intellectual tradition which contains not only tensions but also the resources to deal with those tensions, and in writing this book I have become more and more convinced that liberal principles are our best hope for achieving just outcomes in a modern, mobile, multicultural world.

Bibliography

Ahmed, Leila, 1992, *Women and Gender in Islam*, Yale University Press.
Alibhai-Brown, Yasmin, 2014, *Refusing the Veil*, Biteback.
Alibhai-Brown, Yasmin, 2015, 'As a Muslim Woman I See the Veil as a Rejection of Progressive Values', *The Guardian*, 20 March.
Allais, Lucy, 2016, 'Kant's Racism', *Philosophical Papers* 45(1–2): 1–36.
Anderson, Joel, and Axel Honneth, 2005, 'Autonomy, Vulnerability, Recognition and Justice', in *Autonomy and the Challenges to Liberalism*, 127–49, Cambridge University Press.
Ansari, Usamah, 2008, ' "Should I Go and Pull Her Burqa Off?": Feminist Compulsions, Insider Consent, and a *Return to Kandahar*', *Critical Studies in Media Communication* 25(1): 48–67.
Appiah, K. Anthony, 1994, 'Identity, Authenticity, Survival: Multicultural Societies and Social Reproduction', in *Multiculturalism: Examining the Politics of Recognition*, ed. Amy Gutmann, 149–63, Princeton University Press.
Arberry, Arthur J. (trans.), 2008, *The Koran*, Oxford University Press.
Aristotle, [c. 340 BCE] 2004, *The Nichomachean Ethics*, trans. Thomson J. A. K., revised by Hugh Tredennick, Penguin Classics.
Arneson, Richard J., 1980, 'Mill versus Paternalism', *Ethics* 90(4): 470–89.
Arneson, Richard J., 2007, 'Freedom and Desire' in *Freedom: A Philosophical Anthology*, ed. Ian Carter, Matthew H. Kramer and Hillel Steiner, 138–47, Blackwell.
Baehr, Peter, and Daniel Gordon, 2013, 'From the Headscarf to the Burqa: The Role of Social Theorists in Shaping Laws against the Veil', *Economy and Society* 42(2): 249–80.
Barry, Brian, 2011, *Culture and Equality*, Polity Press.
Baubérot, Jean, 2016, 'La loi de 1905, étape fondamentale de la laïcisation de la République française, est libérale et tolérante', Interview in *Le Monde*, 13 October.
Berlin, Isaiah, 1998, 'Two Concepts of Liberty', in *The Proper Study of Mankind: An Anthology of Essays*, ed. Roger Hausheer and Henry Hardy, 191–242, Pimlico.
Blackford, Russell, 2012, *Freedom of Religion and the Secular State*, Wiley-Blackwell.
Bogart, Kathleen R., and David Matsumoto, 2009, 'Living with Möbius Syndrome: Adjustment, Social Competence, and Satisfaction with Life', *Cleft Palate-Craniofacial Journal* 47(2): 134–42.
Canetti, Elias, 1992, *Crowds and Power*, Penguin.
Chambers, Clare, 2005, 'All Must Have Prizes: The Liberal Case for Interference in Cultural Practices', in *Multiculturalism Reconsidered*, ed. Paul Kelly, 151–73, Polity Press.

Chambers, Clare, 2008, *Sex, Culture and Justice: The Limits of Choice*, Penn State Press.
Chesler, Phyllis, 2010, 'Ban the Burqa? The Argument in Favour', *Middle-Eastern Quarterly* 17(4 Fall): 33–45.
Christman, John, 2004, 'Relational Autonomy, Liberal Individualism, and the Social Construction of Selves', *Philosophical Studies* 117: 143–64.
Christman, John, and Joel Anderson, 2005, 'Introduction', in *Autonomy and the Challenges to Liberalism*, 1–23, Cambridge University Press.
Colburn, Ben, 2010, *Autonomy and Liberalism*, Routledge.
Conly, Sarah, 2013, *Against Autonomy*, Cambridge University Press.
Darwin, Charles, [1872] 1965, *The Expression of Emotion in Man and Animals*, University of Chicago Press.
de Marneffe, Peter, 2006, 'Avoiding Paternalism', *Philosophy and Public Affairs*, 34: 68–74.
Donatelli, Peirgiorgio, 2006, 'Mill's Perfectionism', *Prolegomena* 5(2): 149–64.
Dworkin, Gerald, 2007, 'from *The Theory and Practice of Autonomy*', in *Freedom: A Philosophical Anthology*, ed. Ian Carter, Matthew H. Kramer and Hillel Steiner, 333–7, Blackwell.
Dworkin, Ronald, 1985, *A Matter of Principle*, Harvard University Press.
Dworkin, Ronald, 1988, *The Theory and Practice of Autonomy*, Cambridge University Press.
Ekman, Paul, 2015, *Darwin and Facial Expression: A Century of Research in Review*, Los Altos, CA: Malor Books.
Elster, Jon, 1983, *Sour Grapes: Studies in the Subversion of Rationality*, Cambridge University Press.
Esposito, John, and Ibrahim Kalin, 2011, *Islamophobia: The Challenge of Pluralism in the 21st Century*, Oxford University Press.
Etzioni, Amitai, 2004, *The Common Good*, Polity Press.
Feinberg, Joel, 1980, *Rights, Justice and the Bounds of Liberty*, Princeton University Press.
Feinberg, Joel, 1984, *Harm to Others*, Oxford University Press.
Feinberg, Joel, 1985, *Offense to Others*, Oxford University Press.
Feldman Barret, Lisa, 'What Faces Can't Tell Us', *New York Times*, 28 February 2014.
Fernandez-Dols, J.-M., and Russell, J. A. (eds), 2017, *The Science of Facial Expression*, Oxford University Press.
Flanders, Judith, 2015, *The Making of Home*, Atlantic.
Foucault, Michel, 1995, *Discipline and Punish*, trans. A. Sheridan, Vintage.
Fraser, Nancy, 1989, *Unruly Practices*, University of Minnesota Press.
Friedman, Marilyn, 2005, 'Autonomy and Male Dominance', in Christman, John, and Joel Anderson (eds), *Autonomy and the Challenges to Liberalism*, ed. John Christman and Joel Anderson, 15–73, Cambridge University Press.
Galeotti, Anna Elisabetta, 2002, *Toleration as Recognition*, Cambridge University Press.
Gaus, Gerald, and Richard Vallier, 2009, 'The Roles of Religious Conviction in a Publicly Justified Polity', *Philosophy and Social Criticism* 35(1–2).

Gordon, Daniel, 2008, 'Why Is There No Headscarf Affair in the United States?', *Historical Reflections* 34(3 Winter): 37–60.
de Haan, Michelle, and Charles A. Nelson, 1997, 'Recognition of the Mother's Face by Six-Month-Old Infants: A Neurobehavioural Study', *Child Development* 68(2): 187–210.
Habermas, Jurgen, 2011, 'Reconciliation through the Public Use of Reason: Remarks on John Rawls's Political Liberalism', in *Habermas and Rawls: Disputing the Political*, ed. G. F. Finblayson and F. Freyenhagen, 25–45, Routledge.
Hamilton, Marcia, 2014, *God vs the Gavel*, Cambridge University Press.
Henley, William Ernest, [1888] 2016, 'Invictus', in *A Poem for Every Night of the Year*, 268, Macmillan.
Al-Hibri, Azizah. Y., 1999, 'Is Western Patriarchal Feminism Good for Third World/Minority Women?' in *Is Multiculturalism Bad for Women*, ed. J. Cohen, M. Howard and M. Nussbaum, 41–6, Princeton University Press.
Hirsch, Andrew von, 1996, 'Extending the Harm Principle', in *Harm and Culpability*, ed. A. P. Simester and A. T. H. Smith, 259–76, Clarendon Press.
Hunter-Henin, Myriam, 2012, 'Why the French Don't Like the Burqa: *Laïcité*, National Identity and Religious Freedom', *International and Comparative Law Quarterly* 61(3): 613–39.
Hurka, Thomas, 1993, *Perfectionism*, Oxford University Press.
Iacobono, Marco, 2008, *Mirroring People: The New Science of How We Connect with Others*, Farrar, Straus and Giroux.
Jennings, B., 1996, 'Beyond the Harm Principle: From Autonomy to Civic Responsibility', in *Moral Values: The Challenge of the Twenty-First Century* (Vol. XVII in the *Andrew R. Cecil Lectures on Moral Values in a Free Society*), ed. W. L. Taitte, University of Texas at Dallas.
Kahneman, Daniel, 2011, *Thinking Fast and Slow*, Farrar, Strauss and Giroux.
Kant, Immanuel, [1785] 2008, *Groundwork of the Metaphysics of Morals*, ed. Mary Gregor, Cambridge University Press.
Kanwisher, Nancy, Josh McDermott and Marvin M. Chun, 1997, 'The Fusiform Face Area: A Module in Human Extrastriate Cortex Specialised for Face Perception', *Journal of Neuroscience* 17(11): 4302–11.
Kargar, Zarghuna, 2012, *Dear Zari*, Vintage.
Kemp, Anna, 2010, *Voices and Veils (Feminism and Islam in French Women's Writing and Activism)*, Legenda.
Khader, Serene J., 2011, *Adaptive Preferences and Women's Empowerment*, Oxford University Press.
Kukathas, Chandran, 2003, *The Liberal Archipelago*, Oxford University Press.
Kukathas, Chandran, 2010, *Reconciling Modernity and Tradition in a Liberal Society*, CIS Occasional Paper 121, Centre for Independent Studies.
Kymlicka, Will, 1995, *Multicultural Citizenship*, Clarendon.
Laborde, Cécile, 2008, *Critical Republicanism*, Oxford University Press.

Laborde, Cécile, 2017, *Liberalism's Religion*, Harvard University Press.
Locke, John, [1689] 2013, *A Letter Concerning Toleration*, ed. K. Walters, Broadview Editions.
MacCallum, Gerald C., 2007, from 'Negative and Positive Freedom', in *Freedom: A Philosophical Anthology*, ed. Ian Carter, Matthew H. Kramer and Hillel Steiner, 70–8, Blackwell.
Mackenzie, Catriona, 2008, 'Relational Autonomy, Normative Authority and Perfectionism', *Journal of Social Philosophy* 39(4): 512–33.
Maclure, Jocelyn, 2011, 'Reasonable Accommodations and the Subjective Conception of Freedom of Conscience and Religion', in *Identity Politics in the Public Realm*, ed. Avigail Eisenberg and Will Kymlicka, 260–80, UBC Press.
Maclure, Jocelyn, and Charles Taylor, 2011, *Secularism and Freedom of Conscience*, Harvard University Press.
McConnell, Michael, 2010, 'Religion and its Relation to Limited Government', *Harvard Journal of Law and Public Policy* 33(3).
Mill, John Stuart, [1859] 2005, *On Liberty*, Cosimo Classics.
Mill, John Stuart, [1869] 2008, *On the Subjection of Women*, Hesperus.
Napier, William, 1851, *History of General Sir Charles Napier's Administration of Scinde*, Chapman and Hall.
Narayan, Uma, 2002, 'Minds of Their Own: Choice, Autonomy, Cultural Practices and Other Women', in Antony, Louise. M. and Charlotte E. Witt (eds), *A Mind of One's Own*, ed. Louise. M. Antony and Charlotte E. Witt, 418–32, Westview.
Nozick, Robert, 1969, 'Coercion', in Morgenbesser, S., Suppers, P., and White., (Eds.) *Philosophy, Science and Method: Essays in Honour of Ernest Nagel*, ed. S. Morgenbesser, P. Suppers and M. White, 440–72, St Martin's.
Nussbaum, Martha, 2001, *Women and Human Development: The Capabilities Approach*, Cambridge University Press.
Nussbaum, Martha, 2007, *Frontiers of Justice*, Belknap.
Nussbaum, Martha, 2008, *Liberty of Conscience*, Basic Books.
Nussbaum, Martha, 2010, 'Veiled Threats', *New York Times*, 11 July 2010.
Nussbaum, Martha, 2012, *The New Religious Intolerance*, Belknap.
Okin, Susan Moller, 1999, 'Is Multiculturalism Bad for Women?', in *Is Multiculturalism Bad for Women*, ed. J. Cohen, M. Howard and M. Nussbaum, 7–24, Princeton University Press.
Orwell, George, 2000, 'Politics vs. Literature', in *Essays*, ed. B. Crick, 370–87, Penguin.
Oshana, Marina, 1989, 'Personal Autonomy and Society', *Journal of Social Philosophy* 29(1): 81–102.
Oshana, Marina, 2006, *Personal Autonomy in Society*, Ashgate.
Parekh, Bikhu, 1999, 'A Varied Moral World', in *Is Multiculturalism Bad for Women?*, ed. J. Cohen, and M. Howard and M. Nussbaum, 69–75, Princeton University Press.
Parfit, Derek, 1987, *Reasons and Persons*, Clarendon Press.
Persak, Nina, 2006, *Criminalising Harmful Conduct*, Springer.

Phillips, Anne, 2007, *Multiculturalism without Culture*, Princeton University Press.
Pinker, Steven, 2011, *The Better Angels of Our Nature*, Penguin.
Plato, [c. 380 BCE] 2008, *The Republic*, trans. Robin Waterfield, Oxford World's Classics.
Quong, Jonathan, 2011, *Liberalism without Perfection*, Oxford University Press.
Rawls, John, 1971, *A Theory of Justice*, Belknap.
Rawls, John, 2005, *Political Liberalism*, Columbia University Press.
Raz, Joseph, 2009, *The Morality of Freedom*, Oxford University Press.
Reynolds, Joel, 2016, 'Toward a Critical Theory of Harm: Ableism, Normativity, and Transability (BIID)', *Philosophy and Medicine* 16(1).
Robert, Naima B., 2006, *From My Sisters' Lips*, Bantam Books.
Rosen, Michael, and Jonathan Wolff, 1999, *Political Thought*, Oxford University Press.
Ross, Lee, and Richard E. Nesbitt, 2011, *The Person and the Situation*, Pincher and Martin.
Sardar, Z., 2016, *Reading the Qur'an*, Hurst.
Sen, Amartya, 1999, *Development as Freedom*, Oxford University Press.
Shakespeare, Tom, 2014, *Disability Rights and Wrongs Revisited*, Routledge.
Shakespeare, William, [c. 1606] 1987, 'Macbeth', in *The Complete Works of William Shakespeare*, 999–1027, Collins.
Shiffrin, Seana, 2000, 'Paternalism, Unconscionability Doctrine, and Accommodation', *Philosophy and Public Affairs* 29(3): 205–50.
Siedentorp, Larry, 2015, *Inventing the Individual: The Origins of Western Liberalism*, Penguin.
Song, Sarah, 2007, *Justice, Gender and the Politics of Multiculturalism*, Cambridge University Press.
Swift, Adam, 2001, *Political Philosophy*, Polity.
Taylor, Charles, 1994, 'The Politics of Recognition', in *Multiculturalism: Examining the Politics of Recognition*, ed. A. Gutmann, 25–73, Princeton University Press.
Taylor, James S., 2009, *Practical Autonomy and Bioethics*, New York: Routledge.
Thaler, Richard H., and Cass R. Sunstein, 2003, 'Libertarian Paternalism Is Not an Oxymoron', Working Paper No. 43, University of Chicago Public Law and Legal Theory.
Thomas, Laurence, 2012, 'Evil and the Norms of Society', in *Thinking towards Humanity*, ed. Stephen de Wijze and Eve Garrard, 89–106, Manchester University Press.
Treacher, Amal, 2003, 'Reading the Other: Women, Feminism and Islam', *Studies in Gender and Sexuality* 4(1): 59–71.
Vernon, Richard, 1996, 'John Stuart Mill and Pornography: Beyond the Harm Principle', *Ethics* 106(3): 621–32.
Voltaire, 1962, *Candide*, London University Press.
Watson, Lori, and Christie Hartley, 2018, *Equal Citizenship and Public Reason*, Cambridge University Press.
Watts, Michael, 2009, 'Sen and the Art of Motorcycle Maintenance: Adaptive Preferences and Higher Education', *Studies in Philosophy and Education* 28(5): 425–36.

Westermarck, Edvard, 1932, *Ethical Relativity*, Kegan Paul, Trench, Trubner.
Wolff, Jonathan, and Avner De-Shalit, 2007, *Disadvantage*, Oxford University Press.
Yaffe, Gideon (2003), 'Indoctrination, Coercion and Freedom of Will', *Philosophy and Phenomenological Research* 67: 335–56.

Internet sources

Agerholm, Harriet, 2016, 'Dutch Parliament Approves Partial Burqa Ban in Public Places', *The Independent*, 29 November, http://www.independent.co.uk/news/world/europe/dutch-burqa-veil-ban-holland-votes-for-partial-restrictions-some-public-places-a7445656.html. Accessed on 20 January 2020.

Anderson, Scott, 2017, 'Coercion', *Stanford Encyclopaedia of Philosophy*, Winter Edition, ed. Edward N. Zalta, https://plato.stanford.edu/archives/win2017/entries/coercion/. Accessed on 17 May 2017.

ANRI, 2010, 'Rapport d'information au nom de la mission d'information sur la pratique du port du voile integral sur le territoire nationale', Assemble´e Nationale document no. 2262, Rapport d'information, http://www.assemblee-nationale.fr/13/pdf/rap-info/i2262.pdf. Accessed on 10 May 2018.

BBC News website, 2014, 'Gang Jailed for Selfridges Smash-and-Grab Robbery', 19 August, http://www.bbc.co.uk/news/uk-england-london-28853340. Accessed on 15 March 2016.

BBC News website, 2015a, 'Cameroon Bans Islamic Face Veil after Suicide Bombings', 16 July, http://www.bbc.co.uk/news/world-africa-33553041.

BBC News website, 2015b, 'Chad Bans Islamic Face Veil after Suicide Bombings', 17 June, http://www.bbc.co.uk/news/world-africa-33166220. Accessed 15 March 2016.

Baghariam, M., and J. A.Carter, 2017, 'Relativism', *Stanford Encyclopedia of Philosophy*, Summer Edition, ed. Edward N. Zalta, https://plato.stanford.edu/archives/sum2017/entries/relativism.

Bergo, Bettina, 2017, 'Emmanuel Levinas', *Stanford Encyclopedia of Philosophy*, Fall Edition, ed. Edward N. Zalta, https://plato.stanford.edu/archives/fall2017/entries/levinas/. Accessed on 18 January 2018.

Boffey, Daniel, 2019, 'Dutch "Burqa Ban" Rendered Largely Unworkable on First Day', *The Guardian*, 01 August, https://www.theguardian.com/world/2019/aug/01/dutch-police-signal-unwillingness-enforce-new-burqa-ban. Accessed on 25 June 2019.

British and Irish Legal Information Institute, 2007, http://www.bailii.org/uk/cases/UKEAT/2007/0009_07_3003.html. Accessed on 20 January 2020.

British Medical Journal, 2013, 'Long Term Effect of Reduced Pack Sizes of Paracetamol on Poisoning Deaths and Liver Transplant Activity in England and Wales: Interrupted Time Series Analyses', 07 February, http://www.bmj.com/content/346/bmj.f403. Accessed on 16 January 2018.

Burke, Darren, and Danielle Sulikowski, 2013, 'The Evolution of Holistic Processing of Faces' *Frontiers in Psychology* 4(11), https://www.ncbi.nlm.nih.gov/pmc/articles/PMC3560284/. Accessed on 20 January 2020.

Burr, Amelia, 2013, 'Mosque Condemns Veil Ban at Whipps Cross Hospital', *Waltham Forest Guardian*, 20 September, http://www.guardian-series.co.uk/news/10687985.Mosque_condemns_hospital_veil_ban/. Accessed on 20 January 2020.

Dworkin, Gerald, 2017, 'Paternalism', *Stanford Encyclopedia of Philosophy*, Winter Edition, ed. Edward N. Zalta, https://plato.stanford.edu/archives/win2017/entries/paternalism/. Accessed on 11 February 2018.

ECHR Judgement in the case of *S.A.S v France*, 2014, http://hudoc.echr.coe.int/eng?i=001-145466. Accessed on 20 January 2020.

ECHR Press Release 241 in the case of *Belcacemi and Oussa v Belgium*, 2017, https://www.femmesforfreedom.com/wp-content/uploads/2019/08/Judgment-Belcacemi-and-Oussar-v.-Belgium-ban-on-wearing-face-covering-in-public-areas-Law-of-1-June-2011.pdf. Accessed on 20 January 2020.

Ekman, Paul, 2014, 'Darwin's Claim of Universals in Facial Expressions Not Challenged', https://www.paulekman.com/uncategorized/darwins-claim-universals-facial-expression-challenged. Accessed on 9 September 2017.

Gerin, André, 2010, 'Avant-Propos, Rapport d'Information', http://www.assemblee-nationale.fr/13/pdf/rap-info/i2262.pdf. Accessed on 10 May 2018.

The Guardian, 2013, 'How Many Women Wear the Niqab in the UK?', 20 September, http://www.theguardian.com/politics/reality-check/2013/sep/20/how-many-wear-niqab-uk.

LOI n° 2010-1192 du 11 octobre 2010 interdisant la dissimulation du visage dans l'éspace public, https://www.legifrance.gouv.fr/affichTexte.do?cidTexte=JORFTEXT000022911670&categorieLien=id. Accessed on 14 April 2019.

McNeil, Jane E., and Elizabeth K. Warrington, 1993, 'Prosopagnosia: A Face-Specific Disorder', *Quarterly Journal of Experimental Psychology* 46(1), http://www.tandfonline.com/doi/abs/10.1080/14640749308401064. Accessed on 14 April 2019.

McIntyre, Alison, 2014, 'Doctrine of Double Effect', *Stanford Encyclopedia of Philosophy*, Winter Edition, ed. Edward N. Zalta, https://plato.stanford.edu/archives/win2014/entries/double-effect/. Accessed on 15 March 2015.

Malverde, Jesus, 2014, 'The Women of the University of Cairo over the Years', https://www.democraticunderground.com/10024727575. Accessed on 20 January 2020.

Pew Research Poll, 2014, 'How People in Muslim Countries Prefer Women to Dress in Public', http://www.pewresearch.org/fact-tank/2014/01/08/what-is-appropriate-attire-for-women-in-muslim-countries/. Accessed on 20 January 2020.

Reuters, World News, 2016, 'Bulgaria Bans Full-Face Veils in Public Places', 30 September, https://www.reuters.com/article/us-religion-burqa-bulgaria/bulgaria-bans-full-face-veils-in-public-places-idUSKCN1201FV. Accessed on 20 January 2020.

Stoljar, Natalie, 2015, 'Feminist Perspectives on Autonomy', *Stanford Encyclopedia of Philosophy*, Fall Edition, ed. Edward N. Zalta, https://plato.stanford.edu/archives/fall2015/entries/feminism-autonomy/. Accessed on 1 December 2015.

The Times, 2010, 'Judge Orders Muslim Witness to Remove Burqa', 19 August, https://www.thetimes.co.uk/article/judge-orders-muslim-witness-to-remove-burqa-0s9wq273dss. Accessed on 20 January 2020.

Wainwright, Martin, 2006, *The Guardian*, https://www.theguardian.com/uk/2006/oct/20/politics.schools1. Accessed on 2 January 2020.

Index

accommodation, cultural 9, 24–6, 139–40, 142–5, 151–2
adaptive preference (AP) 1–2, 8–10, 16, 112, 117–30
Aesop 235
Afghanistan 96, 109, 162–3, 172, 192, 228
Against Autonomy 85
agenda 2
Agerholm, Harriet 4
Ahdar, Rex 5
Ahmed, Leila 129, 190–1
Alibhai-Brown, Yasmin 196, 205, 223
Allah 124, 204
Allais, Lucy 94
American Declaration of Independence 71
Amin, Qassim 129, 191–2
Anderson, Joel, and Alex Honneth 132, 147–9, 150–2, 159–61, 163
  see also Christman, John
Anderson, Scott 218–19
ANRI 13–14, 55
Appiah, Anthony K. 154–5
Aquinas, Thomas 79
Arberry, Arthur 43, 174
Aristotle 49, 122–3
Arneson, Richard 70
Assemblée Nationale 12
Assemblée Nationale Rapport d'Information see ANRI
Assyrians, ancient 190
Ataturk, Kemal 192
Atkins, Kim 161
Australia 179 (*see also* Perth, Australia)
Authenticity Condition (for autonomy) 104, 106, 108
autonomy (*see also* personal autonomy) 2, 6, 56–61, 74, 81, 93–115, 150–1, 163
  autonomy, comparison with intelligence 98–103
  autonomy, content-neutral 93, 98, 102, 104–6

autonomy, substantive vs. proceduralist accounts 104–9
autonomy deficits 123
Autonomy-Protecting Requirement 154–6
first-order autonomy 8, 93, 109–14, 118
relational autonomy 93, 117–18, 128, 150, 161
second-order autonomy 8, 56, 93, 109–14, 118
Autonomy and Liberalism 56
Azmi, Aisha 4, 146

'Baby Face' (song) 28
Bach's Cello Suites 57
Baehr, Peter, and Daniel Gordon 18–20, 211–12
Bagharian, M., and J. A. Carter 138
Barry, Brian 21, 96–7, 102, 138, 141, 144
Baubérot, Jean 12–13
Belgium 4, 6, 179, 236–7
  v. Belcacemi and Oussar 2017 14
Bellamy, Richard 18
Benin, Kingdom of 28
Bergo, Bettina 28
Berlin, Isaiah 94–5
Better Angels of Our Nature, The 177
BIID *see* Body Integrity Identity Disorder
Blackford, Russell 5, 22, 38, 206
Body Integrity Identity Disorder (BIID) 71, 210
Boffey, Daniel 237
Bogart, Kathleen R., and David Matsumoto 91
Boko Haram 216
Book of Common Prayer, The 110
Bourdieu, Pierre 2
breast enhancement surgery 167
breast implants 187, 189
British Medical Journal 89
Bulgaria 4, 179, 236
Burke, Darren and Danielle Sulikowski 29

Burr, Amelia 228
burqa 1–11, 14, 16–17, 19–21, 23, 26, 38, 48–9, 54, 69–70, 87, 117, 139–40, 152, 155, 159, 166–6, 175, 193, 228
  and coercion 217–24
  and disadvantage 194–6
  and exemptions 147
  and freedom of choice 178–9
  and gender 167–97
  genealogy of 190
  and harm 207–31
  and health 89–92
  and misogyny 204
  and personal autonomy 93–115
  and social influence 190–3
  and tolerance 133–4
burqa ban 1, 4, 7–9, 13, 19–21, 39, 61–2, 70, 103, 117, 129, 133, 167, 179, 213, 237
Burr, Amelia 5
Butler-Sloss, Elizabeth 161

Cairo University 130
Cameroon 216
Canada 25, 179
Candide 102
Canetti, Elias 180
capabilities 51–3, 93, 120, 186
Carter, J. A. *see* Bagharian, M.
Cass R. Sunstein *see* Thaler, Richard H.
Chad 215
chador 140, 196
Chambers, Clare 9, 93, 97–8, 110–13, 117, 167–8, 179–81, 184–90, 194, 196–7
character planning 119, 125
Chesler, Phyllis 205–6
child marriage 175, 179
Chirac, Jacques 224
Christians 135
Christianity 22, 156
  Christian Europe 186
  Christian theocracy 5
Christman, John and Joel Anderson 104, 161
Church of the New Song 145
circumcision 113–14
citizenship 19, 212
clitorodectomy (*see also* FGM) 152–3, 175
coercion 2, 10, 16, 87–8, 118, 124, 126–8, 147, 165, 207, 233–5
Colburn, Ben 56–61, 93, 95–7

colonialism 192
communication 4, 8–9
communitarianism 211–13
Competency Condition (for autonomy) 104, 106, 108, 128
comprehensive doctrine 41–2
Congo Brazzaville 216
Conley, Sarah 69, 85–8
Convention for the Protection of Human Rights and Freedoms 15, 17
Cranmer, Thomas 234
crime 17, 36, 165, 200, 212, 214–15, 217, 225
Crowds and Power 180
crucifixes 21
cultural accommodation *see* accommodation
cultural affirmation 194
cultural resources 1

Darwin, Charles 29
Dawkins, Richard 156
Dean, Shauna 4
Dear Zari 162
de Marneffe, Peter 76–7, 79–80
deliberative intervention 122–3
Denmark 4, 236–7
De-Shalit, Avner *see* Wolff, Jonathan
disadvantage 185–90
  see also burqa and disadvantage
Disadvantage 186
Discipline and Punish 182
divorce 175, 178–9, 191
Dorkenoo, Efua 188
Dworkin, Gerald 80, 94
Dworkin, Ronald 111–12, 141

ECHR 6–7, 11, 14–17, 212–13
efficacy 10, 233, 236
Egypt 129, 192–3
Ekman, Paul 29
Elster, Jon 119, 125
Endowment Effect 86
ethical consistency 90, 216
Etzioni, Amitai 213
eudaimonia 122
Europe 179, 216
  European states 207
  European Court of Human Rights *see* ECHR

exemptions 2, 21
Expression of Emotion in Man and Animals, The 29

face, significance of 7–8, 27–38
face-covering 6–9, 11, 18–19, 21, 26, 27–38, 133, 139–40, 142, 144–5, 165, 167, 212, 214–15, 236
facial mirroring 30
Feinberg, Joel 10, 33, 48, 159, 201–4, 206, 208–10, 221, 229
Feldman-Barrett, Lisa 29
Female Genital Mutilation (FGM) 113–14, 152, 164, 173, 176, 178, 187–9, 196–7 (*see also* clitorodectomy)
feminism 4, 6, 168–71, 179, 204
  feminist principles 204
  see also liberal feminism; misogyny; and gender
'First Time Ever I Saw Your Face' (song) 28
Flanders, Judith 186
flourishing 8–9, 121, 125–6, 129, 186
  Flourishing Claim 122
forced marriage 173, 175–6, 179
Foucault, Michel 180–4, 190
France 4, 6, 11, 174, 179, 212–13, 236–7
Fraser, Nancy 183–4
freedom
  and autonomy 94, 99
  of choice 178–9
  of conscience 22, 24, 26
  of expression 5, 23
  to make experiments in living 5, 23
  to pursue different forms of sexuality 5
  see also religious freedom
Freedom of Religion and the Secular State 22, 38
French ban 6–7, 11–20
French Declaration of the Rights of Man 19
French government's policy on polygamy 171
French Revolution 14
French schools 224
Friedman, Marilyn 170
Frontiers of Justice 60

Galeotti, Anna 132, 147–50, 152–3
Gaus, Gerald and Richard Vallier 43

gender 1, 9
  gender equality 6, 11, 14
  gender and the burqa *see also* burqa, and gender
Gerin, André 14
Germany 186
Give-'Em-Enough Rope Tendency 44, 64
Gordon, Daniel 2
  see also Baehr, Peter
Great Britain 45, 186, 193, 196, 229
Greek busts and statues 28
group rights 9, 139–42, 153, 171–2

de Haan, Michelle 28
Habermas, Jurgen 45, 64
Hadith 168
Hamilton, Marcia 145
harm 2, 35, 73
  and the burqa 10, 49, 87, 207–31
  problem of defining 209–11
  remote harm 225–6
harm principle 46–8, 65, 74, 208–9
Hart, H. L. A. 218
Hartley, Christie *see* Watson, Lori
Hegel, Georg Wilhelm Friedrich 49
Henley, W. E. 101
Heraclitus 102
Al-Hibri, Azizah Y. 173–6
hijab 3, 12, 21, 194, 230
Hindu theocracy 5
Hirsch, Andrew von 225–7
History of Sir Charles Napier's Administration of Scinde 136
Honneth, Alex *see* Anderson, Joel
Honoré, Tony 218
Hunter-Henin, Myriam 12–13
Hurka, Thomas 49

Iacabono, Marco 30
Identity-Protecting Commiments (IPCs) 25
immigrants 2
Inappropriate Adaptive Preference (IAP) 9, 117, 122–5, 128–30, 162, 185
India 136
individuality 47
Inventing the Individual 22
Iran 192
Iraq 193
Islam 5–6, 20–1, 156, 169
  Islamic headscarf 149

Islamic feminism, weak and
    strong 168–70
Islamic, Salafist theocracy 5
Islamic scholars 14
Islam and condition of women 191
Islamic world 3
    political Islam 205
It's a Wonderful Life 82
'I've just Seen a Face' (song) 28

Japanese art 28
Jehovah's Witness 25
Jennings, B. 209
Jennings-White, Chloe 71–3, 106, 210
Jews 135
Juliet 83
Justice, Gender and the Politics of Multiculturalism 224

Kahneman, Daniel 86
Kant, Immanuel 50, 94, 134
Kanwisher, Nancy 29
Kargar, Zarghuna 162
Kemp, Anna 169
Khader, Serene 9, 117, 120–3, 125, 143, 162, 165, 185
Khala, Hamida 230
King Lear 60
Kirklees Metropolitan Borough Council 146
Koran, The 43, 174 (*see also* Qu'ran)
Kukathas, Chandran 132–7, 139, 142, 147–8, 152
Kymlicka, Will 9, 132, 135, 139–44, 171

La Fontaine 119
Laborde, Cécile 22, 24–6, 152
laïcité 12–13
Latimer, Hugh 234
Leigh, Ian 5
Lerner, Gerda 191
Letter Concerning Toleration 5, 22
Levinas, Emmanuel 28, 30
Liberal Archipelago, The 132
liberal feminism 168–70, 180
Liberal Paternalist Principle *see* paternalism
liberal perfectionism (*see also* perfectionism and perfectionist liberalism) 7, 17, 39, 50–1, 53–5, 149, 165
liberal state 1–4, 37, 151, 154, 160, 164–6, 185
liberalism 1–3, 5–7, 9, 22, 39–67
    not culturally neutral 156
Liberalism without Perfection 16, 61
liberalism, definition of 3–4
Liberalism's Religion 22, 24
Libertarian Paternalism 86–7
Liberté, Egalité, Fraternité 14
liberty, individual 7, 11
    positive liberty 94–5
living together see *vivre ensemble*
Locke, John 5, 22
Loi no 2010-1192 11
Lone Face-Coverer, the 33–5

Macbeth 31
Mackenzie, Catriona 161
Mackie, Gerry 188
Maclure, Jocelyn 23–5, 142–6
    see also Taylor, Charles
Malverde, Jesus 130
Marx, Karl 49
Marxist state 5
    Marxist feminism 168
Matsumoto, David *see* Bogart, Kathleen R.
Matter of Principle, A 141
Mayflower and *Speedwell* 19
McConnell, Michael 23
Mcntyre, Alison 79
McNeil, Jane E. and Elizabeth K. Warrington 31
Michigan University 193
Mill, John Stuart 39–41, 46–8, 65, 74, 76–7, 80, 82, 100, 169–70, 208
millet system 135
misogyny 204
Moebius syndrome 91
moral relativism 137–8
Morality of Freedom, The 53
Müller, Sabine 72
Multicultural Citizenship 140
multiculturalism 2, 4, 6, 9, 131–2, 139–43
    bad for women? 172–8
    weak multiculturalism 139, 142, 147
Multiculturalism 148
Muslim Council of Great Britain 228

Muslim girls 140, 143, 224
Muslim women 3, 92, 193, 196, 200, 228, 234
  Muslim Women's Network UK 228
Muslims 12, 20, 131, 135, 168, 174, 215, 217
  liberal Muslims 235

Napier, General Sir Charles James 136
Napier, William 136
Narayan, Uma 126-8
Nasif, Malak Hifni 129-30
Nasser 130
Nedelsky, Jennifer 150
Nelson, Charles A. 28
Netherlands 4, 179, 236-7
neutrality (of the state) 13, 41, 59
New Religious Intolerance, The 21, 207
New York Times 216
niqab 3, 5-6, 14, 19, 70, 124-5, 146, 193, 228
North America 216
Nozick, Robert 218-19
Nudge 86
nun, Roman Catholic 109-13; (monks and) nuns 125
Nussbaum, Martha 4, 21-2, 24, 51-3, 60, 89-90, 93, 111-14, 120-2, 127, 168, 186, 207, 215-17, 221-4, 230

OC *see* overlapping consensus
offence, and the burqa 10, 199, 204-6
  offence principle 10, 33, 201-4, 206
Okin, Susan Moller 9, 132, 167-8, 170-9
On Liberty 39, 48, 80, 100
Orwell, George 60
Oshana, Marina 95, 102-9, 161
Ottoman Empire 135
overlapping consensus (OC) 41, 43-5, 62-4

Pakistan 192-3
Parekh, Biku 176-8
Parfit, Derek 83-4
Parmenides 102
paternalism 1, 6, 8, 17, 64-5, 69-92
  autonomy-based paternalism 95-6
  hard and soft paternalism 80-3, 88-9, 93

Liberal Paternalist Principle 33, 69, 88, 125, 179, 200, 208
  weak and strong paternalism 80-4, 88
patriarchy 127, 169
perfectionism 17, 49-50, 64, 98, 154, 161, 214
perfectionist liberalism (*see also* liberal perfectionism) 39, 53-5, 66, 101, 121, 142
personal autonomy (*see also* autonomy) 1, 8, 54, 69, 93-115, 117, 150, 154
  necessity of socially supportive conditions for 159
Persak, Nina 211
Personal Autonomy in Society 103
personal choice 1
Perth, Australia 4
Peter Pan 60
Petit Prince, Le 108-9
Pew Research Poll 193
Pinker, Steven 177
Pirzada women 126, 128-9
PL *see* Political Liberalism
Plato 49-50, 71
pluralism 15, 41, 46, 54
Political Liberalism (PL) 7, 39-42, 46-9, 51, 55, 61-4, 66-7, 96, 121, 142, 154, 214
  Political Liberalism and the burqa, 48-9
Political Liberalism 41
politics of recognition 147-9
  limits of 152-66
polygamy 171, 173-6, 178, 191
portraiture 28
positive liberty *see* liberty, individual
prosopagnosia 31
public reason 45
purdah 128, 230

Quebec 148
Quong, Jonathan 3, 8, 16, 45-6, 55, 61-7, 74-5, 81
Qu'ran 168, 174

Raj, the 136
Rawls, John 41-7, 50, 55, 59, 62, 64, 133, 234-5
Raz, Joseph 49, 53-6, 64-5, 67, 96-8, 102
Reasons and Persons 84

recognition 26, 148–52
    mutual recognition 150
Refusing the Veil 196
religion 2, 6, 21–6
religious freedom 5, 7, 11, 20–1, 23–4
religious obligation 3, 5, 21
religious tolerance 1
republicanism 18, 26
    contrast between French and American forms 19
    French republican tradition 18, 211
Reynolds, Joel 71
Ridley, Nicholas 234
Rights-Protecting Requirement 154–6
Robert, Na'ima B. 124–6
Roman busts and statues 28
Roman Catholic Church 19
Romeo 83
Rosen, Michael, and Jonathan Wolff 71
Ross, Lee and Richard Nesbitt 99
Rushdie, Salman 56–7

safety belts *see* seat belt law
'S.A.S.' 14
Salafist 5
Sardar, Z. 20, 175
Sarközy, Nicolas 11
Saudi Arabia 172, 192–3, 228
seat belt law 21, 77–9, 80–1, 89
secularism 4, 13
Secularism and Freedom of Conscience 24
security 4–5, 9
Sen, Amartya 119–20, 122, 159, 186
Selfridges 215
Sex, Culture and Justice 179
Shakespeare, Tom 72–3
Shakespeare, William 31
sharia law 213
Shiffrin, Seana 8, 74–81
Siedentorp, Larry 22, 156
smoking 86
social influence 9, 187–8, 193–4
Song, Sarah 22, 139, 142–3, 224
Stasi, Bernard 224
Stewart, James 82
Stoljar, Nataalie 118
Sulikowski, Danielle *see* Burke, Darren
Summa Theologica 79
Sunstein, Cass R. *see* Thaler, Richard H.

suttee 136
Swift, Adam 95
Swiss parliament 236
synchronic/diachronic fork 157

Tahrir Al-Mara (The Liberation of Women) 129, 191
Taliban 96, 109, 205, 228; 'Taliban Woman' 103, 107–9
'Tasneem' 4
Tasneem, Umm 124, 126
Taylor, Charles 24–5, 132, 145, 147–8, 153–8
    and Jocelyn Maclure 156
Taylor, James 118, 123
terrorism 17, 214–17
Thaler, Richard H., and Cass R. Sunstein 86–7, 181–2
Thomas, Laurence 193–4
The Times 5
theocracy 5
Theory of Justice, A 50
throffers 219
Ticino 236–7
tolerance 131–2, 134, 137
    as recognition 148–9
toleration 132–3, 135, 137, 139
    'maximal' toleration 132
    minimal level of toleration 136, 139
    as recognition 149–50
Toleration as Recognition 149
Totality and Infinity 28
Treacher, Amal 168
tribunal(s) 145–6, 185
turbans 21
Turkey 192–3

Unconscionability Doctrine 78
unfair imputation 225–7
United Kingdom 179, 215
United States 45, 179, 186
Unruly Practices 183

Vallier, Richard *see* Gaus, Gerald
veil 2, 14, 129–30, 191
    veiling 128, 143, 191
Veil-of-Ignorance thought experiment 177, 182
Vernon, Richard 46

vitamin D deficiency 49, 89–90
vivre ensemble 14, 17, 207, 211–13
Voices and Veils: Feminism and Islam in French Women's Writing and Activism 169
Voltaire 102
Voluntary Slave 105

Wahhabist women 3, 12, 70, 234
   Wahhabist community 24
   Wahhabist girls 144
Wainwright, Martin 4, 146
Warrington, Elizabeth K. *see* MacNeil, Jane E.
Watson, Lori and Christie Hartley 45, 213–14
Watts, Michael 120
Weil, Patrick 224
Westermarck, Edward 138
West, the 109
Western liberal states 4, 205, 212, 236

Western burqa-wearer 110–11
Western civilisation 192
Western countries 215
Western cultures 172, 191
Western democracies 177
Western liberalism 5
Western liberal feminism 168
Western liberal societies 172–3
Western liberal values 205
Western Muslims 228
'Western Patriarchal Feminism' 173
Whipps Cross Hospital 5
Wolff, Jonathan and Avner De-Shalit 53, 186–7
Wolff, Jonathan *see* Rosen, Michael
Women and Human Development 230

x-ray spectacles 36–7

Yaffe, Gideon 220
'You're Beautiful' (song) 28

www.ingramcontent.com/pod-product-compliance
Lightning Source LLC
Chambersburg PA
CBHW072140290426
44111CB00012B/1927